ONE OF OUR ROYAL MARINES IS MISSING

The enduring mystery of the disappearance of Alan Addis

David Miller

In memory of Sarah Anne Addis
who tried so hard to discover what happened to her son

CONTENTS

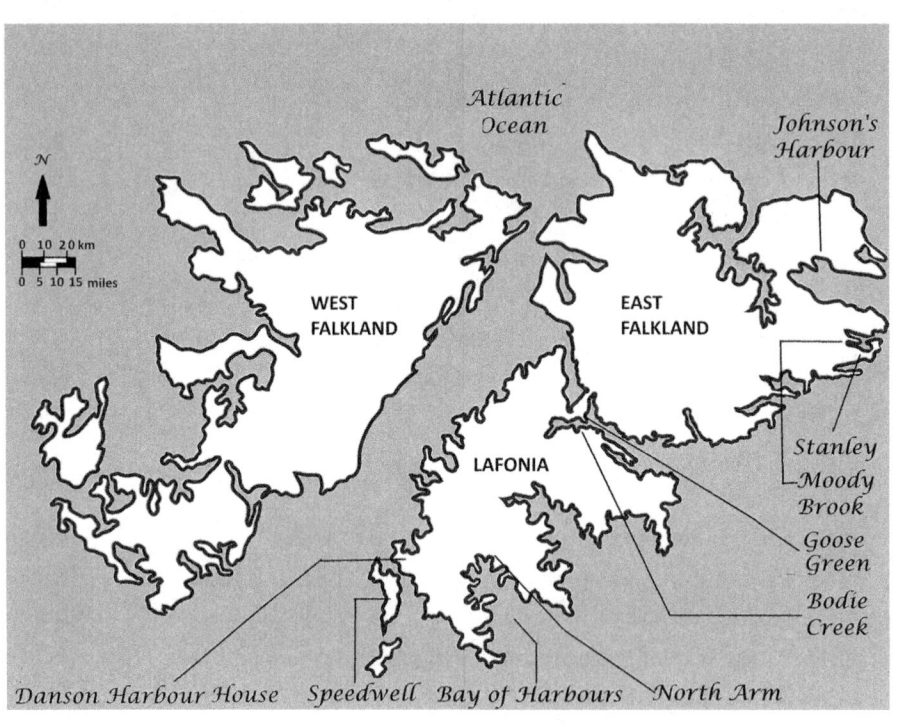

Atlantic
Ocean

Johnson's
Harbour

N

0 10 20 km
0 5 10 15 miles

WEST
FALKLAND

EAST
FALKLAND

LAFONIA

Stanley

Moody
Brook

Goose
Green

Bodie
Creek

Danson Harbour House   Speedwell   Bay of Harbours   North Arm

CHAPTER ONE

Introduction

There is a peculiar fascination about people who disappear. Sometimes whole groups have vanished, one of the more notorious being the Roman Legion IX Hispana, composed of over one thousand men and three hundred horses, which disappeared without trace somewhere in North Britain in 122CE. Their fate has kept scholars and archaeologists occupied for years. In a completely different case, the sailing brigantine, *Mary Celeste*, was found on the high seas totally deserted on 4 December 1872. She had been carrying a crew of seven, together with the Captain's wife and infant daughter, was well stocked with provisions, and was in reasonable sailing order. There was no sign of fighting and people's personal property seemed untouched. Despite that, there was no indication whatsoever as to what had happened to the nine souls known to have been on board, nor has any clue ever been found.

There are many more cases involving individuals. Some are understandable: a child running away from abuse, a wife escaping a violent husband, a vagrant. But in other cases, a fit, healthy person with no obvious problems simply disappears, causing family and friends great distress. Some of these are solved within days, a few within weeks, but others, seemingly, never. Perhaps the highest profile of current enduring cases is that of Madeleine McCann, aged three, who disappeared on 3 May 2007 from a holiday apartment in Praia da Luz, Portugal. But, as will be discussed later, there are many more.

Many of those cases, particularly those involving children, can require huge efforts and expense by the police, and a few keep the media and authors busy for years. They are akin to the old-fashioned disappearing lady illusion in music-hall acts where a pretty girl walks through a doorway on the stage and vanishes, to the total mystification of the audience, only to reappear minutes later, again without explanation. The difference is that in real life, the person often does disappear, permanently.

Nineteen-year-old Royal Marine Alan Addis vanished in the Falkland Islands in 1980, which has proved to be another of those unsolved mysteries that just will not go away. The circumstances are so bizarre, the setting so unusual, and so many of the subsequent investigations have been poorly conducted, coupled with strong evidence of both local and governmental cover-up, that it continues to capture the imagination. But, forty-five years later, it seems to be as far from a solution as on the day after it occurred.

There is little doubt that Alan was killed, almost certainly by accident, and that his body was then disposed of in a way that has never been discovered, but both must have involved one or more Falkland Islanders. That some islanders should have covered up the death of a Royal Marine, a corps whose members died for their freedom in 1982, is a disgrace of which all islanders should be thoroughly ashamed and needs to be resolved before the last of those with knowledge of what happened die. Alan's mother fought valiantly over many years to discover what happened, but died in 2011, since when, nobody has fought her corner; his family seem to have given up, the Royal Marines do not seem interested, and the authorities in the Falklands appear to be doing their best to sweep it under the carpet.

The outline facts are simple. At 0130 on 8 August 1980, Alan was seen to leave a party at North Arm Settlement on East Falkland Island and, from that time to this, not a single trace of him has ever been found – not a bone, not a scrap of clothing, not the torch he was carrying, nor the very expensive watch he was known to be wearing. Apart from Alan, there were some sixty people at the party, of whom five were fellow Royal Marines, leaving over fifty Falklanders, and a tiny minority of those must have either participated in or known what happened, but they have kept remarkably and consistently quiet. In blunt terms, some villains – and almost certainly more than one – have got away with it.

AUTHOR'S COMMENTS

This review follows the principles employed by Air Accident Investigators that all possibilities, no matter how seemingly far-fetched, are considered, until each is ruled out, leaving, hopefully, just one.

Reported speech from the various enquiries has been recorded and analysed. However, it must be borne in mind that some people were being interviewed many years after the event, so that times and dates may have been changed, perhaps sometimes unwittingly. Also, the Falkland Islands are known for their gossip, with salacious stories being repeated endlessly and often being enhanced for effect in the retelling. Such gossip was not only within Settlements, but also between them, using the two-metre band wireless and the telephone, both of which were of the 'all-informed' type in which every listener heard everything that was being said.

It is also important to recall that the initial investigations were conducted by amateurs, who had little experience of murders. At the time of Addis's disappearance, the operational staff of the Falkland Islands Police consisted of a fatally ill inspector and an inexperienced Constable, while none of the members of the Royal Marines Board of Inquiry had any previous experience of such matters. Thus, as was to be pointed out by a later Chief Police Officer, Superintendent Greenwood, they did not pursue anything concerning foul play; indeed, if it did cross their minds, it was quickly dismissed.

The major source for background information on the Falkland Islands used here is the Annual Report for 1974–1975. It has been confirmed by the excellent Jane Cameron National Archive in Stanley that these reports were published some three-to-four years in arrears due to the time taken to assemble all the data, so this was the most recent to 1980. Further issues did not appear due to the war of 1982 and the reports were discontinued thereafter. Nevertheless, the rate of development in pre-1982 Falklands was so slow that the 1975 report is considered to be an adequate reflection of the situation in 1980.

AUTHOR'S CONVENTIONS

The author has employed the following conventions:
- Where names are listed, they are placed in alphabetical order by surname, regardless of rank or importance.
- Measurements and quantities are given in imperial units followed by the metric equivalent, both rounded to the nearest whole number.

- All timings are local, using the twenty-four-hour clock.
- Direct quotes are in italics.
- Two groups, each of three Marines, were involved. For ease of reference AND FOR THIS BOOK ONLY, they will be referred to as: Team A (Sgt Howden plus two) and Team B (Cpl Davis plus two).

In a case such as this, much is a matter of recorded fact, which cannot be disputed. Many of the statements by witnesses corroborate each other, but some either contradict each other or are plainly fanciful and the author has had to exercise judgement as to which is the more probable. Finally, some aspects come down to a matter of personal opinion, upon which not all can agree. Where that occurs here, the opinions are those of the author, for which he takes full responsibility.

ACKNOWLEDGEMENTS

The author wishes to acknowledge with gratitude the unstinting help in research, advice and comments by Professor John Hunter, and Philip Davis, Robin Goodwin, Eric Goss and Ken Greenland.

CHAPTER TWO

The Falkland Islands in 1980

Almost everything about the people and their way of life in the Falkland Islands changed following the Anglo-Argentine war of 1982. Thus, in order to appreciate the circumstances of Alan Addis's disappearance in 1980, it is first necessary to outline the pre-war environment in which these events took place. The history and geography of the islands are well documented elsewhere, so this chapter concentrates on the elements relevant to the Alan Addis story.

The Falkland Islands are located in the South Atlantic Ocean some 400 miles (650km) from Cape Horn, 4,000 miles (6,500km) from Cape Town and 7,900 miles (12,700km) from London. Many people in the UK consider the Falklands to be on the verge of the Antarctic, but the capital, Stanley, is actually 895 miles (1,440km) North of the Antarctic Circle, whereas London is 902 miles (1,450km) South of the Arctic Circle – a marginal difference.

The archipelago consists of some 778 islands of widely varying sizes, with a combined area of 4,700 square miles (approx. 12,172 sq. km). There are two large islands – East and West Falklands – although it should be noted that Lafonia[1] – the setting for these events – is effectively an island on its own, being separated from East Falkland by Grantham and Choiseul Sounds and only joined to East Falkland by a narrow isthmus at Goose Green.

---

1 The area was named after Samuel Lafone, a wealthy British merchant, who purchased it in 1845.

Population

NATIONAL ORIGIN	STANLEY	EAST FALKLAND (less Stanley but including Lafonia)	WEST FALKLAND	TOTALS
UK (Notes 1, 2)	982	430	311	1,733 (95.6%)
South American (Note 3)	50	5	5	60
United States	13	5	6	24
Other European	5	1	0	6
TOTALS	1,050 (58%)	441 (24%)	322 (18%)	1,813

Table 1. Falkland Islands Population by National Origin; Census 1980

Notes:

1. Excluded Naval Party 8901 and British Antarctic Survey.
2. Included UK-based contract employees; e.g., nurses, doctors, teachers.
3. Most of the fifty South Americans in Stanley were Argentine nationals employed by the airline (LADE). Others in East and West Falklands were Chilean labourers/shepherds.

Islanders born and bred in the Falklands were known as 'Kelpers' and the complexities of relationships within the Kelper community were well illustrated by Governor Hunt during his visit to Beaver Island in August 1980: *"Tony and Vi Felton were there to meet us, with their daughter Faith (later to be a maid at Government House) and Tony's daughter from a previous marriage, Sonia, with her second husband and two children from her previous marriage. These complicated marital relationships were not uncommon in the Falklands and it behoves the newcomer to tread warily lest he find himself maligning an ex-wife or ex-husband, or, worse, someone's mother or father. Both Tony and Vi could trace their ancestry back to the original Chelsea pensioners (Vi's maiden name was Short). Tony's first wife had been Winnie Miranda, née Jones, and he was Vi's third husband. Tony and Winnie's daughter, Sonia, had first married Royal Marine Geordie Gill and was currently married to another Englishman, Brian Paul."*[2]

The people were spread over the islands in tiny, self-contained Settlements and major efforts were made to bring them together. The schools at Stanley and Darwin were early opportunities for children to meet others of the same age from other Settlements, while for the adults, there were regular meetings including horse races, sheepdog trials and steer-riding, which were accompanied by evening events, such as dances, simple feasting and considerable drinking.

Foremen in the Settlements were paid a minimum monthly wage of £66.97, while shepherds living in the Settlements earned £56.45 per month, and those in 'outside houses' an additional £3.25.[3] Shepherds and labourers received free quarters, fuel, meat and milk, while bonuses were paid for shearing, fencing and peat cutting. Hands assembled at 0900 daily for allocation of work by foremen and an average of forty-five hours weekly was worked, with Saturday afternoons and Sundays as rest days. All were entitled to an annual holiday of fifteen working days with pay.

With an overabundance of sheep, mutton was the staple diet and was supplied free-of-charge to farm employees, with beef usually available during the winter months.[4] The diet could also include goose and fish, such as smelt and mullet. Poultry thrived. Vegetables, usually grown in householders' own gardens, included potatoes, turnips, carrots, parsnips, radish, lettuce, cabbage, cauliflower and peas.

Expatriates

The Falkland Islands have long had a significant number of expatriates. In 1980, most Settlement managers were expatriates, while many Settlements had one or two shepherds and farm hands from South American countries, particularly Chile. Most expatriates, however, were from the UK and located

---

2   Hunt, p.77.
3   Source: Falkland Islands Report 1972-73. Pp4-5
4   Mutton was delivered to houses in Stanley. The houseowner paid cash for the meat, but delivery was free.

in Stanley. These British officials included: the Governor; legal officers (e.g., Colonial Secretary); some police officers; schoolteachers; medical and dental staff; and the Permanent Staff Instructor with the Falkland Islands Defence Force (FIDF). Many of these were seconded from UK government bodies and on fixed-term tours, while others were recruited by and on contract to the Falkland Islands government.

A major body in Stanley in 1980 were the fifty-strong staff of Líneas Aéreas del Estado (LADE), the Argentine government-owned airline, which was staffed by the Argentine air force and operated air force aircraft. This detachment supposedly provided servicing, fuel supply and administration for the LADE aircraft operating the airlift to Argentina. The Falklands' government maintained that these numbers were excessive, but they had little control.

The Capital

The capital, Stanley,[5] with a population of just over a thousand, was chosen in the nineteenth century for its excellent harbour and its convenience to sailing ships rounding Cape Horn. In modern times, however, its situation at the easternmost tip of East Falkland is less than ideal and a central site would be more convenient, but there is no move to change. Inhabitants of Stanley in 1980 were mainly government officers, company officials, hospital staff and schoolteachers. There were also many elderly people who had spent their working lives in the Settlements in 'tied' accommodation, i.e., the houses belonged to the proprietors of the farm and were only available to bona fide workers for the duration of their employment. This meant that they had to vacate on retirement, leaving them with no option but to move to Stanley. The life there was less demanding and more sociable, but, more importantly, medical and care facilities were readily available, an important feature for the 'old-and-bold'.

---

5   Sometimes referred to as 'Port Stanley', its correct and legal name at the time was simply 'Stanley', as it remains today.

Governance

The head of government was the Governor and Commander-in-Chief, who was appointed by the Queen on the advice of the Foreign and Commonwealth Office (FCO).[6] The Governor lived in Government House (known locally as 'GH'), a rather grand building by Falklands' standards, situated at the western end of Stanley in a small estate. The Governor in 1980 was Rex Hunt, then aged fifty-six, who was an experienced diplomat and colonial administrator.[7] He was advised by the Executive Council, which consisted of two Appointed Members, two Elected Members and two *ex officio* members (Chief Secretary and Financial Secretary). The next level down was the Legislative Council, consisting of the Governor as President, two Elected Members representing the Stanley constituency, four Elected Members representing the East and West Falkland constituencies respectively, and the Chief Secretary and Financial Secretary, again, both *ex officio*.

The Judiciary

There were six levels:
- **Settlement Managers**. Many Settlements were long distances from Stanley and travel was difficult, so, in an unofficial arrangement, managers tended to deal with minor domestic matters affecting their staff on a local basis. Some, but not all, managers were appointed Justices of the Peace.
- **Summary Court**. This had limited jurisdiction and had fallen out of use in 1971.
- **Magistrates' Court**. In practice, this was the major tribunal. In 1975, there were seventeen Justices of the Peace appointed by the Governor from citizens of Stanley and some farm managers.
- **Supreme Court**. This was presided over by a retired judge brought in from the UK for the occasion and dealt with serious cases specifically designated to it such as murder, rape, manslaughter, divorce and child

---

6   The title changed to Foreign and Commonwealth Development Office in September 2020.
7   Rex Masterman Hunt (29 June 1926 – 11 November 2012) was appointed Governor, Commander-in-Chief and Vice-Admiral of the Falkland Islands on 14 January 1980. He was appointed Knight Bachelor on 11 October 1982.

custody. There were no qualified lawyers in either government or private practice in the colony, so the government employed a part-time legal adviser in the UK. This meant that, for their part, defendants had to fly in their own lawyer, either from South America or the UK. Appeals from the Magistrates' Court were dealt with in the first instance by the Supreme Court.

- **Court of Appeal**. This body, which was shared with St Helena and the Seychelles, was presided over by a UK-based judge.
- **Commissioners for Oaths**. There were also fifteen Commissioners for Oaths who were appointed to facilitate witnessing legal documents in remote Settlements.

Camp

The term 'Camp' frequently arises in Falklands conversations and, since its use differs from that in the UK, it needs to be explained. In the UK, 'camp' describes a specific, populated, well-defined and usually relatively small area, such as an Army camp, holiday camp or tented camp. In the Falklands, however, the word is derived from the Spanish *campo,* which simply means the countryside; in Stanley, this covered all areas outside the capital, while, within Settlements, it meant all areas outside that particular Settlement.

Settlements

In 1980, there were thirty-three Settlements, and, without exception, these were sheep-farming communities based on a number of considerations. Firstly, there had to be sufficient grazing for sheep and other animals. Secondly, the animals or their products, such as wool, had to be exported, which meant a site accessible to ships. Thirdly, there had to be a guaranteed supply of drinkable water and, finally, access to peat beds was needed for cooking and heating. This meant that Settlements were invariably close to the coast, with a jetty extending into the sea for ship access, although some otherwise suitable harbours could not be settled due to the absence of peat. A supply of drinkable water was also a problem in some Settlements.

A few of these farms were owned and operated by families, but vast areas were owned by absentee companies, most importantly the Falkland Islands Company (FIC), which, among other properties, owned the whole of Lafonia.[8] The FIC had been founded in 1851 and had changed hands several times since then; in 1980, it was owned by the Coalite Group, which had its headquarters in Bolsover in Derbyshire.

These companies employed the manager, who was responsible not only for the employment of farmhands and day-to-day operations of the farm, but also, as described by Governor Hunt: *"… the manager of a Settlement did much more than run the farm. He was in effect the old-time colonial District Officer, responsible for the lives and welfare of all his charges."*[9] The companies were liable for capital expenditure and some were generous, while others were niggardly – Governor Hunt, for example, being particularly critical of Hamilton Estates who owned most of the western islands, including Weddell.[10] Farms ranged in size from a single family of perhaps four-to-six people to Settlements of fifty-to-sixty.

How individual Settlements were organised and run depended on the parent company and the manager, but, in general, in the larger Settlements, the manager and his family lived in rather grand style in a separate building known always, and quite simply, as the 'Big House'. One necessary reason for the large size was that the manager (and his wife!) were obliged to provide accommodation for short-term visitors, such as clergy (of various faiths), doctors, dentists, itinerant schoolteachers, directors from the company base in the UK and government officials, sometimes even the Governor in person. The manager's wife was often assisted by maids, found from among the young women on the Settlement, and a gardener, but usually did the cooking herself. In most cases, she also acted as the Settlement nurse, which included maintaining and dispensing from the Settlement medical chest, as well as consulting a doctor over the radio where necessary. She also sometimes acted as counsellor to couples with marital difficulties.

Families occupied company-owned houses, which were sited in a higgledy-piggledy cluster, while unattached workers and lower-level visitors lived in bunkhouses (hostels) and ate in cookhouses, which were

---

8   Lafonia was purchased by the Liverpool-based Lafone brothers in 1845, hence the name. They sold it to the FIC in 1851.

9   Hunt, op. cit., p.17.

10   Hunt, op. cit., p.76.

often known, naval-style, as galleys. The larger Settlements had a sheep-shearing shed, killing shed (slaughterhouse), shop, school, generator shed and a community hall. Apart from the manager, his wife and children, a typical Settlement comprised: one or two foremen, a number of shepherds, a mechanic, carpenter/odd-job man, a number of handymen, cowman, engineer/electrician (for the generator), gardener and a cook, who looked after the occupants of the Bunkhouse.

Some of the shepherds, and in some cases their families also, lived in remote areas, in what were known simply as 'outside houses'. These could be some 10-20 miles (24-32km) from the Settlement and had to have a ready supply of water and peat, but, if permanently occupied, may also have had cows, horses and a garden. It was a lonely life, but alleviated by regular visits to their parent Settlement, to pick up supplies, to receive instructions from the manager or foreman and last, but by no means least, for some company and opportunity to catch up on gossip.

The houses were warm and relatively comfortable, but the Falklanders were used to a hard way of life. Cooking and heating were provided by a cast-iron stove, usually a Stanley Range No. 8, Rayburn or Aga, which were fired by peat, ensuring that the entire house had a very pleasant aroma, while a huge black kettle usually sat on one of the hot plates, providing a constant supply of ready-brewed tea. Each household was required to cut its own peat (often done by the wives), which was transported by horse cart or farm tractor and then piled outside the house. One remarkable feature of Falklands' life was moving houses, quite literally, when buildings were raised by powerful jacks and mounted on wooden sleds. They were then towed by horses or a fleet of tractors to the new site, sometimes many miles away and were seldom the worse for the experience.

The cycle of life in the Settlements revolved around the sheep, the major activities being (months are approximate): October – lambing; November – marking, i.e., cutting identification marks on sheep's ears; castrating males and clipping tails; November-to-February – driving sheep to home paddocks, which involved all the men, plus wives and the older children.

Shearing was an important part of the year and was carried out either by men on the Settlement or by travelling contract shearers. The 'clips' were then bundled, taken to the jetty and shipped by one of a number of coasters, such as the Motor Vessel (MV) *Forrest* or *Monsunen*, to Stanley, and then onward by an ocean-going ship to the UK.

Land usage was almost entirely devoted to sheep farming and, with the exception of 20,500 acres of Crown Land, the colony was divided into freehold farms varying in size from 3,600 to one million acres, carrying a total of about 640,000 sheep. The table shows typical annual exports of wool and hides, and indicates how vulnerable the Falklands were to international wool prices.[11]

Product	1974		1975	
	Quantity	Value (£)	Quantity	Value (£)
Wool	1,973tons (2,004,740kg)	2,225,262	2,175tons (2,209,948kg)	2,209,948
Skins	74.4tons (72,595kg)	11,443	66.2tons (67,251kg)	17,174

Table 2. Exports of wool and hides

Education

As at 31 Dec 1975	Male	Female	TOTALS
Stanley Schools	78	71	149
Darwin School	34	27	63
Camp	54	49	103
TOTALS	166	147	315

Table 3. Children undergoing education, 1975

Children were entitled to free education up to age fifteen. There were two schools in Stanley and, in 1975, ninety-five children attended the junior school, forty-five the senior school. There was also a boarding

---

11   Source: Falkland Islands and Dependencies, 1974 and 1975 p.18. (The most recent to 1980 available)

school at Darwin, catering for up to forty-two boarders. Some of the larger Settlements, including North Arm in 1980, had a resident teacher, but the smaller Settlements and the outlying houses were a particular problem. To cope with this, the government employed 'Camp teachers', each of whom was assigned a beat of three or four houses, which were covered by Land Rover, horse, or, in a few cases, by boat, although by the mid-seventies aircraft were also being used. The teacher stayed with each family for about two weeks at a time before moving on to the next, leaving children sufficient homework to keep them occupied until the next visit.

Weather

Falklands' seasons are the reverse of those in the northern hemisphere; i.e., summer occurs from December to March and winter from late June to August. High winds and moderate cold are inescapable features of life on the islands, with temperatures ranging from about 36°F (2°C) in July to 49°F (9°C) in January. One of the most noticeable features of Falklands' weather is that it changes rapidly, gales can blow up within minutes, and UK visitors sometimes remark that they experience all four seasons in a single day. Fog/mist, frequently dense, can also appear without warning and is more likely in spring and early summer, and usually associated with wind from the North or East.[12]

Land Travel

In 1980, there were only sixteen miles (26km) of metalled roads, all of which were in and immediately around Stanley. Elsewhere, all overland travel was on tracks by horse, Land Rover or, occasionally, motorcycle.

Outside Stanley, there were vehicle tracks, which had, perforce, to take account of the terrain, obstacles such as rock outcrops, and streams. Lafonia was a special case with very shallow soil atop extremely hard slate stone, where the driver was more likely to get lost or suffer a mechanical breakdown

---

12   The difference between the two is that 'mist' has visibility of 5,500 > 1,100yd (5000 > 1000 metres), while 'fog' is less than 1,100yd (1000m).

rather than get bogged. The major routes between Settlements were well-known to regular users, but even so took a long time. For example, in 1980, a Land Rover took nine hours to travel the 6miles (105km) from Darwin to Stanley, an average speed of 7mph (11km/hr), while Governor Hunt took two hours each way to travel the fifteen miles (24km) from Stanley to Bluff Cove.[13] Local drivers knew the tracks well and regularly drove as a single vehicle with a solitary driver, but always accompanied by a 'debogging kit' consisting of a full complement of tools, such as heavy-duty jacks, steel pickets, tow ropes and several wooden planks, together with warm clothing and enough food for several days should the driver get stuck and not be able to get the vehicle out. By 1980, many vehicles also carried a 2m band radio to call for help, if needed. People who did not know routes outside Stanley, such as the police, would tend to travel in two- or three-vehicle convoys. One curiosity was that, as Governor Hunt described, "*Distances were measured more by gates and fences than miles and kilometres.*"[14]

Unique to the Falklands were the 'standing men' – tall cairns built from local stones and rocks, which were sited at prominent points to mark a route. For example, there was one such some three miles (5km) from North Arm on the track to Goose Green.

Most shepherds and labourers had their own horses. They knew their areas intimately and were able to follow much more direct routes than vehicles, particularly in using gates and gaps in fences.

Sea Travel

All Settlements were close to the sea and had a jetty for government and FIC ships. The vessel involved in this story was MV *Forrest,* which had been designed and built in England for the Falkland Islands government.[15] The ship arrived in Stanley in 1967, and her tasks were to transport wool clip and meat to Stanley, to deliver supplies to the Settlements, and to move limited numbers of passengers and animals. There was a two-berth cabin for passengers and any in excess of that number had to sleep in the hold, which was accessed by

---

13   Hunt, p.49.
14   Hunt, p.67.
15   The ship was named after a popular and effective Roman Catholic priest.

a 2ft (61cm) square hatch and a vertical ladder. *Forrest* also carried a Gemini inflatable outboard-powered dinghy for use when it could not berth alongside a jetty. The ship was frequently used by Governor Hunt to visit remote Settlements and there was also an annual charter to the Ministry of Defence to transport Royal Marines of NP8901 as and when required.

There were several other vessels operating in 1980. The Danish MV *Monsunen* was on charter to the Falkland Islands government, while the Falkland Islands Company operated two small auxiliary ketches, both somewhat aged: *Ilen*, which had been delivered in 1927,[16] and *Penelope.*

Air Travel

The Falkland Islands Government Air Service (FIGAS) started in 1948 and in 1980 was operating float-equipped de Havilland Canada Beaver 'bush' transport aircraft. Single-engined, these rugged, reliable and well-liked aircraft could carry six passengers or 2,100lb (953kg) freight and loads could include small animals and mail. They were also essential for evacuating sick or injured patients from the Settlements to the hospital in Stanley and sometimes the reverse, taking doctors to patients. Camp teachers were flown regularly around their beats on the main and outer islands, and Camp children attending boarding schools in Stanley or Darwin travelled mainly by aircraft. In 1979, FIGAS decided that the successor should be a twin-engined landplane and the first Britten-Norman Islander arrived in 1980.

Stanley airport was completed in 1972, which enabled an international air service to be introduced that November by Líneas Aéreas del Estado (LADE), the military-owned and operated Argentinian airline. This service provided a weekly schedule, usually on a Monday,[17] between Stanley and Comodoro Rivadavia Military Air Base in Argentina, using twin-turboprop Fokker F27 Friendship aircraft. Passengers then had to transfer by bus to Ezeiza International Airport at Buenos Aires for onward travel. The short length of the Stanley Airport runway restricted passengers to a maximum of twenty-two, with similar limits on mail and freight.

While the LADE service was welcomed as a much improved and faster

---

16   *Ilen* returned to Ireland in 1996, where she was rebuilt and is still in use as a training vessel.
17   This was later increased to two flights per week.

de Havilland Canada Beaver 'bush' transport aircraft
(Courtesy Philip Davis)

method of travel to and from the Falklands, the islanders had three major complaints, the most important of which concerned the large size of the resident LADE team (a vice-Commodoro[18] plus some fifty staff) was far in excess of what was needed. Associated with this was the Argentine demand for ever-increasing fuel storage tanks, which was far beyond what was needed for the limited service provided by LADE. A more personal complaint was that at both Rivadavia and Ezeiza airports in Argentina, Falklanders were treated by Argentine officials with disdain, with frequent 'problems' introduced to make their journeys as difficult as possible. They also had to undertake a lengthy bus journey between the two airfields.[19]

Kelp

Parts of the Falkland coasts are homes to large beds of kelp (*Laminariales*), a type of sea growth with long fronds, so dense and heavily intertwined

---

18 In 1980 it was ViceCommodoro Hector Gilobert. RAF equivalent rank was wing-commander.
19 Conversation Tim Blake (Hill Cove)/Miller 1986.

that individual areas are known as 'kelp forests'.[20] These areas are avoided by ships as they can slow down or even stop progress, as fronds can get sucked into and eventually block water intakes, or become wrapped around propellers, bringing them to a standstill. Low Island is virtually surrounded by dense kelp forests.

So widespread was this kelp that within the Falkland Islands those who had been born there were known as 'Kelpers'.

Animal Husbandry

In 1980, the economy of the Falkland Islands depended almost entirely on the export of its high quality wool, production in that year amounting to 2,080 imperial tons (just over 2 million kg), although the actual value of the 'clip' varied according to world prices, which fluctuated wildly. The sheep were primarily (but not exclusively) of the Corridale breed, which had originated as a cross between Lincoln and Merino sheep in New Zealand. Not only was the wool of high quality, but so, too, were their carcasses.[21]

Much of the Camp was criss-crossed by fencing, which was used to control the sheep and to move them from one area to another to conserve the vegetation. Fencing was installed by the Settlements, but with some financial support from the government. Of necessity, there were gates to allow sheep, humans and vehicles to pass through, and in the absence of normal recognition features, such as hills or woods, these gates also served as navigation points. So important was the fencing that it, together with the gates, was marked on the maps.

There was a particular problem with dogs. The Settlements needed large numbers for use with the sheep, but the dogs could also act as transmitters for *echinococcosis*, a parasitic tapeworm disease, also known as hydatid disease, which, if untreated, could prove fatal. As a result, sheepdogs had to be regularly treated and when not working were kept in a wired-off kennel and not allowed to roam freely around the Settlement. In other words, they were working dogs and not pets. There was an animal quarantine facility at Navy Point.

Not surprisingly, in islands with so many animals, the government

---

20   There are some thirty types of kelp, a large brown seaweed.
21   A Corridale features prominently on the Falklands coat-of-arms.

also employed a Chief Veterinary Officer, who was based in Stanley, but travelled all over plying his trade. His many responsibilities included: health inspections; blood testing of rams for brucellosis; oversight of dog dosing to eliminate hydatid cyst; and treatment of damage to animals of all kinds.

Wildlife

Lafonia had an abundance of birdlife, but only four species were relevant to this story. The turkey vulture (*Cathartes aura falklandica*) is unique to the Falklands. Large birds, with an adult wingspan of up to 28 inches (70cm), they are carrion feeders, soaring high above the ground in search of virtually any type of carcass that they can discern, particularly dead or dying sheep or cows, but humans, too, if given the opportunity.

The crested caracara (*Polyborus plancus plancus*) has a wingspan of 47–52in (120–132cm) and, like the turkey vulture, is primarily a carrion feeder, seeking out the carcasses of livestock and birds. It is known to the Falkland Islanders as 'Johnny Rook'.

Southern giant petrel (*Macronectes giganteus),* also known as 'the stinker', is, as its name implies, a large bird with a wingspan of 6ft – 6ft 9in (185–205cm). A voracious predator, it can operate over land and is known to eat carrion.

Natural mortality amongst the many tens of thousands of sheep that roam all over the Falklands provides an abundant supply of food for these birds. Expected sheep losses are about 10% per year, which for a population of some 600,000, means a lot of carcasses. The significance in the Addis mystery is that a circling vulture, caracara or giant petrel would have been a certain sign of a dying or dead body, whether animal, or, in this case, human, but none was ever seen.

Also deserving mention due its large numbers is the upland goose (correctly termed *leucoptera* or greater Magellan goose), which is only found in the Falklands. They are herbivores with males weighing between 8 and 10lb (4–5kg) and females 6–8lb (3–4kg). One of their most remarkable characteristics is their total disregard for humans, who can approach to within touching distance without causing them to flee.

Telecommunications

With Settlements spread out in penny packets across a vast area, telecommunications were vital for emergency and medical purposes, as well as for social cohesion, and at the higher level were the responsibility of the Falkland Islands government.

In 1980, each Settlement had a number of landline telephone terminals; for example, North Arm had four, one each in the houses of the manager, the foreman, the head shepherd and the galley/cookhouse. Most 'outside houses' were linked to the Settlement telephone system, but some were not, such as Danson Harbour House, which was without telecommunications of any kind.

There were also overland telephone line routes on the two major islands – East and West Falklands – linking the Settlements. These were all Single-Wire Earth-Return (SWER) systems using a single connecting wire, with the second terminal in each telephone set connected to a metal earth spike, which was driven firmly into the ground. These single wires were normally mounted on poles some 8–10 feet (2–3m) high and originally used copper wire, although this was steadily replaced in the Falklands by single-strand wire as used in their sheep fences, which was both practical and economical, but did little to contribute to the speech quality. Further, breakages in the overhead wire were usually repaired by a section of new fence wire, which was simply twist-jointed to the original wires, resulting in poor electrical connections, detracting yet further from the quality of speech.

Such SWER links were originally used in the trenches in World War One, but were discontinued when it was discovered that the enemy could easily listen in to what was being said. In the pre-1982 Falklands, the enemy was not a problem, but neighbours could (and most certainly did!) easily listen in and there was little real privacy.

There was a government telephone exchange building in Stanley, completed in 1957, which housed a four-position manually operated switchboard, providing a twenty-four-hour service. Landline telephone systems linked the East Falkland Settlements into Stanley exchange, while on West Falkland, the lines converged on Fox Bay, which had radio telegraph (i.e., teleprinter) and radiotelephone (voice) links to Stanley.

By 1980, all Settlements also had 4.5m[22] radiotelephone links to Stanley, the equipment being provided and maintained by the government and installed in the managers' houses.[23] There was also a set for the Royal Marines in their barracks at Moody Brook. The control station was located in an office adjacent to the fire station in Stanley. This was a major improvement on the telephone system, but was still liable to static (i.e., atmospheric) interference, while faults at outstations required a wait until a technician arrived from Stanley, who usually simply swapped the faulty set for a working one he had brought with him.

Almost all families had small transceivers on the 2m[24] amateur (ham) band, and many had two sets, one in the home and the other a 'mobile' in their Land Rover. Known to the Falklanders as '*diddle-dee radios*', these operated in the VHF band and were supposedly line of sight, although a lot depended on the siting and design of the antenna and some users were able to obtain remarkable ranges.

The Falkland Islands Broadcasting Service (FIBS) was a government-owned system based in Stanley, providing local news and entertainment, usually only in the evenings. Located in John Street, it had a 5kW AM (amplitude modulated) transmitter, installed in 1954 and was avidly listened to throughout the islands.[25] During times when FIBS was not broadcasting, most islanders tuned their domestic radios to BBC World Service.

The government-owned ship, MV *Forrest*, had a mandatory maritime Marconi set. Operating around the islands, the ship was usually also able to communicate with a station in the Customs shed, but the ship was frequently out of range or screened. There was also a daily schedule (0800–0830) to the Royal Marine-manned 4.5m set at Moody Brook.

The Royal Marines brought their normal short-range British Army infantry radios with them, but these could only be used within NP8901 itself.[26] Thus, when away from Moody Brook and needing to communicate with base, the

---

22   4.5m = 66.6 megahertz (MHz).

23   For the technically minded, the set was the AEL 3000 (AEL = Acro Electronics Ltd), a single sideband set, covering 2–16MHz in four crystal-controlled channels, selected by a rotary switch on the front of the box.

24   144–148Megaherz.

25   In 2005, ownership was transferred to an 'arms-length' trust and the name changed to Falkland Islands Radio Service (FIRS).

26   Typically, these were Radio Sets A40 and A41, which operated on exclusive military frequencies in the VHF band.

Marines had to use whatever civilian means were nearest and operating.

The link to the outside world was provided by a Cable & Wireless radio telegraphy station at Stanley, with daily schedules to Portishead in England, to Buenos Aires and to any passing ships.

Electrical Supply

There was a government-operated 'mains' electrical supply within Stanley, where a 1,280kW diesel generator provided 230 volts AC on a twenty-four-hour basis. In the Settlements, the situation was different, usually a generator with a maximum output of 12kW providing 230 or 110 volts, mostly AC, although some still used the antiquated DC system. A significant feature of these Settlement systems was that they operated strictly within hours prescribed by the manager, typically closing down at 2200, 2300, or 2330, but with extensions for special occasions. Many outside shepherds' houses had a lighting system, mostly with batteries charged by wind-driven generators, although some, such as Danson Harbour House, had small 1.5kW diesel generators.

Currency

The Falkland Islands government issued currency whose value was pegged to the pound sterling. British currency was equally acceptable. One curious feature, which applied in most Settlements, was that actual money was rarely handled. The Settlement store, which was the sole source of supplies, ran individual accounts, which were credited with each person's weekly wage and, when the individual bought goods from the store or from the bar in the Social Centre, the account was duly debited. The only time an individual Settler drew actual currency was to visit Stanley.

Military Activity

The Falkland Islands Volunteer Corps was formed in 1892 from Settlers and was mobilised from 1914 to 1919 to man strongpoints around the islands. Renamed the Falkland Islands Defence Force (FIDF) in 1920, it was again mobilised in 1939, although once the German pocket battleship *Graf Spee* had been disposed of in December 1939, there was no serious German threat. However, the situation changed dramatically on 7 December 1941 when the Japanese attacks on Pearl Harbor and Malaya gave rise to a perceived threat of Japanese penetration into the South Atlantic. So, a British garrison was hastily despatched, consisting of some 1,700 officers and men of 11th Battalion West Yorkshire Regiment and supporting services. This force remained in the islands from early 1942 to 1945, with its base camp and HQ just outside Stanley.

Strength of the FIDF varied but was usually about 100–150,[27] mostly from Stanley, but some were in outlying Settlements and unable to contribute to a significant mobilisation. They were equipped with rifles, light machine guns, and mortars and, in military terms, were equivalent to a small, infantry company. As would be shown in 1982, the FIDF could not cover more than one invasion landing site and its main purpose was in reassuring the Falklanders that they were doing something to contribute to the defence of their islands. They also provided a very smart guard-of-honour, adding to the dignity of events in Stanley.

Following the departure of the West Yorkshires, defence reverted to the FIDF until 1966 when an Argentine airliner landed on Stanley racecourse and, although the brief 'occupation' was quickly resolved, the British government deemed it necessary to station a small permanent garrison of Royal Marines on the islands. Designated Naval Party 8901, this is described in Chapter Three.

The Governor was *ex officio* Commander-in-Chief of all military and naval forces defending the Falkland Islands.

Weapons

There was no question of a firearm being used in the Addis disappearance, but the subject is mentioned here for completeness. It was a legal requirement that all civilian-owned firearms had to be licenced by the police, and many people, particularly those in the Camp, had shotguns for use in hunting

---

27   On the Argentine invasion in 1982, the FIDF comprised some 130 men of whom thirty-two responded to the mobilisation order.

game. In addition, a few men were allowed to carry handguns, and it is known that Tony Blake, the manager at North Arm, possessed a sizeable armoury, including 0.22in and 0.410in revolvers. The Marines did, of course, carry weapons, which were carefully stored in an armoury at Moody Brook, while aboard *Forrest* the weapons cabinet was in Capt. Sollis's cabin and ammunition was stored separately in the Chief Engineer's cabin,[28] both being secure.

Virtually all men in Camp carried a 'shepherd's knife'. These were of various makes but the general pattern was a single, highly sharpened steel blade. Some had a 4–5in (10–13cm) long blade, which folded into a steel housing some 5–7in (13–17cm) long, which was usually cased in decorated wood or bone, and carried in a pocket. Others had fixed longer blades, which were carried in a leather or canvas sheath slung from the belt, similar to a soldier's bayonet frog. These knives had a wide variety of uses at work, ranging from cutting through wool to release a sheep from wire, through skinning dead lambs to clothing a live lamb to enable adoption, to killing an injured or ailing sheep by cutting its throat, but there were many other uses.

Medical

Medical treatment for Falkland Islanders was free at the point of delivery, being financed by fishing licences and income tax. The only hospital was the King Edward VII Memorial Hospital in Stanley. It was equipped with twenty-seven beds and had a staff of one matron, three nursing sisters and six nurses, together with domestic staff and a clerk. There were three doctors, all expatriates on limited length tours. The hospital treated medical, surgical, obstetric and geriatric cases, but serious cases had to be transferred by air or sea to the highly regarded *Hospital Británico* (British Hospital) in Montevideo, Uruguay. There was no facility in the islands for post-mortems.

At the primary level, there was a Settlement medical chest, often maintained by the manager's wife, and all Settlements in East and West Falkland could communicate with a doctor by radio or landline telephone, while inhabited islands were supplied with radiotelephones. The Government Air Service (FIGAS) could either take doctors to patients or

---

28   Chief Engineer was 'Nutt' Goodwin.

patients to Stanley, while if travelling overland, doctors normally used a Land Rover, although some still occasionally rode on horseback. There were four doctors, all on secondment from the UK. Until the mid-seventies, there were two in Stanley, with one each in Darwin and Fox Bay, but the latter two were then centralised in the capital.

There was a dentist at Stanley Hospital, also seconded from the UK, with a fully equipped surgery and laboratory, who also undertook Camp tours, endeavouring to visit each Settlement in the course of the year.

'Wild West'

Outsiders sometimes liken the pre-1982 Falkland Islands to the United States' Wild West. It is true that, Stanley apart, Falklanders lived in small, widely separated Settlements, but these were relatively peaceful and law-abiding by comparison with the United States. In the Falklands, the manager combined the roles filled by the sheriff and the mayor in the USA, although he was appointed by the company owning the Settlement, not elected by the inhabitants. There was also a properly constituted, if not particularly efficient or well-manned police force in Stanley.

There were no pre-existing indigenous Falklanders to challenge ownership of the land and, finally, although there was the occasional crime, there was nothing like the gun culture that was so characteristic of the frontier zones of the nineteenth century United States. So, there was no justification for using the phrase 'Wild West' in the context of the Falklands and it will not be used again in this book.

CHAPTER THREE

Naval Party 8901

A Naval Party is a small unit formed by the Royal Navy or Royal Marines overseas for the conduct of a specific shore-based task. For example, in 2025, the current Naval Party 1022 (NP1022) is the permanent Royal Navy unit at the British Defence Singapore Support facility. In the Falklands case, the story started on 8 September 1964 when an Argentine civilian pilot landed his Cessna 185 single-engined light aircraft on the Stanley racecourse, just a short distance outside Stanley, the Falklands' capital. To deter a repeat, a small group of Royal Marines was despatched to the Falkland Islands aboard the Ice Patrol Ship, HMS *Protector*.[29] Designated Naval Party 8901 (NP8901), their task was to serve as a 'tripwire' against Argentine invasion, to provide enhanced training to the FIDF and to reassure the Falkland Islanders that the UK government took their defence seriously.

The first garrison comprised one officer and five Marines, who were relieved by six more in March 1965 and those by another six in March 1966. The situation changed on 28 September 1966 when a hijacked *Aerolineas Argentinas* Douglas DC-4 airliner was forced to land at Stanley, also on the racecourse. That situation was resolved but led to NP8901 being enhanced to some forty-to-fifty men, commanded by a Major. This officer was under military command of the Governor, in the latter's capacity as Commander-in-Chief, but administratively he reported to Headquarters Training and Reserve Forces Royal Marines (HQTRF) located in Portsmouth, UK.

The actual strength and composition of NP8901 differed marginally from year-to-year, while the internal organisation depended upon the officer commanding, but was typically: one officer (Major); second-in-command

---

29 HMS *Protector* (A146), a former net-layer, served as the Royal Navy's Antarctic patrol vessel from 1955 to 1968.

(Captain/Lieutenant);[30] Quartermaster-Sergeant; Platoon Weapons Sergeant; and Signals Sergeant. The remainder of the unit was split into sections, each of six-to-eight Marines led by a non-commissioned officer (Corporal or Lance-Corporal).

In 1980, NP8901 comprised forty-three Marines,[31] all volunteers, who had flown by BOAC to Montevideo in Uruguay and then sailed aboard HMS *Endurance* to Stanley.[32] They assumed responsibility on 1 April 1980 under the command of Major CR Gilding, Royal Marines (RM), with Captain P Whitcomb, RM, as his second-in-command, and were due to be relieved on 31 March 1981.

The unit was based at Moody Brook at the head of Falkland Harbour and some three miles (5km) outside Stanley. Some of these buildings had originally been constructed for the government wireless station in 1916, but they had been lying empty for some time. The main buildings comprised an accommodation block, a combined Officers' and Sergeants' Mess, a galley (combined cookhouse and mess hall), a signal office and miscellaneous stores. When the barracks was inspected by Governor Hunt shortly after his arrival in January 1980, he "*… was shocked at the state of the buildings*," most of which had been condemned many years previously.[33] There was also hard-standing for the few vehicles and a garage for maintenance.[34]

The Ministry of Defence had long agreed in principle to build a new barracks, but as so often happens where troop accommodation is concerned, the Ministry had ruled that financial constraints meant repeated postponements. However, in 1980, there was a step forward when a Warrant Officer Class Two (WO2) of the Royal Engineers – Clerk of Works – was sent South and attached to NP8901 while he designed a new barracks for the Royal Marines.

In broad terms, the tasks of NP8901 were to:
- Deter illegal landings by Argentine troops/Marines.
- Patrol the outer islands, including a small detachment on South Georgia.
- Foster good relations with the Falkland Islanders.

---

30 The 2IC post may have been introduced later; certainly in post from 1979–80.
31 Figure from Falkland Islands Census 1980, p.2.
32 HMS *Endurance* (A171) relieved HMS *Protector* in 1967 and served until 1991.
33 Hunt, p.27.
34 Some married senior NCOs with Falklands' wives were allowed to 'live out' in Stanley.

- Give military training to the FIDF, both in Stanley and in the Settlements.
- Perform non-military tasks as requested by or agreed with the Governor.

The Marines did their best to fit into the local community, taking part in many ceremonial and social activities, which included being presented with the freedom of Stanley in 1976. They also proved convenient for a number of miscellaneous tasks ranging from an officer to carry the diplomatic pouch to and from Montevideo, to manning the fire unit at the airport. Less glamorous tasks included backing up the police by providing stand-in warders at the civil jail and, on one occasion, escorting a civil prisoner to Montevideo.

Organisation of duties within NP8901 varied between detachments but typically involved a weekly cycle, which included activities ranging from patrols and weapon training for the FIDF to administrative duties within the barracks. Medical cover was provided by a Royal Marines first-aider, but after that there were GPs at Stanley civil hospital. Domestic tasks were also shared out. Alan Addis, for example, was in charge of captive birds – geese, ducks and chickens – which were a source of meat (generally tough and stringy), and of eggs, which seem to have been few and far between, possibly, as he himself admitted, due to forgetting to feed the hens.[35]

One notable contribution came in 1974 when a four-man concert party of Marines from that year's NP8901 toured nine Settlements, transported by MV *Forrest*. Their one-night shows came at a time when there was no television, and few Settlements even had cinema projectors, so that the Marines' efforts were greatly appreciated.[36]

The Marines' contribution to Falklands' life was mostly positive, but there was a particular point of friction. The number of women of marriageable age among the Falklands' population was not great and the young commandoes tended to attract a disproportionate number of them. The Marines were young, fit and well-paid by Falkland standards and seemed very worldly-wise compared to the Falklander men, few of whom had ever left the islands. It is estimated that, prior to the war of 1982, no less than seventy-five Falkland girls married sailors and Marines of NP8901 and then departed to the UK with their husbands, rarely to return, apart from a few whose husbands

---

35 Letter to his mother.
36 Information from Philip Davis, a member of the group.

MV *Forrest*

volunteered to return to NP8901 as 'married accompanied' and to 'live out' in Stanley.

Secondly, there were a few examples of poor discipline, particularly where alcohol was concerned. Unfortunately, this had resulted in some unpleasant incidents aboard MV *Forrest* which led Major Gilding, the commander in 1980/81, to issue a very firm order, which left no member of his detachment unaware of the strength of his feelings on the subject or of his reaction to any misbehaviour – see Annex E.

Movement

Movement among the islands and between Settlements was not easy. NP8901 had a few vehicles, which provided transport between Moody Brook and Stanley, but for movement further afield, they had no choice but to rely on the government's ships and aircraft. The Marines had a standing contract to use MV *Forrest*, which was skippered by Captain Jack Sollis, MBE, BEM, then aged sixty-five. The ship could carry a small number of passengers. In 1980, FIGAS operated two float-equipped de Havilland Canada Beaver 'bush' transport aircraft and the first Britten-Norman Islander twin-engined landplane was being brought into service.

Telecommunications

NP8901 normally included a signals Sergeant who was in charge of telecommunications. When Marines were deployed from Moody Brook aboard MV *Forrest*, there was a daily schedule (0800–0830) on the ship's 4m net. The Royal Marines also brought their short-range Army infantry radios with them, which in 1980 were Radio Sets, A40 and A41, but these operated on military frequencies that could only be used between these particular sets. This meant that, when away from Moody Brook, the Marines had to use whatever civilian means were nearest and operating. Communications from NP8901 back to the UK were via the Cable & Wireless radio telegraphy station at Stanley.

Training FIDF

Moving now to the events of August 1980, the plan was for the Marines to provide on-the-spot training in weapons, fieldcraft and minor tactics for local members of the FIDF. This was to be done at two Settlements, North Arm and Fitzroy, where each session would comprise two days in which the visiting teams would reconnoitre the ground and prepare their training programme, followed by five days with the FIDF. This was to be conducted by two separate three-man Marine teams, which, for convenience **in this narrative only,** are designated:

- **TEAM A.** Training at North Arm Settlement 4–7 August 1980.
- **TEAM B.** Training at Fitzroy Settlement 11–15 August 1980.

Since the Falklanders were not allowed to retain their weapons on-site, Team A took the weapons (rifles, light machineguns and ammunition) with them on 1 August and these were to be handed over to Team B on board MV *Forrest* on 8 August.

Team A

This consisted of three Royal Marines – Sergeant Fred Howden and Marines Andy Corrie and Geordie Gill – who trained FIDF volunteers at North Arm

Moody Brook (Courtesy Philip Davis)

from 4–7 August 1980. Howden plus one Marine were accommodated in the Big House (i.e., the manager's house), the third with another family. They arrived at North Arm aboard MV *Forrest* on 1 August and their training programme started on 4 August, culminating in an all-day exercise on Thursday 7 August, which ended at about 2000. All three Marines then joined a party at the Social Club, which was in their honour to thank them for the training.

These three men left the party at an unknown time and, as far as is known, spent the night, as throughout their visit, with North Arm families. They boarded MV *Forrest* in the early morning of Friday 8 August and handed over the weapons and other equipment to Team B. The ship sailed at ≈0710 for the return to Stanley, intending to call at Fitzroy en route to drop off Team B.

Team B

This team was also three strong: Corporal Roger Davis, with Marines Alan Addis and Chris Johnson. Their task was to carry out one week's training at Fitzroy Settlement, arriving on the afternoon of 8 August, conducting reconnaissances and detailed planning on 9–10 August, and starting the training programme on Monday 11 August.

On 7 August, MV *Forrest* duly sailed from Stanley, the plan being that the ship, carrying Team B, would go directly to North Arm, spend the night alongside the jetty there, embark Team A the following morning, sail to Fitzroy, drop off Team B and then return with Team A to Stanley. The people of North Arm had arranged to hold a party to thank Team A for the training and all three members of Team B were also invited, rather than spend a dull night aboard *Forrest*. The three Team B Marines, none of whom had visited North Arm before, duly attended the party at the Social Club, walking there in darkness and arriving at about 2000. Sunset had been at 1638, but the houses in the Settlement would have had some lights on and the Social Club was one of the first buildings on their route and easy to pick out, so the walk would not have been difficult.

The Social Club was a single, open-plan room, with bar and stockroom, stage, tables and chairs. Music at the popular Saturday dances was often provided by a local group, consisting of a guitar and an accordion, with the manager (Blake) thumping the floor with a 'lagerphone', which consisted of a broomstick sprouting arms of varying length festooned with metal bottle tops.[37] Music was normally country and western, while dances ranged from the Circassian Circle to old-fashioned waltzes.

Two members of Team B (Corporal Davis and Marine Johnson) left the party at about 2300, returned to *Forrest* and stayed aboard overnight. They reported later that they had asked Addis to leave with them, but he had declined.

The three members of Team A boarded *Forrest* in the morning of 8 August and two locals arrived at the jetty in time to cast-off at the planned time of 0630. Captain Sollis was known to be a stickler for timing, but on this occasion and for unknown reason, *Forrest* did not sail until about 0710. The ship followed the zigzag around the kelp beds, then South into the open sea before heading East for Fitzroy.

Addis is Missing

Soon after the ship sailed, Marines Corrie and Gill from Team A took their kit to the sleeping accommodation in the hold, where they noticed that Alan Addis's bunk had not been slept in. Their first reaction was to search the ship for their missing comrade and, only when they could not find him, did they tell Sergeant Howden, who then told Captain Sollis. It is not clear exactly when this took place; one account says ten minutes, another thirty minutes after sailing, but it is certain that *Forrest* was well clear of the entrance to North Arm and in the open waters of the Bay of Harbours. Captain Sollis

---

37   This sophisticated musical instrument was invented in Australia.

was the master and responsible for his ship, and he decided, presumably after discussion with Sergeant Howden, that he would not return to North Arm, but continue the voyage, leaving Addis to find his own way from North Arm to Fitzroy.

COMMENTS

It is sometimes questioned as to why the voyage was planned in this way, i.e., could *Forrest* not have dropped off Team B at Fitzroy on Thursday 7 August? The reason is quite simple. The weapons for the FIDF were carried to North Arm by Team A and had to be signed over to Team B, which meant that they had to meet. If Team B had disembarked at Fitzroy on 7th, *Forrest* would still have had to bring the weapons there on its way back to Stanley. However, such alternative possibilities are not relevant, since what actually happened is as described above.

It is not clear why the senior NCO (Sergeant Howden) did not hold a headcount prior to sailing from North Arm. After all, there were only six to be counted – not a large number for a roll call – and it was only a small ship. It seems a careless oversight, but these things do happen. Once it was realised that Addis was missing, none of those aboard suspected foul play; indeed, there was no reason to, as they were among friends. The Marines' guess at this stage was that Addis had found a bed for the night, possibly with a woman, and had not got up in time to board MV *Forrest*. As the Royal Marine Board of Inquiry later remarked, he would not have been the first sailor or Marine to miss his ship.

The decision to leave Addis to find his own way to Fitzroy is hard to understand. It was approximately 30 miles (48km) from North Arm to Goose Green by track and a further 40 miles (64km) to Fitzroy. Perhaps two days walking alone, in freezing weather, along well-marked vehicle tracks was considered no real test for a young, fit, healthy Royal Marine, although he was dressed in civilian clothes, his military gear all being aboard MV *Forrest*. He might even have been given a lift, although traffic was light. Perhaps it was intended to teach him a lesson – not to be absent from parade? A more practical solution would have been to instruct him to remain at North Arm until the next visit by MV *Forrest* or the FIGAS aircraft.

CHAPTER FOUR

North Arm Settlement in 1980

The location of these events in 1980 was North Arm Settlement, an isolated hamlet on the southern coast of Lafonia, where the inhabitants earned a living based almost entirely on sheep ranching and the export of wool, together with a small trade in mutton, beef and hides. As the name implies, the Settlement was situated on the northernmost arm of the Bay of Harbours, on an inlet known locally as 'the Creek'.

The Settlement itself consisted of some thirty buildings, which included accommodation for both married and single staff, various stores and barns, shop, post office, school, generator shed, blacksmith's smithy, carpenter's workshop, pigsty and stables. There was also an ancient stone shed with a Norman-style arched entrance but no windows, whose original purpose has been lost in the mists of time but may have been religious.[38] An important building was the Social Club, which was used for socialising and the Saturday-night parties. The shearing shed, by far the largest building in the Settlement, was located away from the Settlement at the landward end of the jetty, whose doors were always open, revealing a deep, cavernous and unlit interior. Near the shearing shed was the killing shed, where sheep and cattle were slaughtered for human consumption.[39] There was also a cemetery.

The majority of buildings were for married workers. These buildings had the usual facilities, except that the fuel used for heating and cooking was peat. All houses also had a small garden for vegetables, while geese, ducks and chickens were bred for their eggs and meat. The only domestic

---

38 Spruce, op. cit., p.197.
39 The killing shed in 1980 was demolished in the period 1983–85 and replaced by a refurbished Bunkhouse No 4. Information from Robin Goodwin.

pets were cats. There were many dogs, but these were exclusively kept for working the sheep and, by Falkland Islands law, had to be kept in fenced-off kennels due to the risk of hydatid disease; there was no question of a dog being kept as a pet in a Settlement. There was a conspicuously larger house for the manager, set some distance to the North of the others, which had twenty-four rooms and was known, as in all Falkland Islands Settlements, as the 'Big House'.

Apart from the family houses, there were four bunkhouses, each with four bedrooms, a common room, bathroom, toilet and a hallway. Bunkhouses Nos 1 and 2 were for unmarried or unaccompanied navvies who worked and lived in the Settlement. Bunkhouse No 3 was for outside shepherds to use during their routine visits, such as restocking supplies, shearing, etc. Bunkhouse No 4 was for casual workers on short-term engagements. These bunkhouses had a Rayburn stove to provide main heating and hot water, which was fuelled by peat and in permanent operation. Each occupant would be 'tallyman' for a week, when his job would be to keep the living area clean and tidy, fill the peat buckets and keep the furnace alive and stoked, and dispose of the ash.

The jetty was some 400 yards (370m) South of the Settlement. It was ≈100 yards (90m) long with two steel rails running along its length for trolleys to transfer bales of wool from the shearing shed to the ship. There were electric lights at either end of the jetty.

There was deep water close to the jetty, and it was used by vessels up to the size of MV *Forrest*. But, because of the shape of the channel and the kelp reefs around the entrance to the Creek, ships had to follow a tricky 'S-shaped' course when entering and leaving, and care was required. A direct approach was impossible, and the reef was avoided by sticking close to the starboard side of the channel until the jetty could be clearly seen. While interfering with ships, the kelp had the benefit of preventing any large waves coming into the Creek and provided an almost wave-free stretch of water, an ideal landing/take-off area for the FIGAS Beaver floatplanes.

North Arm estate was huge, roughly 44 miles (70km) from East to West and 37 miles (60km) from South to North, a total of over 270,000 acres (109,300 hectares). The primary activity centred on the ≈68,000 wool-bearing sheep, providing them with good pasture, shearing them and exporting the wool to world markets.[40] There were also: 677 cattle; 114 dogs; 267 horses; two pigs; and 269 hens.[41]

Outside the Settlement, the land consisted of a vast area of flat, featureless and bleak heath interspersed with peat bogs, tussac grass and a few gorse patches. No trees grew and while there were a few rocky outcrops, these were neither as many nor as high as elsewhere in East and West Falklands; there was only one feature deserving the name of a hill. There were many short rivers and numerous areas of standing water labelled, with typical Falklander understatement, as 'ponds' – none seemed sufficiently large to be labelled a lake.[42]

The Manager

In the pre-1982 Falklands, the Settlement manager occupied an almost medieval – indeed, baronial – control over his people and their lives. He (and it was always a man) was appointed by the landowner, which, in the case of North Arm, was the Falkland Islands Company. There was neither a policeman nor an elected mayor in the Settlement, the manager filling all those functions, although the legal holders of similar offices were available, but they were in Stanley, which was a long way away. The only official government employee normally resident in the Settlement was the schoolmaster.

In addition to organising and running the agricultural activities, the manager also ran the daily lives of those in the Settlement, which meant that he not only knew everything that went on, but also that no decision of any importance could be made without him being involved. As Blake himself described it to a visitor: "*People hold you up as a paternal figure and come to you with every problem ... from filling in their taxes to marrying them, to sending emergency medical messages over the radio to Stanley.*"[43]

---

40   Actual sheep population in 1979 was: rams – 640; ewes – 30,975; wethers – 22,981; hoggets – 13,729; Total 68,325.

41   Farming statistics, Falklands Government Dept of Agriculture.

42   The largest on Lafonia was 'Laguna Pond' (51º 58'S, 59º23'W), which measured some 2,200 x 270yd (2,000 x 250m).

43   'A Lonely but Free Life at the Southern Edge of the World' by Fred Strebeigh http://www.strebeigh. com/falkland-islands-smithsonian-1981.html

The manager in North Arm in 1980 was Anthony Thomas (Tony) Blake, usually known as 'ATB'.[44] He was born in Kesteven, England in April 1940, but his family emigrated to New Zealand in 1953, so that he matured and regarded himself as a New Zealander. He graduated from Lincoln College in 1961.[45] After early farming experience, he became a lecturer at the Telford Farm Training Institute at Otanomomo in the South Island. While there, he became friends with Brook Hardcastle, who had worked in the Falklands from 1951 to 1962 and then went to New Zealand before returning to the Falklands in 1971.[46] Hardcastle persuaded Blake of the attractions of the Falklands and, in 1972, Blake tended a large shipment of sheep from New Zealand when, prompted by Hardcastle, he applied for and was granted first the post of assistant manager at Goose Green, and after a few years was moved to North Arm, this time as general manager. This was one of the largest of the Falkland Island Company's farms and he remained there until October 1983.

Blake's wife was Lyndsay (née Rae), always known as Lyn. Also a New Zealander, she was a trained children's nanny. She was widely known to be devoted to her husband and family of two children, Heidi and Thomas Patrick (Tom).

Although this occurred after the Addis disappearance, a later event throws interesting light on Blake's character. On receiving news of the Argentine invasion in 1982, Blake went round to every house demanding, presumably on his own authority, that the owners hand in all radios and firearms, although not all did so. Argentine officers paid a brief early visit but assessed the Settlement as offering no threat and left the people relatively undisturbed. However, this was to change on 21 May 1982 when Blake and David Clarke chanced upon Lieutenant Alberto Phillippe, an Argentine Navy pilot, who had been flying a Douglas A-4Q Skyhawk against HMS Ardent in Grantham Sound. His aircraft was hit and damaged by a Sidewinder missile from a Royal Navy Sea Harrier and, unable to return to the mainland, he ejected over the Thyssen Islands. He landed in the sea and swam ashore to take shelter in a nearby unoccupied 'outside house' known as the Congo

---

44 By coincidence there was another manager at this time, named Tim Blake, at Hill Cove. The two were unrelated and Tim Blake does not feature in the Addis story in any way.

45 From 1961 to 1990, New Zealand's Lincoln College was part of the University of Canterbury, but achieved autonomy in 1990 under its present title of Lincoln University.

46 Hardcastle (1930–2003) was manager at Darwin from 1971 to 1991.

House.[47] The following day, Tony Blake and several farm shepherds were out with tractors and sledges working sheep in the area, when Phillippe, thinking they were Argentine troops, attracted their attention, only to find himself in British hands. He was taken back to North Arm and accommodated in the Big House. Against the wishes of some of his people, Tony Blake informed the Argentine HQ at Goose Green, who sent a helicopter to collect him, and he was then flown to Stanley and CASEVACed to Argentina. He and Tony Blake remained friends, maintaining contact by amateur-band radio (Tony was call-sign VP801) and visiting each other's homes on several occasions after the war.[48]

Blake was a member of the legislature, one of those representing the Camp constituency, and a member of the Legislative Council from 1980 to 1984, less the seventy-four days of the 1982 Argentine invasion. He remained at North Arm until October 1983 when he moved on, being replaced by Eric Goss, previously manager at Goose Green. In the post-war redistribution of land, Blake purchased Little Chartres in 1984, which he and Lyn ran until she died in 2003. He then sold up and moved to Stanley. He remarried, this time to a Paraguayan woman, Marella, and on occasions acted as guide for Spanish-speaking visitors, when his command of their language was invaluable. He also established a fishing company, RBC Ltd, in partnership with a Spanish company, remaining as director until his death on 1 October 2019, when his son, Tom, took over.

Outside Houses

There were a number of 'outside houses' located ten or more miles (16km+) from the Settlement, which provided accommodation for individual shepherds and sometimes their families. These were properly built and with a modicum of facilities, such as heating, lighting, drinking water, furniture, toilets, etc. Some were occupied on a semi-permanent basis, others only for the annual 'gather' or for visitors, if required. Some were on the landline telephone system, others were not. Danson Harbour House was 12 miles

---

47   Congo House was an unoccupied 'outside house' located some 11 miles (18km) at 310⁰ from North Arm. The derivation of the name is not known.

48   The story is told in *Penguin News* 21 November 2003, p.9.

(19km) from North Arm and stood entirely on its own. The Bethune family lived there in the 1890s where Mrs Bethune gave birth to three children between 1892 and 1897; she must have been a hardy and brave woman.[49]

Serial	Outlying House	Occupied August 1980	Occupant	Landline telephone
1.	Cattle Point	No		No
2.	Congo	No		No
3.	Danson Harbour	Yes	Jimmy Biggs Hector Tellez	No
4.	Fanny Cove	Yes	José Ruiz	No
5.	Lion Creek	No		No
6.	Mapa	No		Yes
7.	Moffat Harbour	No		No
8.	North West Arm	Yes	Sydney Smith Joan Browning	Yes
9.	Sound	No		Yes
10.	Wreck House	Yes	Jimmy Miller plus wife	Yes

Table 4. North Arm – 'Outside Houses' 1980

People

	Adults at NA	Children at NA	FIC Employ-ees	Outside House; present in NA	Possibly Visiting	Royal Marines	MV Forrest; crew	TO-TALS	Outside House; NOT present in NA
Men	21		1	1	2	6	6	37	2
Women	19		1					20	
Chilean	2							2	1
Children		14						14	
TOTALS	42	14	2	1	2	6	6	73	3

Table 5. North Arm – Estimated Population Night 8 August 1980

---

49 Spruce, op. cit., p.194.

There were an estimated sixty Settlement people at North Arm on the night of 8 August 1980, plus the six Royal Marines training team and six crew of MV *Forrest*. Not all can now be positively identified but known staff were the manager Tony Blake and his wife Lyn, plus the foreman Alec Jaffray and his wife Elliot.[50] The remainder were as listed in the table above, although not all would have attended the party. In particular, by no means all of the children would have attended – nor, indeed, have been allowed to attend.

As is normal in such small and isolated communities, gossip was prevalent, both within and between Settlements. This was partly due to the telephone system and later the radios, none of which possessed any form of privacy, so that whatever was spoken into a microphone could be heard by anyone bothering to listen. However, some information did remain within the Settlement, because, as with isolated rural communities the world over, the inhabitants of North Arm closed ranks when faced by 'outsiders', whether the latter were from the elsewhere in the islands or (even worse) from abroad.

Entertainment

Entertainment was basic, with great reliance on the radio provided by BBC World Service and the domestic Falkland Islands Broadcasting Service (FIBS); there was no TV. There were very occasional visiting entertainers, such as the Royal Marines group in 1974, but otherwise it was all homemade. Like other Settlements, North Arm had a 16mm projector, with films supplied by the central library in Stanley and brought in by FIGAS Beaver or MV *Forrest*; Westerns were by far the most popular. There were regular drinking evenings on a Friday night and any excuse could be found for other celebrations, such as the Queen's birthday, Battle Day,[51] Commonwealth Day, sports days and, as described here, visits by the Marine training teams. Much alcohol was consumed and there were regular performances by the Settlement's own group, which included the manager on his lagerphone. As, indeed, happened on the night of 7 August 1980.

---

50 Their daughters, Valerie and Joan, were maids at Government House in Stanley.

51 This commemorated the Battle of the Falklands on 8 December 1914.

A curious incident is described in Annex D. It seems to show that Titch Jaffray was a somewhat aggressive character, always spoiling for a fight, but frequently so much the worse for drink that he was unable to go through with it. Why he should have tried to start a fight with visiting Marine Philip Davis is not at all clear.

Travel

North Arm was in contact with Stanley and the remainder of the Falklands by land, sea and air, albeit with varying degrees of difficulty. There was a land track (it could scarcely be termed a road) from North Arm running North-eastwards by way of either Bodie Creek Suspension Bridge or the Orqueta Track to Darwin/Goose Green. The distance was some 30 miles (48km) and in a Land Rover with a skilled driver would take about three-to-four hours. Within the Settlement, there were a number of Land Rovers, tractors, motorcycles and horses.

As described above, there was a jetty that could accept small vessels such as *Ilen* and MV *Forrest*. The latter vessel could carry cargo and a number of passengers, and, depending on tides and weather, took about twelve hours from Stanley.

The FIGAS Beaver floatplanes took about forty minutes between Stanley and North Arm, landing at the latter on the Creek immediately North of the jetty. Each aircraft could carry a maximum of six passengers (fewer if carrying impedimenta, e.g., diving equipment), and up to 2,100lb (953kg) freight.

There were several dinghies. The pram[52] was considered unstable and seldom used, while the 18ft (5m) dinghy was normally stored near the blacksmith's shop and also seldom used. The 12ft (4m) dinghy was the most frequently used, its main role being to transport people and stores between the jetty and visiting de Havilland Beaver floatplanes, when the aircraft could not dock alongside the jetty. This dinghy was powered by a British Seagull 5h.p. outboard motor, which could be easily dismounted. When not in use,

---

52 Pram dinghies are normally some 8–10ft (2–3m) long, with a flattened rather than pointed bow. They are used for short journeys in harbours, for example, transporting not more than two or three people between moored yachts and the shore.

the oars, rowlocks, rudder and motor were stored in the workshop, which was normally locked to prevent pilfering. The three keys were held by the foreman, carpenter and blacksmith.

CHAPTER FIVE

Alan Addis and His Mother

Sarah Ann Addis (1941–2011) was a remarkable woman who put up a strong and determined fight to discover her son's fate and bring his body back to England. Her parents, Sidney Longthorp (1914–79) and Edna (née Watson; 1917–65), were married in 1939 and lived in Kingston-upon-Hull in Yorkshire.[53] He was a bus cleaner with East Yorkshire Motor Services. They had five children: June (b.1939); Sarah Ann (b.1941); Kathleen (b.1942); Ralph (b.1946); and Jane (b.1954). Sarah Ann was born on 27 November 1941 at Amounderness in Lancashire. It is known that large numbers of children and pregnant women living in areas such as Hull, which were threatened by German bombers in 1939–41, were evacuated to safe areas, including Lancashire, so it is assumed that this is why Sarah Ann was born there.

Sarah Ann appears to have had a normal childhood and schooling in Hull, but in her early twenties moved to Croydon. Her first (and only) child, Alan, was due in early October 1961, but was actually born three months prematurely on 14 July 1961 at the Mayday Hospital in Croydon.[54] The mother's surname was registered as Young (née Longthorp), aged eighteen, so there is no doubt this is her, but no trace can be found of a Sarah Ann Longthorp marrying or subsequently divorcing a man named Alan Joseph Young.[55]

Sarah Ann did marry Keith Addis in Croydon in April 1971, at which time she was aged twenty-nine with a ten-year-old child but, as with Mr

---

53 This ancient town, sited at the confluence of the Hull and Humber Rivers, was originally Kingston-upon-Hull, but today is always known by its shortened title of Hull, as it will be from here.

54 Addis, *Missing on Patrol*, p.15.

55 The birth certificate lists the father as ALAN JOSEPH YOUNG and the family address as Flat 5, 45 Heathfield Road, Croydon.

43

Young, there is no trace of this man in any record, other than this marriage certificate. However, in 1975, Sarah Ann took the unusual step of not only having her son's surname changed to Addis, but also and, even more unusual, having it published in the London Gazette:

> *"Notice is hereby given that by a Deed Poll dated the 15ᵗʰ September 1975 and enrolled in the Supreme Court of Judicature on the 27ᵗʰ October 1975, SARAH ANN ADDIS of 8 Eastern Road, Gillingham, Kent, as mother, abandoned on behalf of Alan Addis of 8 Eastern Road, Gillingham, Kent, being an infant and a citizen of the United Kingdom and Colonies by birth his former surname of Young and assumed in lieu thereof the surname of Addis.— Dated 13ᵗʰ October 1975."* [56]

Now named Alan Addis, the boy lived with his mother throughout his schooldays, originally in Croydon, but they moved to Gillingham in Kent in 1969 and then to Yorkshire in 1976. His first school was Catford Boys Primary, followed by Woodlands Secondary. He held his own at school and was well-liked by both teachers and fellow pupils, although he does not seem to have been academically inclined, devoting his spare time to typical boys' pursuits of that era: trainspotting, canoeing and swimming. He left school at sixteen and, after a brief and happy spell on a local farm near Sproatley,[57] joined the Royal Marines.

Alan enlisted in the Royal Marines in 1978 when he was just seventeen, receiving the number PO37596K. He carried out the normal recruit training, followed by Arctic training in Norway. He got on well with his fellow Marines who addressed him as 'Addy'. He was naturally slim and fit, with dark brown hair, somewhat above average height at 6ft 2in (1.87m) and weighed 168lb (12 stone, or 76.2kg). He was described by a friend as a good-looking boy and popular with women. No particular girlfriend is known, although he carried a photograph of one of his cousins, presumably female, in his wallet.

Alan and his mother were particularly close and, when he was away from home, they exchanged letters on a regular basis, Alan sending at least two a week from the Falklands, which were, in part, about local news, but mostly

---

56   *London Gazette* 4 Nov 1975 Page 13943.
57   Sproatley is a small village in Yorkshire approximately 7 miles (11km) north-east of Hull.

concerning food – or the lack of its variety and quality. In return, Sarah Ann sent him a seemingly endless series of presents, including a birthday cake, a blanket, many boxes and tins of sweets, shampoo, soap, and even, on one memorable occasion, six raw eggs. His last letter to her was dated 5 August, telling his mother that he was due to sail on his 'training package' in two days' time, a letter which, tragically, she received after the news that he had disappeared.

The Armed Forces usually take great care when informing next-of-kin that their loved one has died, but in this case, Sarah Ann was left bewildered by the contradictory information she was given and the multiplicity of sources. The first she knew of his fate was a telephone call in the evening of 8 August 1980 to tell her that her son "had gone missing on patrol." At 0900 the following morning, two police officers arrived to tell her that he had fallen overboard from MV *Forrest* and drowned. On 13th, she received a letter telling her that it must be assumed that he had died.

Several more letters followed, culminating in one from Governor Rex Hunt dated 14 August 1980, in which he told her that: *"We live in hope that the sea will deliver up that which it appears to have taken away."* Yet another letter told her that, *"Alan had either drowned after falling off the jetty or had wandered inland, collapsed and died of exposure in hours."*

About a week later, she was visited by a lieutenant from the Hull Careers Office, whom she told she needed to go to the Falklands herself and was even prepared to pay her own way. The visitor was less than helpful, even telling her that the Ministry of Defence (MoD) could prevent her visit. She then turned to her MP, who referred the matter to the Minister of Defence, who gave permission for the journey in January 1981 and issued a reprimand to the Royal Marines for the way they had handled her case.

She actually went in March 1981, at which time the Marines who had been with Alan were still at Moody Brook.[58] Talking to these Marines, she first heard suggestions that foul play might have been involved and that the Army's Special Investigation Branch (SIB) should have been called in. She spent all her time in Stanley as she was told that the weather at North Arm was too severe for flying. In view of the ruggedness of the Beaver aircraft and the skill and local knowledge of the pilots, this seems an improbable

---

58   According to Supt Lamb, she was accompanied by a "gentleman companion" (Lamb Report para 6).

story, although the name of its originator is not known. However, she was a stranger and in no position to argue.

After she returned home, Sarah Ann started to receive letters from Falkland Islanders, which contained theories about what had happened, some of them quite upsetting. She was also forwarded a copy of a letter from the new Officer Commanding Naval Party 8901 reporting that there was a great deal of gossip among the islanders. Sarah Ann then went to visit the Royal Marines HQ at Portsmouth, and she must have presented her case very forcefully, as that HQ contacted the MoD, following which, Sarah Ann was told that the case would be taken up by the SIB. She was duly visited and interviewed at length by the SIB case officer, a Captain Jim Gallacher, Royal Military Police (RMP), who later returned to debrief her after his visit to the Falklands. She then received a letter from the MoD telling her officially that the SIB investigation had been inconclusive.

Sarah Ann sold the bungalow she had shared with Alan in happier times and opened a motor accessory shop, living in the flat above. At this point, Sarah Ann became very depressed and took an overdose of tablets, but fortunately was found by a policeman, rushed to hospital and saved, although a full mental recovery took some time.

In 1982, she, like the rest of the country, was dismayed by the Argentine invasion, but the more so, in her case, as she had visited the islands and met many of the people there. What she did not learn until later was that the police records of her son's disappearance had been destroyed.

In 1983, she decided on a complete change in her personal life, sold her business, and moved to California, where she had friends, and on 24 August 1983, married David V Malone in San Francisco.[59] As with the other two known men in her life (Young and Addis), she never mentions this man in her book, nor is she known to have used the surname 'Malone', and it is assumed that she divorced him at some time in the 1980s. In 1985, she was diagnosed with cancer but treatment in the United States led to a long period in remission. In 1991, she bought a bungalow in North Lincolnshire, but she continued to split her time between California and England until she moved back home full time, following which, she found employment as a care support worker with the mentally ill.

---

59   California Marriage Index 1960–1985. She used the surname Addis, but it is not known whether Mr Addis had died, or they had divorced.

Sarah Ann maintained contact with the Falklands and with Marines who had served with Alan and, in 1992, received information from a Sergeant who had been in NP8901 with Alan. He told her that he had been talking to a former member of the Royal Falkland Islands Police (RFIP) in a Portsmouth pub who told him that there was an individual in the Falklands who boasted that he had murdered a Marine and got away with it. That Falklander claimed that he had had a drunken row with Addis over his girlfriend and that they had then gone outside where he had knifed and killed Alan.

In 1993, Sarah Ann held a three-way telephone call with the Sergeant and with Inspector Morris, deputy chief of the RFIP in Stanley. This led to a further call to the Chief of Police, Superintendent Ken Greenland, who proved to be most helpful and sent her a long document, which included the statement that the RFIP now accepted that foul play had been involved.[60] The RFIP also sent her photographs of North Arm Settlement and a sketch they had prepared showing Alan as he had been dressed on the night he disappeared.

This led to an invitation for Sarah Ann to visit the Falklands again, which she did in February 1995, this time hosted by the RFIP. She started by interviewing some dozen people who were then living in Stanley but who had been at the party at North Arm on the night Alan disappeared. The interviews were one-to-one, but with a police officer sitting outside in case Sarah Ann needed assistance. Each interviewee came up with a story of what had happened. Some were simply fantasies, such as that he had been run over by a Land Rover, but others were, at least, plausible. These included that he had been taken to the shearing shed and beaten to death, that he had been knifed and his body dumped in Cow Park Pond,[61] another that his body had been incinerated in the furnace at the Big House. She flew to North Arm on 17 February, where she visited all the places Alan's body might have been and talked to many people, but to no avail.

Meanwhile, other police had travelled to North Arm overland and, together with Sarah Ann, they visited Cattle Point before spending the night at North Arm House. The following morning, they continued southwards

---

60 It is assumed that, from this time on, the case was treated as an 'unsolved murder'.

61 Cow Park Pond is a sizeable stretch of water some 500 yards (457m) inland from the Settlement. It is very shallow, and its extent is greater in winter than summer. It was never searched by divers as there was no perceived need.

to Devil's Point, where they found a cave with a blowhole as had been forecast by a clairvoyant Sarah Ann had consulted in the UK, but there was no trace of a body. Sarah Ann and the police then returned to Stanley, after which she went home to England.

Attempts to find the solution to Alan's fate continued and, in 1994, Sarah Ann was told that a Forensic Search Advisory Group (FSAG) was to be formed, headed by an eminent forensic archaeologist, Professor John Hunter of Birmingham University. A major part of the expense was met by Lion TV, who made a documentary on the subject. Professor Hunter held a meeting with Sarah Ann before leaving for the Falklands, but on this occasion, she did not herself go to the islands, although she was kept in the picture, waiting in England for the good news, which never came.

She was told that the four men arrested and freed by Pennington in 1995 had been invited to take part in the Lion TV documentary, but that one, whom she described as 'Mr X' but was clearly David Clarke, had declined. She contacted his representative in the Falklands and offered to meet 'Mr X' in Chile or the Falklands, but she never received a reply.

Sarah Ann then turned her energies to a book, which was published in 2003 under the title *Missing on Patrol*. A slim volume of sixty-four pages, it sets out her case and the sequence of events but seems to have had little public impact.

Sarah Ann died at her home on 6 May 2011. Her various businesses had clearly been successful as her Will was valued at £300,000. Concerning Alan, she was still hopeful that his body would be found, so she left £2,000 to her niece Joanne Bettson to be invested with the capital, the proceeds to go towards the cost of returning Alan's remains to the UK where they would be buried in her plot at Wrawby Road cemetery. She also bequeathed Alan's gold chain to her brother Ralph, with the comment that it was currently held by RFIP. Interestingly, she was also still in contact with Lt Col Gilding, who had been Officer Commanding NP8901 when Alan disappeared; she made no bequest but did ask that he be informed of her death.

It is of no major consequence, but there is some mystery about the three men in her life and why she did not take the name on marriage to Young in the first place and later retained the surname Addis after marrying Malone in California. Further, it has been impossible to discover how she made her money, apart from a brief spell running a motor spares shop, but whatever it was, it was clearly successful, as her Estate of £300,000+ shows. However, these are of little relevance to her relationship with her son and her efforts on his behalf.

Sarah Ann was clearly a courageous and determined woman. She took on Members of Parliament, the Royal Marines and the Falklands' vested interests with courage and a refusal to be ignored. In the final analysis, however, while she seems to have originally wanted to identify and prosecute his killers, in which she was not successful, in the later years, her only wish was to find his body and bring it back to the UK. Sadly, this dream has not yet been realised.

CHAPTER SIX

The Party at North Arm Settlement

Having arrived at North Arm, MV *Forrest* was secured to the jetty and, after supper aboard, the three Marines (Corporal Davis, Marines Johnson and Addis) walked to the Social Club house, arriving at about 2000. This walk from the ship to the party was short and straightforward; one hundred yards along the jetty to the shore, then turn right and follow the only track to the Settlement, with the Social Club one of the first buildings – about a quarter of a mile (400m) and ten-to-fifteen minutes in all. At this time of the evening, most house lights would have been on, so there were no navigation problems, all they had to do was to head for the lighted and noisy building.[62] None of the three men had either a map or a compass, nor did they need them.

At the risk of stating the obvious, this was their first visit to North Arm, so the three Marines knew none of the Falklanders, nor did the latter know any of these particular Marines. The numbers at the party probably fluctuated during the evening, but one of those present estimated that some fifty Settlers were present, plus the six Marines; this suggests a total of between fifty and sixty.

The three Marines in Alan's group were dressed in civilian clothes and Alan's appearance, as reconstructed by the RFIP, is shown in Figure 1.[63]

In more detail, he was wearing:

- Blue denim, open-necked shirt.
- Dark-blue woollen zip-up fur-lined bomber jacket with letters 'T.R.A.'

---

62 At this time, most Settlements had small generators. They operated after dark, but there was no TV on the islands, so the 'gennies' tended to be closed down at about 2200–2300. The close-down time for the North Arm generator on this particular night is not known, but may have been kept going for the party.

63 Addis, op. cit., p.45. Reproduction of police sketch with comments by Sarah Ann.

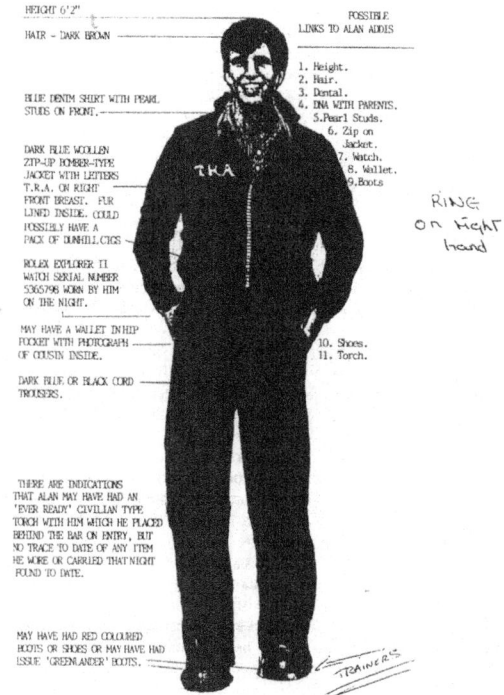

HEIGHT 6'2"

HAIR – DARK BROWN

BLUE DENIM SHIRT WITH PEARL STUDS ON FRONT.

DARK BLUE WOOLLEN ZIP-UP BOMBER-TYPE JACKET WITH LETTERS T.R.A. ON RIGHT FRONT BREAST. FUR LINED INSIDE. COULD POSSIBLY HAVE A PACK OF DUNHILL CIGS

ROLEX EXPLORER II WATCH SERIAL NUMBER 5365798 WORN BY HIM ON THE NIGHT.

MAY HAVE A WALLET IN HIP POCKET WITH PHOTOGRAPH OF COUSIN INSIDE.

DARK BLUE OR BLACK CORD TROUSERS.

THERE ARE INDICATIONS THAT ALAN MAY HAVE HAD AN 'EVER READY' CIVILIAN TYPE TORCH WITH HIM WHICH HE PLACED BEHIND THE BAR ON ENTRY, BUT NO TRACE TO DATE OF ANY ITEM HE WORE OR CARRIED THAT NIGHT FOUND TO DATE.

MAY HAVE HAD RED COLOURED BOOTS OR SHOES OR MAY HAVE HAD ISSUE 'GREENLANDER' BOOTS.

POSSIBLE LINKS TO ALAN ADDIS
1. Height.
2. Hair.
3. Dental.
4. DNA WITH PARENTS.
5.Pearl Studs.
6. Zip on Jacket.
7. Watch.
8. Wallet.
9.Boots

RING on Right hand

TRA

10. Shoes.
11. Torch.

TRAINERS

Figure 1: Police sketch of Alan Addis, 1993

embroidered in white on right chest.[64] (But see next paragraph below.)

- Blue/black corduroy trousers.
- Footwear, either his Marines-issue 'Greenlander' boots or trainers.
- Ever-Ready torch.
- According to the police, he "may have a wallet in hip pocket with photograph of cousin inside."[65] The wallet should also have contained his Armed Forces identity card (MoD Form 90), which included his photograph and personal details.
- According to a manuscript note by Sarah Ann in her book, he would also have had a ring on his right hand.[66]
- He was known to have deposited his jacket and torch at the bar on arrival

---

64 Extensive research has failed to find an explanation for these initials. His mother remembered them from when she laundered his jacket at home in England, which means that the jacket pre-dated his departure to the Falklands. She, too, had no idea what they meant.
65 He had three female cousins, but it is not known which of them this might have been.
66 Addis, ibid. See Annex A.

at the party and is presumed to have collected them when he left, as they were not recovered.

There is conflicting evidence about his parka. According to the police reconstruction and several witnesses he was wearing a civilian parka, as illustrated above. There is also strong evidence, confirmed by Sarah Ann Addis, that his Marine-issue parka was found aboard MV *Forrest* with other items of clothing beside his bunk and returned to Moody Brook.[67] However, there are other reports that the Marine-issue parka was found the following day lying on the ground near the shearing shed, suggesting that it might have been stripped from him in a fight, or taken off by him before the fight started; this cannot be confirmed.

The most intriguing item was a Rolex Explorer II watch. This was a very expensive watch for a nineteen-year-old Marine with just two years' service. It is suggested by the British Institute of Horology that it would have cost in the region of £6,000-7,000 (at today's prices) when bought new in 1978–79 and, depending on condition and provenance, would be worth some £18,000–20,000 today.[68] It seems unlikely that Alan himself could have bought it and it is more probable that it was bought for him by his doting mother, Sarah Ann, a well-off woman, who was known to shower him with presents. The serial number of the watch, given on the police sketch, was 5365798. Since he was wearing it and it disappeared with him, how the police obtained this number is not known, although it may have been either from a presentation case or documents found among his effects, or it may have been provided by Sarah Ann herself. A further curiosity is that the police sketch was included in various Freedom of Information releases from the MoD, but with the watch serial number carefully redacted, whereas in Sarah Ann's book the number is clearly visible.[69] Alan's fellow Marines were fully aware of this expensive watch, but seemingly not envious. They used to tease him by repeatedly asking him the time and he always responded by telling them – according to a respondent – that was just banter.[70]

---

67   Sarah Ann Addis, op. cit., p.32.
68   Telecon Miller-Burtoft 2 August 2023.
69   Addis, op. cit., p.45.
70   Information from Mr Jim Fairfield, Alan's section commander, via Philip Davis.

The Social Club

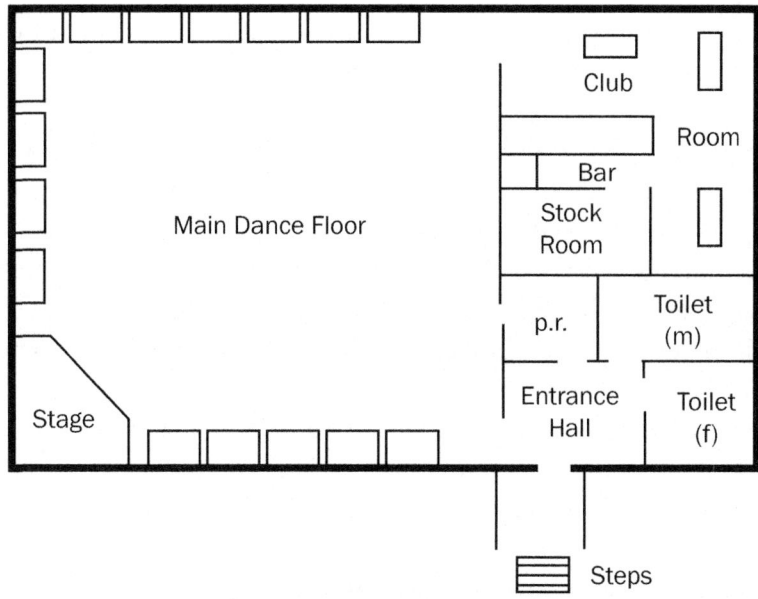

Figure 2. North Arm Social Club

Note:

External windows, internal doors and chairs NOT shown.

p.r. = projection room; m = male; f = female.

The diagram shows a reconstruction of the North Arm Social Club as accurately as is possible after forty-three years. Externally, the building was a pitched-roof design, covering an area approximately 40ft x 30ft (12m x 9m). The building was used for all social events, as well as for general meetings and film shows. Tables are shown against the walls, while chairs are not shown, but both would obviously be arranged according to the specific function.

Internally, the building was subdivided as shown. The main dance floor area had been fitted with a curved ceiling to improve the acoustic quality, which made it look like the interior of a Nissen hut. The walls were decorated with pictures and the flags of the United Kingdom and of the Falkland Islands, and there were public-address speaker units sited high on the end wall.

The club room contained the bar itself, with tables and chairs, and a dartboard on one of the walls. The bar served a wide variety of drinks and was manned by a duty barman, who, on this occasion, was David Clarke, probably assisted by Bernard Peck. Crisps and a few varieties of biscuits were also sold at the bar, but no food. The stock room was annexed to the bar. Payment was by cash or chit. The public-address (PA) control system was on the bar. Lighting, the cinema projector and the public-address system were powered by the Settlement generator.

The function on the night 7 August 1980 was a 'meet-and-greet' affair and took place in the club room, leaving the main dance floor empty. As with all such events, the number of people present would have fluctuated, probably at its maximum between 2100–2200 and steadily reducing from 2300 onwards. This suggests that the last sighting of Alan Addis as reported to the various inquiries was as he passed through the door from the club room/bar to the main dance floor and not as he actually left the building. However, there is no reason to believe that he did not leave the building through the normal entrance porch a few seconds later.

Leaving the Party

The Board of Inquiry (BoI) and subsequent investigations did their best to reconstruct the events at the party, but, as with many parties (and not only in the Falklands) the drink flowed freely, with most of those attending becoming inebriated, and maybe in some cases actually drunk. The majority of Falklanders and Marines were known heavy drinkers, with the result that memories were somewhat confused and contradictory. Mr Blake, the manager of the estate and organiser of the party, reported afterwards that he had never felt it necessary to assert his authority to restore order. He also told the BoI that he and his wife had chatted to Addis, but without noticing anything unusual.

The Board of Inquiry recorded that:

"Addis appears to have been in good spirits throughout the evening and held conversations with a number of people, who report him to have been acting normally but more drunkenly as the evening went on, but that at no time had he drunk so much that he was incapable."

The two other Marines in Addis's group (i.e., Corporal Roger Davis, Marine Johnson) left at about 2315 and said that they invited Addis to go with them, but he declined. They felt no anxiety as to his behaviour or that he might be incapable of making his own way back to the ship later. At some point, someone suggested to Addis that he should spend the night in the Settlement Bunkhouse, which was very close to the Social Club, and rejoin the ship in the morning, but Addis made no known attempt to take up this offer.

Addis's departure from the Social Club was an event of no significance whatsoever at the time and it seems unlikely that more than a very few noticed it at all. Even so, there are a number of contradictory reports about his exit. The Board of Inquiry concluded that he left the Social Club building at about 0130 – apparently peacefully and alone, as there were no reports of shouting, shoving or fisticuffs. It is presumed that he collected his torch and civilian parka as he left, because neither is listed among the effects collected after his disappearance.

There are several other reports about his departure. One witness claimed to the Board of Inquiry that Addis left at 0230, but this witness proved unreliable in other respects, so his statement was disregarded by the Board. A boy, who had been twelve years old at the time, told Sarah Ann during her 1991 visit that he had seen Addis leave carrying a crate/box of beer, but could not say whether this was for consumption at another party elsewhere in the Settlement, or to be taken back to MV *Forrest*. Unfortunately, Sarah Ann did not record the name of her informant, so this story cannot be verified. (As an aside, Governor Hunt also remarked on young children attending such late-night parties, but there can have been little other entertainment for them.)[71] Yet another story is that he left the bar in the company of Lyn Blake with the intention of escorting her in the darkness to the gate of the Big House and leaving her there.

Thus, the situation as Alan left the Club at about 0130 on 8 August 1980 was:

- It was very cold – about freezing. There was no reported snow, but the ground was frosted, suggesting that footprints would have shown up.
- Outside the Social Club it would have been totally silent apart, perhaps, from some muffled noise from the party.
- There were electrical light installations at either end of the jetty, although whether they were on or not is not known.

---

71   Addis, op. cit., p.32.

- He had never visited North Arm before, had not seen it in daylight and probably had little or no idea of the layout of houses and tracks.
- As far as is known, he had not met any of the inhabitants of North Arm before about 2000 on 7 August 1980.
- Immediately on leaving the light and noise of the Social Club building, it is safe to assume that Alan closed the door and found himself in a silent and very dark environment with few electrical lights.
- He had been drinking but was not incapable.
- He was a physically fit and well-trained Royal Marine.
- He was a good swimmer.
- He was dressed as shown in the police sketch, which was suitable for the intended short walk from the ship to the party and back again.
- He was not carrying a map, whistle or compass.
- He was carrying a torch.
- He did not intend to return to the Social Club party.
- The other two members of his team had returned to MV *Forrest* without any reported difficulty.

But he disappeared and not one person in North Arm Settlement has ever admitted to having seen him after he left the Social Club. To put it bluntly, he disappeared without trace.

CHAPTER SEVEN

Alan Disappears

MV *Forrest* was due to sail at 0700 on the morning of Friday 8 August 1980 and at about 0630 two farmhands from the Settlement reported to the jetty, ready to cast-off the lines – a standard procedure. Sergeant Howden and his two Marines also arrived, carrying the weapons and ammunition to be passed over to the Fitzroy party. For an unknown reason, there was a short delay, causing frustration for Captain Sollis, who was famously keen on punctuality. By 0710, however, the ship was at sea with on board Captain Sollis and his five-man crew; Sergeant Howden and his two Marines, Andie Corrie and Geordie Gill (Team A); plus Corporal Davis and Marine Johnson (Team B). But there was no physical head-check of the Marines prior to sailing, and it appears to have been assumed that Alan Addis was in his bunk down in the hold and asleep.

At about 0715–0720 on 8 August 1980, when MV *Forrest* was well out into the Bay of Harbours, the two Marines from Team A took their kit down to the hold and saw that Addis's bunk had not been slept in.[72] This concerned them, so they immediately conducted a search of the ship, and finding no trace of him, reported to Sergeant Howden. It was not a large ship and, by about 0730–0740, the ship had been thoroughly searched from stem-to-stern and it had been established that Addis was not on board.

It is clear that at this stage all aboard *Forrest* considered that Alan must have spent the night ashore, either on his own in some sheltered spot (remember there was a heavy frost) or with a woman, and, in either case, overslept and missed the boat. This was embarrassing, but it would have been by no means the first instance of a seaman or a Marine missing his ship.

---

72 It is important to note that they did not remark that he was simply not in his bunk, but that he had not spent the previous night in it.

They had no reason to suspect anything other than that he was alive and well at North Arm, where he, so they assumed, must be trying to work out how to resolve his predicament. It does not appear that anyone aboard *Forrest* considered the possibility of foul play, nor, indeed, was there any reason they should have done so – they had been among friends.

Captain Sollis and Sergeant Howden next considered what to do, while *Forrest* continued to head away from North Arm, but when Sollis decided that he would not turn back, that meant Howden had to work out what to do about Addis. In the event, he decided that once he had contacted Addis, he would instruct him to make his own way from North Arm to Fitzroy.

Although Sergeant Howden may have been a party to this decision, the responsibility for not turning back lay solely with Captain Sollis. His Captain's log cannot be found, and he left no oral report, but he was a very experienced mariner and had unparalleled knowledge of the Falklands inshore waters, weather and tides, so it must be assumed that he brought all those factors into consideration when reaching his decision. As it happens, of course, had he turned back, it would have made no difference – Addis had disappeared and would not have been waiting on the jetty to be picked up.

Communications

Captain Sollis initially attempted to raise North Arm on the 2m set, but was unable to do so, either due to screening problems, or, possibly, because nobody was manning the set at the Settlement at that time of the morning. However, due to the unpredictability of radio communications in the Falklands, he was able to raise the much more distant Johnson's Harbour Settlement and asked the operator there to use the telephone system to inform North Arm that a Royal Marine was not on board and was believed to be somewhere in that Settlement. That telephone call was received by Lyn Blake who informed her husband, who then organised the searches of the Settlement starting at 'turn-to' at 0900.

This information about Johnson's Harbour was gleaned by Detective Chief Inspector Pennington in 1995 and explains why there were searches of North Arm in the morning, whereas it had always previously been assumed that the telephone call at 1500 was the first time that the people of North Arm knew that a Marine was missing. It also explains how David Clarke could have known this before leaving on his journey to Goose Green, irrespective of whether or not he had played any part in the actual disappearance.

Meanwhile, under his contract with the Royal Marines, Captain Sollis was required that whenever he had their men on board, he had to make a daily radio call to the Royal Marines' HQ at Moody Brook, normally between 0800 and 0830. On this occasion, Howden and Sollis appear to have agreed to make the call, but not to mention Addis's absence and that they would only report what had happened after they had had a chance to speak to Addis and hear his explanation. Whatever the reason, when the morning call was made, Addis's absence was not mentioned.[73]

Back in North Arm, the farmhands attended the routine 0900 'turn-to' where they expected to be allocated their tasks for that day. But, on this occasion, they were told that a Marine was missing. For example, Sandra Hirtl, a farmhand, told Sarah Ann Addis: "*… The next morning, we all went to work and I'd just got in my tractor and was just driving off when someone said to me 'Have you got a Marine in your trailer?'*" To make sure there was no misunderstanding about the time, Sarah Ann asked: "*When was this then?*" And Sandra replied: "*This was in the morning.*"[74]

This is confirmed separately by Robin Goodwin, who records that "*… We were told at 'turn-to' time at 9am that morning to go and check our homes in case Alan was sleeping in a shed.*"[75] He later added: "*Yes, the initial 9am request to check the main buildings for Alan was the order, so we all went back and checked our properties. That took a couple of hours. At that time, we were looking for someone that simply overslept and missed his boat. Not the first time a visitor had missed his mode of transport. Then, after there was no sign of Alan, it was suggested to do a sweep of the other farm buildings and along the gorse wall. While that was going on, someone suggested maybe he fell in the water and was washed up in the Creek on the rising tide.*"[76]

At this stage, the searches were based on the supposition that he had either overslept or suffered some form of accident. The North Armers split into small groups, each following their own theory as to what had happened

---

73   Information from Signals Sergeant via P Davis.
74   Theroux documentary. 0.30 et seq.
75   Robin Goodwin email to author 18 June 2023.
76   Robin Goodwin email to author 8 June 2024.

to him and where he might be. Some Marines arrived the next day to help and carried out their own search, as did the crew of MV *Forrest*. With hindsight, all these searches were carried out enthusiastically, but, unsurprisingly, were uncoordinated and lacking a master plan.

In a separate incident, on the morning of 8 August 1980, one of the farm hands, David Clarke, drove a Land Rover from North Arm to Goose Green, via Bodie Creek Suspension Bridge, a distance of some 25 miles (40km), which he could not have undertaken without the express permission of the manager (i.e., Blake). This may have been a routine journey and, as he was a frequent user of the route, there was nothing odd about him travelling without an escort; he would have carried unditching tools and also had a 2m radio. He left at about 0800 and Eric Goss, the manager at Goose Green, records that at about 1100: "... *there was a knock at my back door... I opened it to find David Clarke on the doorstep, he asked had I seen a Royal Marine as one was missing from North Arm.*"[77]

At about 1500, having gone ashore at Fitzroy, Sergeant Howden was able to make contact using the 2m civilian set, when he informed the duty watchkeeper at North Arm that one of the Marines had failed to board *Forrest* before she sailed that morning. The watchkeeper told the manager, who promptly organised search parties. This was the second, possibly even the third such search, with virtually every inhabitant of North Arm taking part. Closely supervised by Blake, they searched in and around the jetty and Settlement until nightfall and found nothing.

Meanwhile, Sollis and Howden waited at Fitzroy until about 1630, when, in the absence of any good news from North Arm, they had no choice but to 'bite the bullet' and inform Major Gilding at NP8901. The latter immediately made a plan to search for Addis the following day, which included not only the tasks for his own men, but also arrangements with FIGAS and Captain Sollis. He held his 'Orders Group' ('O-Group') at 1900. Gilding also signalled the news back to HQTRF in the UK, at which stage he could only record that Addis was 'missing on patrol', which was passed word-for-word to Sarah Ann Addis.

Early on the morning of 9 August, a FIGAS Beaver floatplane brought in additional Marines, following which, the pilot offered to carry out an aerial search and asked for volunteers to provide extra pairs of eyes. One of these

---

77   Eric Goss to this author 24 Aug 2023.

was Robin Goodwin: *"… the pilot asked for a couple of volunteers to search from the air along the nearby shoreline and water in the area near the entrance to North Arm jetty. I was one of that search. You could see seals swimming in the crystal-clear water and even local mullet fish. If there was a body in that area, one of us would have seen it, I am sure. It also confirmed that the actual Creek was clear…"*[78]

Assessment

Although they are unlikely to have succeeded in finding Alan or his body, there are a number of issues. There can be no doubt that there should have been a proper headcount before *Forrest* left the jetty and either Corporal Davis or Sergeant Howden should have noticed that one man was absent. This was a very serious failure on the part of both Sergeant Howden and Corporal Davis, although it actually made no difference to whether Addis could be found or not.

Captain Sollis' decision not to turn back is more difficult to understand, but he must have had good reason. It would have meant that Alan, had he still been alive, would have had to get himself from North Arm to Fitzroy, which he would have had to achieve either by vehicle or walking. Alternatively, he could have waited at North Arm, until *Forrest* or another ship called in, or a FIGAS Beaver had a spare seat.

The initial reluctance for either Sergeant Howden or Captain Sollis to inform Moody Brook is easier to understand. They had no reason at that point to suspect foul play and it was natural that they should seek to establish the facts before reporting to Major Gilding. There could have been a number of innocent explanations, ranging from cuddling up to an overnight partner, through getting lost in the darkness, to falling over and injuring himself, or even to having drowned.

There is no doubt that the searches were uncoordinated. The Settlers formed a number of separate parties – sometimes just one individual – each following their pet theory as to where he might be. Indeed, one participant suggests that there was a competitive element with each wanting to be the first to find him and solve the mystery. This is perfectly understandable, as for the great majority, there was no reason on that first day to think that

---

78   Goodwin, 8 June 2024.

Addis had done anything other than oversleep. By the third day (i.e., 10 August), the perception changed and most now believed that he might have died of exposure and there was increasing concern that they might have missed his body. Alternatively, some thought, since they could not find him on land, that Alan must have boarded *Forrest* and then fallen overboard.

Summary

Thus, the position at midnight 8/9 August was that:
- Alan had gone missing at 0130 and, the perpetrators apart, nobody knew what had happened to him or where he might be.
- MV *Forrest* was on its way from Fitzroy to Stanley, carrying the remaining five Marines.
- The inhabitants of North Arm had conducted several searches.
- The second-in-command of NP8901, together with a small number of Marines, including a trained diver, were preparing to fly to North Arm as soon after dawn as possible.
- Word that a Marine was missing had been passed to the UK, where Alan's mother was told that he was 'missing on patrol'.
- The Falkland Islands Police appear to have been informed, but did not treat it as a matter of urgency.

CHAPTER EIGHT

Royal Marines Board of Inquiry

The first step in a military investigation into a disappearance such as this is to hold a Board of Inquiry, which normally consists of three officers or warrant officers from the unit concerned.[79] Their task is to call witnesses, set out the facts of the case on paper, and then, but only if asked, express an opinion; there is, however, no requirement for any of them to be legally trained or qualified. Typically, such Boards deal with routine matters, such as *"the absence of any person subject to military law who has been continuously absent without leave for a period of not less than twenty-one days and the deficiency (if any) in the clothing, arms, ammunition or other equipment or any other public or service property issued to him for his use."*

Thus, on 13 August 1980, Headquarters Training and Reserve Forces (HQTRF), located at Southsea in the UK, instructed Major Gilding to convene a Board of Inquiry with the task of: *"Investigating the Circumstances of the Disappearance of PO 3759K Marine Alan Addis on or about 8 August 1980."*[80] This step was in conformity with the Army Act, 1955, and the Board of Inquiry (Army)(Amendment) Rules 1961, and required such a Board to consist of a President not below the rank of Captain, with not less than two other members, both of whom were required to be either subject to military law or in the service of the Crown. Further, one of the members was permitted to be a Warrant Officer or a Quartermaster-Sergeant of the Royal Marines. In the event, this was met, albeit with a slight variation due to the remote station. The Board was presided over by Captain Whitcomb, the second-in-command of NP8901, with two members. One of these was a Warrant Officer, Royal Engineers, who happened to be available,[81] the other

---

79 The purpose and conduct of such inquiries was laid down in 'Boards of Inquiry (Army) Rules'.
80 Signal MGRM TRF 131419Z Aug 80.
81 This Warrant Officer was in the Falklands concerning the long overdue rebuild of Moody Brook barracks.

was Mr Ron Bucket from the island's Public Works Department, who was included to cover the obvious civilian interests in the case.[82]

The Board convened at Stanley on 22 September 1980, where the President and members started by discussing their remit, agreeing on procedures, confirming the list of witnesses and arranging their attendance. The Board then heard witnesses in Stanley before moving to North Arm Settlement on Wednesday 23 September for the final tranche of witnesses.

The actual witness statements have not been released by the MoD, but the summary has, albeit with individual's names redacted. The Board clearly found many witness' contributions to be hazy and contradictory, and they accepted that almost all were *"at the worst drunk, and at best inebriated to some extent."* The Board first investigated the events leading up to Addis's arrival at the party. They established that he had not had any breakfast prior to leaving Moody Brook and noted that he was known to suffer from seasickness and had thus stayed in his bunk throughout the voyage. However, he probably joined his comrades for an evening meal aboard MV *Forrest* before departing for the party ashore.

The Board next looked at the period 2000 to 0130 and concluded that there were no fights requiring intervention by the manager, who was the nominal host, and that while Addis had discussions with various people, nothing out of the ordinary had ensued. Addis did not return to the ship with his two comrades at 2315, leaving him as the sole remaining Royal Marine, and at some stage he was offered and refused a bed in a nearby Bunkhouse. The Board also heard two versions of the time that Addis left the building, and they chose to believe 0130. However, the Board received no evidence that Addis was incapable of looking after himself nor could any reason be found to suggest that he might not have been able to make his way back to MV *Forrest*. The Board established that the lights of the *Forrest* and on the jetty could be seen from two paces forward from the doorway of the Social Club, although they do not seem to have confirmed that those lights would actually have been on at the time Addis left the club.

The Board concluded that Addis had consumed alcohol, but only a small amount after MV *Forrest* arrived at North Arm, and more in the Club. This is surprising because Addis was known to his friends always to drink soft drinks. The Board also noted that there were two unopened bottles

---

82 There would also have been a senior NCO, who would have been responsible for marching in military witnesses and general administrative duties.

of whisky in his kit. These may have been for his own consumption, but it is also possible that they were intended as a 'thank you' to his hosts in his forthcoming visit to Fitzroy. In this writer's experience, Kelpers were very generous with their hospitality, for which they refused to take any payment, but would accept bottles of whisky, gin, or the latter's inseparable companion, Schweppes Indian Tonic Water.[83]

The Board said that Addis was first missed at about 0715 aboard MV *Forrest* when she was already at sea. It was assumed that he had overslept and missed his ship, an event which the Board commented was "*a situation common to sailors and Marines for centuries.*" That left Addis responsible for making his own way to Fitzroy. It is of interest that the Board made no mention of any witness telling them that people in the Settlement were told at about 0800–0900 that 'a Marine was missing'.

The Board compiled a useful timetable of events:

DATE	TIME	ACTIVITY	COMMENT
8 August	1500	North Arm alerted.	By radio from Fitzroy
	1500–1730	Settlement searched. Jetty examined.	North Arm Settlers
	1630	Major Gilding alerted at Moody Brook.	By radio
	1900	Major Gilding holds Orders Group at Moody Brook.	Plans for next day
9 August	0730	Search teams fly to North Arm.	FIGAS Beaver
	0820–1700	Search by divers, glass-bottomed boat, air search. Tracks near outside houses searched.	Combined Marines and Kelpers
	1730	MV *Forrest* arrives at North Arm with stores.	Direct from Stanley
10 August	All day	Divers at work. Land search by men on foot, horses, dogs. Three boats with glass-bottom boxes.	Combined Marines and Kelpers
11 August	Morning	Search continues	Combined Marines and Kelpers
	1200	Major Gilding calls off search.	

Table 6. Board of Inquiry Timetable of Events

---

83   This author's experiences. For some reason, the tonic water was very difficult for civilians to obtain.

The Board also noted that, despite Major Gilding's instructions, unofficial searches continued from 11 August onwards. Boats, harbours and coastlines were visited; inland areas up to 5 miles (8km) radius from the Settlement were patrolled twice a week. The 'outside houses' were also repeatedly searched. Finally, all inhabitants were instructed to generally keep their eyes open.

Findings of the Board

The Board considered that Addis might have mistakenly wandered into Camp, sobered quickly and taken shelter until daylight. In that case, he should have found his way back to North Arm or been discovered by one of the many search parties, which had not happened.

Therefore, the Board concluded that Addis must be dead, although his actual fate could not be determined until the body was found. However, the possibilities were that, either, he had wandered into Camp where he took shelter, for example, behind a peat bank, fallen asleep and *"perished in his sleep through exposure"* or, alternatively, that he had fallen into the sea and drowned, either on his way to MV *Forrest,* on the jetty, while boarding the ship, or once on board. The latter was considered by the Board to be the more likely. The Board's finding that Addis could have wandered into Camp, lost his bearings and perished there may seem surprising, but, although unusual, there were numerous precedents in the Falklands, which were generally attributable to the lack of geographical reference points and fog. Some of the better-known examples are described in Chapter Sixteen.

One important finding by the Board was that Alan Addis had been on duty: *"Addis was sent by the OCRM as part of a training team to Fitzroy Settlement. He was on his way to Fitzroy Settlement, and had he disappeared from MV Forrest at sea there would be no doubt that he was on duty. That he happened to be ashore for a few hours' relaxation before continuing to Fitzroy, the Board feels makes no material difference. Without wishing to create a precedent, the Board consider that at the time of his disappearance Mne Addis was on duty."*[84] This finding was never challenged by the chain-of-command.

The third member of the Board, Mr Ron Bucket, when interviewed

---

84   Board of Inquiry Record of Proceedings, para 15.

for the TV programme *Missing in the Falklands* in about 2015, said: *"During the course of the inquiry, I began to feel uneasy listening to the evidence that was being given, and I felt that there was something that wasn't being said. I put my feelings and suspicions to the other members of the Board, off the record. They felt that I was being melodramatic. In a way, I feel that I was right and there was something that wasn't said that should have been said. But that makes me feel guilty that I didn't do more about it at the time."*

Once signed by the members, the Board's findings were the basis for the succeeding steps:

- 5 October 1980. The inquest at Stanley reached an 'open verdict', which meant that a death had taken place, but that the Coroner found it impossible at that stage to specify the cause or allocate responsibilities.
- 13 October 1980. The proceedings of the Board of Inquiry were signed off by the Governor, Rex Hunt, in his capacity as Commander-in-Chief.
- 4 February 1981. Alan Addis's death certificate was issued in Stanley, agreeing with the Board of Inquiry that he had either *"Drowned or perished from exposure."*

The findings of the Board were accepted by the chain-of-command in the UK, few of whom would have had any experience of the Falkland Islands. Nowhere in the Board's findings is there any suggestion that Alan's death could have been due to foul play and, to be fair, at that stage, nobody in Stanley or the UK seems to have had the slightest suspicion that Addis's disappearance might have been due to third parties. This was understandable, as the Marines were on British territory, among vociferously loyal British subjects, and had been guests at a party thrown in their honour.

There were also unconfirmed rumours that the President had been unduly influenced by Blake, the North Arm manager. These rumours arose mainly because the Captain stayed at the 'Big House' during the Board's visit to North Arm; indeed, it would have been customary in the Falklands for a visiting Royal Marines Officer to stay with the manager and his wife. In this case, there can be little doubt that Blake would have wanted the Board to find that there were just two possibilities: that Addis fell off the jetty and drowned or walked off into the countryside and, for whatever reason, died. Whether Blake did try, or even succeeded in influencing the inquiry cannot now be determined, but, admittedly with the benefit of hindsight, it was perhaps unwise of the Captain to stay with someone who might be involved, and he should have been accommodated elsewhere.

Sarah Ann Addis Visits the Falklands

As described elsewhere, in the months immediately following Alan's death, Sarah Ann became dissatisfied with her treatment by the Royal Marines and felt it her right to visit the scene of her only son's disappearance. Thus, she demanded a personal visit to see where it had all taken place and visited the Falkland Islands 4–11 March 1981. Up to this point, she believed, as she had been officially informed, that her son had suffered some form of accident.

It is clear, however, that Sarah Ann became aware of the groundswell of disquiet in the Falklands, among both Royal Marines and Kelper communities, and as she talked to them, she became aware for the first time that there may have been foul play. There were also allegations that the Falkland Police's investigation had been less than thorough and specific complaints were made by some Marines that the Board of Inquiry "*did not reflect the true circumstances of [Marine] Addis's disappearance.*" In particular, it was alleged that "*during the night in question, heated discussions took place between [Marine] Addis and [name redacted] a North Arm shearer.*"

On her return to the UK, Sarah Ann received a letter from HQTRF Royal Marines (RM) on Monday 20 July 1981. This enclosed a copy of a letter from a Major currently serving in the Falklands[85] in which: "*He outlined his concern about the persistent rumours and undercurrents circulating there, which suggested that because of Marine Addis's liaison with a married woman at North Arm, his disappearance was more of design than accident.*"[86]

By June/July 1981, there was distinct unease at HQTRF RM, mainly based on these reports from civilian sources in the Falklands and from Marines who had been serving there at the time of Alan Addis's disappearance. In particular, it was felt that, since a year had passed, if he had died by accident, either by drowning or in the Camp, his body should have been found.

---

85   The letter has not been seen, but presumably 'the Major' was the then current (i.e., 1981–82) Officer Commanding NP8901; i.e., Major Gary Noot, RM.

86   Addis, op. cit., p.28.

Comments

It is sometimes claimed that the Board of Inquiry failed to take cognisance of the death of Jimmy Biggs on 20 August 1980, which had taken place a full month before they visited North Arm. There were two reasons why it would have been improper for the Board to have done so. First, their Terms of Reference confined them exclusively to the disappearance of Alan Addis and, secondly, Biggs's death was a civilian matter and totally outwith consideration by a military board. Because these are unrelated issues, Biggs's death is not included here in this narrative but is described separately in Annex C.

The Board of Inquiry was a necessary legal requirement and was properly conducted within those rules, i.e., Army Act, 1955, etc. It should be stressed, however, that none of the members had any legal or investigative training, nor were they able to call on any expert witnesses; all they could do was to apply common sense and rely on their own past experience. The members appear to have concluded from the start that Addis must have either drowned or perished in the Camp and went on to adhere to those premises throughout, without giving any consideration to the possibility that foul play could have been involved, although they may have done so 'off the record'. Mr Bucket seems to have had some doubts, but failed to persuade the other two members.

It is of interest that the Board made no mention of any alerts being raised in North Arm Settlement at breakfast time on the morning of 8 June (i.e., after MV *Forrest* had sailed) nor of Dave Clarke's journey to Goose Green. However, as these involved only civilians, it may be that either they were not aware of them, or that they did know but considered them to be outside their remit.

Over time, the Board's failure to cover the possibility that Addis might have been killed, whether deliberately or accidentally, gained credence, so that the Board's proceedings and findings were increasingly ignored to the point that they became irrelevant. This led directly to the involvement of the Special Investigation Branch, as will be discussed in the next chapter.

There are records of a single Constable of the FIP taking statements at North Arm, but there does not seem to have been a serious police investigation until Sarah Ann became involved in March 1981. Captain Gallacher of the SIB started his investigation in June 1981, but did not visit the Falklands until November, i.e., well over a year after Addis's disappearance.

CHAPTER NINE

The Special Investigation Branch and Lamb Investigations

FIRST GALLAGHER REPORT

Although it was initially accepted by officialdom, the Board of Inquiry was criticised by junior ranks in the Royal Marines and, when Sarah Ann Addis received her copy, she became extremely agitated. She contacted her MP, James Johnson (1908–95)[87] who, in turn, wrote to the Parliamentary Under-Secretary of State (Royal Navy), Keith Speed, who had no hesitation in authorising a visit by Mrs Addis to the Falkland Islands at public expense.

She duly visited Stanley 4–11 March 1981, where she was able to discuss matters with Falkland civilians and with Royal Marines of NP8901 who had served with Alan and were still at Moody Brook pending their relief in the following month. She was refused a Beaver flight to North Arm on the grounds of 'bad weather', which sounds like a rather weak excuse to prevent her meeting too many people at the Settlement where her son had disappeared. Considering the rugged design of the de Havilland Canada Beaver, the skill and experience of the pilots and the sheltered North Arm Creek where it would have landed and taken off, that just does not seem plausible. As a stranger to the Falklands, she was in no position to argue, but it would seem a deliberate and cynical act by someone.

Nevertheless, she returned to the UK convinced that, if her son's death had been accidental, his body would almost certainly have been found by this time, which suggested that 'foul play' might have been involved. She also received letters from Falklanders concerning rumours that were

---

87   He was MP for Rugby (1950–59) and then for Kingston-upon-Hull West (1964–83).

circulating in the Falklands, several of which concerned a Chilean labourer named Perez.

She concluded that the response of the Falkland Islands Police had been less than adequate. She accordingly visited HQTRF at Southsea on 10 June 1981, which coincided with that HQ receiving a letter from Major Gary Noot, RM, who had taken over as Officer Commanding NP8901 on 31 April. Noot reported that there were widely held doubts in the Falklands. So, as the situation was now beyond the capabilities of the Royal Navy or Royal Marines, HQTRF sought the help of the Army's Special Investigation Branch (SIB).

The SIB was quick to respond and their designated investigator, Captain James Gallacher,[88] started his work in the UK. The first person he interviewed was Sarah Ann Addis, who not only repeated what she had already told HQTRF, but also produced two letters she had received from the Falklands, the most recent being from a Mrs Mazely, dated 27 June 1981, who had apparently been at the party of 7/8 August 1980.[89] Gallacher then went on to interview Major Gilding and the President of the Board of Inquiry, all five Marines who had been at North Arm that night, together with the specialist divers, all of whom had returned to the UK in April. There was one further witness, a Royal Marine who had been a member of NP8901 (1981–82) but had been returned to the UK in June 1981. Unfortunately, his name has been redacted.

Captain Gallacher summarised his first impressions from these interviews:

- Many Marines were dissatisfied with both the original enquiries and the findings of the Board of Inquiry.
- There had been 'heated discussions' between Addis and a 'North Arm shearer'.
- When Addis left the Club, he was accompanied by another man.
- Clarification was required concerning the movements of one man (name unspecified).
- There was confusion over Addis's parka.
- A 'Chilean man' was seen digging in the peat banks of North Arm Settlement during the night of 7 Aug 80.

---

88 His name is redacted in MoD documents, but he is named in *Penguin News* 29 November 1981.

89 Recent research indicates that there was nobody of that name in the Falklands at the time, so it must be assumed that it was a *nom de plume*.

- A North Arm resident departed the Settlement the day following Marine Addis's disappearance and was seen driving inland on a motorcycle.
- Both sub-aqua divers employed in the search for Marine Addis considered that, had he drowned, they would have recovered his body from the sea or on the surrounding shoreline in the immediate vicinity of North Arm Settlement.
- Neither sub-aqua diver was aware of the inland lake – Cow Park Pond – adjacent to North Arm Settlement.

At this stage, Captain Gallacher had only interviewed Royal Marines in the UK, so, as the only Marine at the North Arm party after 2330 had been Addis, quite how he reached some of these conclusions is not clear:

- It was dark from about 1730 to 0730, so how the digging man was seen, let alone recognised as 'a Chilean', is not clear.
- The only known resident to drive out of the Settlement on 8 August was David Clarke, who was driving a Land Rover and left at about 0730.
- It is correct that Cow Park Pond had never been searched – but while occupying a large area at some times of the year and a much smaller area at others, it is also very shallow and thus a most unlikely place to hide a body.

Captain Gallacher ended his report with a request for authorisation for a visit to the Falkland Islands.[90]

SECOND GALLAGHER REPORT

Meanwhile, Rex Hunt, the Governor, had also become anxious about the Addis case. A new Chief of Police, Superintendent Ronnie Lamb, formerly of the Strathclyde Police, arrived from Glasgow on 21 September 1981, and one of his early tasks, as directed by the Governor, was to review the Addis case.

Captain Gallacher subsequently visited the Falklands from 5–11 November 1981, where he handed over all his papers. Gallacher and Lamb

---

90   His report is letter SIB RMP UKLF dated 30 July 1981 (obtained under FoI).

worked well together. They started in Stanley by interviewing members of the current NP8901, who had not been in the Falklands when Addis disappeared, but this was an attempt to see whether any had relevant information. They also interviewed civilians, including Captain Sollis and his crew.

They then spent several days at North Arm, where they conducted extensive interviews and carried out some of their own searches in pursuit of the rumours. Among these, they drained a sheep dip, had a forty-ton stack of peat moved and searched the loft of the cinema, but all to no avail. Thus, they returned to Stanley concluding that nobody at North Arm could explain Addis's disappearance but there was no evidence to support the theory that he had been the victim of foul play.

SIB involvement ended with Gallacher's return to the UK, leaving continuation of enquiries in the hands of Superintendent Lamb.[91] *Penguin News* was also brought into the picture, issuing a full commentary in its issue of 29 November 1981.[92] Gallacher told his superiors that Lamb's further investigations would be protracted, but that a copy of the latter's eventual report would be sent to the Royal Marines in the UK.

Lamb continued his work after Gallacher had left and, by March 1982, had conducted some fifty-odd interviews and had pursued the many rumours to their sources and disproved them all. There were only three men he failed to interview, although they were all only remotely concerned with the case. One was the Chilean, Quan, who was something of an eccentric, practising 'oriental martial arts skills' at unusual times and places, and travelled extensively on a motorcycle. He did not speak English and, as he did not fit in with the others in North Arm, he was discharged by the manager. The other was the Colombian, Gonzalez, who had simply come to the end of his contract and returned to Stanley aboard MV *Forrest* on 8 August. Lamb thought that both might have contributed to his enquiries, but, in the event, they had returned to their home countries, and he decided not to contact their relevant national police forces.

The third was a British yachtsman who was sailing around the world but took a break in the Falklands and was earning some money by serving as a

---

91 SIB Western Region letter 01281/1 dated 27 November 1981.
92 *Penguin News*, 'Marine Addis case re-examined' 29 November 1981.

deckhand aboard MV *Forrest*. He was one of the crew during the voyage to North Arm. By the time Lamb undertook his investigation, this man had left the Falklands and, at Lamb's request, Gallacher tried to find him in the UK, but all that could be established was that his passport had expired and his family had had no contact with him for several years.

Lamb completed his report in late March 1982 and was awaiting the typing of a covering letter to the Governor when the Argentines invaded. On the evening prior to their arrival in Stanley, Lamb ordered his staff to destroy by fire all the most sensitive documents, which included the report on Addis. He was then among those deported by the Argentines in April 1982.[93] On the evening prior to their surrender, the Argentines undertook 'an orgy of destruction', burning all documents, and they even threw the typewriters on the bonfire. Thus, all copies of the original report had been destroyed in the police station and the promised copies had not been sent to the Royal Marines and SIB in the UK.

THE LAMB REPORT

Back in the UK, Sarah Ann Addis had become increasingly sceptical of the findings of the Royal Marine Board of Inquiry, a view reinforced by several letters from friends she had made in Stanley during her visit, which repeated some of the many rumours sweeping the islands, and she was again in contact with her MP. Lamb returned to Stanley shortly after the British victory on 14 June 1982 and initially had many much more pressing matters to deal with. However, the political pressure from the UK was such that Rex Hunt, now Civil Commissioner, instructed Lamb to endeavour to recreate his report from memory, which he did, submitting his new report on 29 July 1982.[94]

In essence, Lamb covered the ground already examined by the original police and Royal Marines investigations. He did not have the original statements in front of him, but seems to have had a good memory and was able to revisit many of his original observations and conclusions, which included:

---

93 Hunt, op. cit., p.222.
94 Letter Police HQ Stanley dated 29 Jul 1982.

- A lack of control of his subordinates by Sergeant Howden, but this was a matter for the Royal Marines.
- Criticism of Captain Sollis was misplaced. He was a very experienced sailor and totally responsible for his ship.
- The movements of the manager were all accounted for by witnesses.
- There was criticism of the Board of Inquiry by one of its members (in fact, Mr Ron Bucket), who asserted that "... *it was just a gut feeling that the inquiry was on the wrong track.*" However, Lamb observed that there was no note of such dissent in the written record.[95]
- There was an irreconcilable difference in accounting for their movements on the night of 7/9 August 1980 concerning Mr Peck of North Arm and Mr Goodwin, first mate of the MV *Forrest*. However, neither had had any contact with Addis nor had they ever exhibited any propensity for violence, so the matter was not pursued.
- One lady said that the manager had forbidden her to graze her horses on a particular island in the Bay of Harbours. She inferred that Addis's remains might have been buried there. Again, Lamb did not pursue this matter.

It is of interest that Lamb's report makes no mention of the 0900 search of the entire Settlement, for which there are several independent witnesses.

Lamb closed his report saying that he had: "... *no hesitation in advising that nothing has been discovered to suggest that Addis's death was other than accidental, and that HM Coroner's verdict was other than the correct one.*" This led Hunt to issue a very firm and authoritative conclusion:

> GOVERNMENT HOUSE,
> PORT STANLEY,
> FALKLAND ISLANDS.

To Whom It May Concern

The enclosed report by the Chief Police Officer on the death of Marine Addis confirms previous reports that his death was accidental and that there was no suspicion of foul play. Nothing

---

95 Lamb also observes that Mr Bucket's wife was one of those who wrote to Sarah Ann Addis.

new has emerged from the exhaustive enquiries conducted by the Chief Police Officer to suggest that the death was anything other than accidental.

28 August 1982
(signed)
R M Hunt CMG
Civil Commissioner[96]

Rex Hunt and others may have thought, quite sincerely, that that closed the matter, but it signally failed to do so.

---

96   Government House, Stanley 'To Whom It May Concern' 28 August 1982. Also FCO 7/5509.

CHAPTER TEN

Sarah Ann's Second Visit and the Pennington Inquiry

Superintendent Ronnie Lamb's plans were overtaken by the invasion of April 1982, when the Argentine Military Police were quick to take over the police HQ on Ross Road, while Superintendent Lamb himself, along with Governor Hunt, was extradited via Uruguay to the UK. When he returned to the Falklands after the war, Superintendent Lamb reported that prior to the occupation he had ordered FIP officers to destroy many papers, including those concerning the Addis case. Secondly, the Argentines had destroyed many more papers during their brief occupation, particularly when their defeat had become inevitable. Thirdly, it appeared that some papers may also have been destroyed when a British missile hit the building on 12 June 1982. Whatever the truth of the matter, the pre-1982 papers on the Addis case have never been found.

In the period immediately following the Anglo-Argentine war, the authorities, for totally understandable reasons, concentrated on islands-wide recovery and rehabilitation. Nevertheless, the FIP still found time to continue their investigation into Addis's disappearance and, after Eric Goss took over as manager at North Arm in October 1983, he: "… *often had members of the FIP stay with us as they continued the search for Addis.*"[97] Also, knowing that David Clarke had crossed Bodie Creek Suspension Bridge on 8 August 1980, two FIP divers set out to search the water beneath the bridge but the tides proved too dangerous and they had to abandon this particular attempt.

In 1992, Sarah Ann was contacted by a serving Royal Marine Sergeant who told her that he had been in a pub in Plymouth, Devon, where he

---

97   Email Goss-Miller 25 August 2023.

was told that there was a man in the Falklands who boasted that he had murdered a Royal Marine and got away with it. It was suggested that the man claimed that he had had a row with Alan over his girlfriend and that the two men had gone outside where the Falklander 'knifed' Alan. After telephone conversations and an exchange of correspondence, the then Chief of Police, Superintendent Ken Greenland,[98] invited her to visit and she flew out in February 1995 for her second visit to the Falkland Islands.

Sarah Ann started her visit in Stanley with one-to-one interviews with twelve Falklanders who had been at the party in North Arm on 7/8 August 1980. She was disturbed by the numerous and contradictory suggestions of how Alan had died and of how his body had been disposed of, including:

• Stabbed and body hidden under a peat stack.
• Buried in an old sheep dip.
• Interred in a cavity in the walls of the Social Club.
• Cremated in the furnace in the Big House (i.e., the manager's residence).
• Taken to the shearing shed and beaten to death.
• Deliberately run over by a Land Rover.
• The body was in Cow Park Pond, which had never been searched.

On this occasion, nobody was able to provide a valid reason for Sarah Ann not to visit North Arm, so she flew there on 17 February 1995. This was her first visit there and she could not help bursting into tears as she realised she was somewhere near where her son had been killed. She looked at the Social Club, the jetty, the storage shed, the shearing shed and the killing shed, and she walked around to see the site and meet the people, but all to no avail.

Meanwhile, a number of FIP officers drove overland to join her. There were more interviews with locals and collectively the group spent the night at North Arm House[99] before going on to visit Garden Point (due South of the shearing shed). They also visited Devil's Point, which, to their surprise, checked out exactly with the predictions of the clairvoyant, Nella Jones, even to having a blowhole in the roof.

On 1 March, all, including Sarah Ann, returned to Stanley to hold discussions; a result of which, the following day, a small group (Chief of

---

98   Greenland was a former Major in the Royal Military Police, who had originally served as Provost Marshal in the post-war garrison. He was Chief Police Officer from 1983–99.

99   Despite its name, North Arm House was several miles due West of the Settlement.

Police, CID, some military but not Sarah Ann) returned to recheck the blowhole at Devil's Point, but nothing was found.

Sarah Ann returned to the UK. Her visit left her very sad, but she was comforted by the knowledge that the police were still working on the case. She then made a three-and-a-half-minute video for Forces TV, which was broadcast on 8 August 1995, the fifteenth anniversary of Alan's disappearance, again with no relevant response from the public.

THE PENNINGTON INVESTIGATION

The Royal Falkland Islands Police (RFIP) had only limited resources, so on occasions, found it necessary to request assistance from the Home Office, which would then arrange for help from a UK-based police force.[100] Thus, in mid-1995, Superintendent Greenland discussed the case with the Chief Constable of Devon & Cornwall Police (DCP), as a result of which, the case papers were sent to the Head of CID at Exeter, with the question: "*Have we missed anything?*" This led to the offer of a four-man team led by Detective Chief Inspector (DCI) Bob Pennington and comprising Detective Sergeant Steve Turpin, and two Constables whose task was to link, via satellite, with the Home Office's major incident computer system. All team members were from CID backgrounds and had been involved in the investigation of many other serious incidents including deaths and drug-related operations. It was designated Operation Lioness.

Full of high hopes, Pennington and his team started work by interviewing some fifty people in the UK, including Royal Marines who had served in NP8901 alongside Alan Addis, as well as former civilian residents of the Falklands now living in the UK. The team also met Sarah Ann Addis and arranged for her to make yet another emotional three-and-a-half-minute video appealing for help in solving what was now a fifteen-year-old mystery. This video was broadcast on Forces TV worldwide and in the Falklands just before the DCP team arrived in Stanley, but as far as is known, it attracted no significant responses.[101]

---

100 Along with several other British Overseas Territories, the FIP was awarded the prefix "Royal" on 1 January 1992.

101 Addis, op. cit., p.49.

Prior to leaving for the Falklands, the DCP team held a very upbeat press conference at their headquarters in Exeter where a spokesman said: "*A lot of people on the Falklands have been harbouring a secret for a long time and we are now hoping that we can get to the bottom of it; we are not sending officers on an 8,000-mile journey for nothing.*"[102]

On arrival in the Falkland Islands in August 1995, Pennington installed his team in an 'incident room' at Stanley Police Station and, since he appears to have been keen to keep the public informed, he called a press conference where he explained the purpose of his team's visit. Their task, he confirmed, was to investigate the disappearance in 1980 of Royal Marine Alan Addis; he stressed that his team was in support of Superintendent Greenland and had brought with them sophisticated equipment enabling direct access via satellite to the best computerised detection system available.

When asked if there were specific suspects, DCI Pennington said that: "*We have certain individuals we will be focusing on,*" adding that, "*we already have a number of interesting lines of enquiry to pursue and we will remain here until the enquiry is finished. We intend seeing numerous people who, I have good reason to believe, have information quite relevant to the enquiry, but, for whatever reason, have not come forward yet.*" He closed by commenting that "*… there are also one or two individuals who were close to the incident, and without doubt it has been playing on their minds.*"[103] It was also announced that a confidential police line would be set up between the hours of 1700 and 1900, which would be personally manned by a DCP officer until Thursday 14 September, after which it would have an answerphone facility. It is not known whether any member of the public took advantage of this facility. A spokesman closed the meeting by emphasising that the police were hopeful that they would bring the matter to a definite conclusion, and, at the very least, would recover Alan's body, bringing some comfort to his mother. Pennington held another press briefing on Monday 25 September 1980 where he said that he was pleased with progress to date and publicly thanked those people who had come forward to assist, but without, of course, naming them.

The DCP team was completely independent, although the RFIP provided

---

102 "Final act in a Falklands drama; Marine Alan Addis disappeared from a Falklands social club 15 years ago." *The Independent*, 28 August 1995.

103 "We will remain until the enquiry is finished say Devon & Cornwall Police;" *Penguin News*, 11 September 1995.

transport, manpower for searches and liaison with the local community. Pennington seemed ideal for the task, being described by Superintendent Greenland as an *"affable, congenial and conscientious colleague."*[104]

The team divided its activities between Stanley, North Arm and Mount Pleasant Airport[105] and appears to have concentrated on interviewing people rather than physical searches. Soon after he had set up for business, Pennington held a formal meeting with the Attorney-General where he presented new evidence. As a result, the Attorney-General authorised the arrest of four men to *'help the police with their enquiries'*: Tony Blake; David Clarke; Robin Jaffray, nicknamed 'Titch'; and Bernard Peck, nicknamed 'Frog'.

These men were arrested in North Arm on Wednesday 27 September 1995 and flown in an RAF Chinook helicopter to Mount Pleasant Airfield, where the RFIP had a sub-station. On the way, Tony Blake was heard to tell the other three: *"Answer all questions with 'no comment' – no names, no packdrill."*[106] They were held for twenty-four hours based on the original warrant, followed by a further thirty-six hour extension. Presumably they offered nothing to help the police as they were released on police bail on Friday 30 September, although that bail was later cancelled, and it was announced that no charges would be pressed.

There was one surprising postscript to the DCP enquiry, as they announced at their final news conference on 1 October 1995:

"On 1 October, acting on the authority of a warrant issued by Her Majesty's Coroner, Royal Falkland Islands Police officers investigating the disappearance of Marine Alan Addis exhumed human remains from an unmarked grave in Stanley cemetery. The remains are believed to have been discovered in the area of North Arm in 1983 and are unidentified. Preliminary enquiries indicate that the remains are of at least two people. There is little likelihood that the remains are in any way connected with the Addis case and they will now be the subject of a separate enquiry. A full report will be made to HM Coroner in due course."[107]

---

104 Email Greenland-Miller 8 Aug 2024.
105 The RFIP had its own civil police station, including cells, inside the military complex.
106 Email Goss-Miller 9 Sep 2023.
107 *Penguin News* 4 October 1995.

This was an astonishing admission, which perhaps indicates that there might be further homicide cases in North Arm, although not in this particular finding, as discussed in Chapter Fourteen.

PENNINGTON VISIT REPORT

There is no record of the date the Pennington team left the Falklands, but it can be assumed to have been in mid-to-late October 1995. DCI Pennington later submitted a report to Devon & Cornwall Police and the Royal Falkland Islands Police. A Freedom of Information request to the Devon & Cornwall Police resulted in the release of the Executive Summary given below, but not the Parts One and Two referred to:[108]

"**EXECUTIVE SUMMARY**
Sir,
This file details the Devon & Cornwall Constabulary investigation into the disappearance in 1980 of Royal Marine Alan ADDIS.

Part one of the report details the enquiry leading up to the arrests, interviews and bailment of four suspects on the Falkland Islands.

Part two provides a précis of the outstanding lines of enquiry and it can be seen that the theory of accidental death cannot be ruled out.

The position now with the enquiry is that the investigation team is satisfied that the four suspects arrested were unlikely to have been involved in the Marine's disappearance, acting with each other in any combination. The probability of just one of the suspects committing the crime alone is remote. Therefore, to encompass a single one of them in any involvement would mean that there would most likely have to be another, as yet unknown, person implicated. Again, the probability of this is remote. An investigation of the scene highlights accidental death as the one scenario remaining which cannot be ruled out.

Appendices to the report include transcribed interviews, documents and operational orders.

Ancillary items such as situation report logs together with other generated material will follow once the Devon & Cornwall Constabulary involvement is completed in its entirety.

---

108 Pennington enquiry as supplied by DCP Dec 2022 under FoI.

CONCLUSION

Despite the many enquiries made following the disappearance of Royal Marine Alan ADDIS over the 15 years since August 1980, there has been no explanation to suggest how he met his death.

His body has not been recovered.

There is no evidence to connect any person with his death.

In the absence of evidence, there is no more support for a foul play explanation than there is an accident theory, which must remain a possibility.

(sgd) Detective Chief Inspector R PENNINGTON"

Comments

Pennington stated that: *"The probability of just one of the suspects committing the crime alone is remote."* This is agreed up to a point. Alan Addis was 6ft 2in tall (1.88m), weighed 12 stone (76kg), and was both fit and well trained. Thus, it was unlikely that one person acting on his own could have killed him without recourse to a knife (or a firearm, although that has never been suggested). This does not preclude a 'sucker punch', let alone disposal of the body.

However, Pennington then goes on to absolve all four arrested men of any involvement in the disappearance of Alan Addis, either individually, or collectively in any combination with the other three, nor indeed any one of those four in combination with unidentified others. The corollary must be that the crime, if crime there was, was committed by unnamed fifth and sixth persons, with the assistance of one or more others, also unidentified.

Pennington's final conclusion is, therefore: *"An investigation of the scene highlights accidental death as the one scenario remaining which cannot be ruled out."* Unfortunately, the DCP will not release their reasoning for this conclusion and Mr Pennington declined to be interviewed for this book.

As described above, Pennington started full of confidence, with several very public promises to succeed where previous efforts had failed. But, despite that early confidence, he ended with precisely the same conclusions as his predecessors, that Alan Addis had left the Social Club at 0130 and that if anyone knew what happened to him after that they had not admitted to it. Thus, the anti-climactic participation of the DCP can be described as: *"In like a lion, out like a lamb."*

CHAPTER ELEVEN

Operation Lioness II[109]

Following the Pennington debacle, the RFIP kept up the pressure. In January 1996, a routine infantry patrol in the Danson Harbour area saw what they thought was a grave and four police Constables were immediately sent out to mark the spot. This was followed by a comprehensive search by twenty-four members of the FIDF but, once again, to no avail.

The next investigation was the most ambitious to date and took some months to organise and assemble all the elements, the most pressing of which was finance. Fortunately, Lion TV came up with most of the money, provided they could film the whole project for a programme, the MoD waived charges for the air fares, while the Falkland Islands government provided the remainder.[110] No team members were paid as such.

Diving Team

The first step was to map and understand the tidal system and the underwater landscape beneath and around the jetty. This was undertaken between 15 and 17 August 1996 by a professional diving team, which was coincidentally resident at Mount Pleasant Airport. The team produced detailed charts and briefed the RFIP on 19 August 1996. Naturally, during this work, they also searched for any traces of Alan, but they found none.

The diving team said that, at the time Alan was reported to be returning to MV *Forrest* (i.e., between 0130 and 0200), there was a neap tide (i.e., high

---

109 Sources.
    1.   *Operation Lioness. Summary Report of J Hunter and M Swindells, January 1998.*
    2.   *Alan Addis – Search Feasibility Study, same authors.*
110 The resulting documentary was screened on Channel 4 in 1998.

tide was a little lower and low tide a little higher than average), which meant that the water was not moving in any significant manner. Further, the shape of the channel and the reef across most of the entrance to the Creek would have combined to keep his body in the area. Thus, the original diving search in August 1980, combined with this new search in 1996, should have found his body – if it was there, which it was not.

There is no record of any follow-up to this diving team's research, nor of any communication between them and the Lioness II (FSAG) team. There has been no known further investigation into the possibility that Alan Addis might have drowned.

Forensic Science Advisory Group (FSAG) – Phase One

The next step consisted of two visits by the Forensic Science Advisory Group (FSAG), a unique body, which had been established in 1995 by Professor John Hunter.[111] One of the pioneers of forensic archaeology,[112] his group worked with the Home Office and many police forces in the UK, as well as in Bosnia and Iraq, but this was their first involvement with the Falkland Islands.

Hunter decided that a feasibility study was necessary in order to save time and effort during the full team's visit. He started in the UK by familiarising himself with the existing evidence, including previous search data, photographs and statements. He also discussed the case face-to-face with Sarah Ann Addis, and with LPCs Burston and Elliott who had accompanied Pennington during his abortive visit. He was also briefed on the various theories on what had happened on 8 August 1980 and on some of the characters involved. Naturally, this meant that he would be particularly interested in the layout and character of North Arm Settlement and its surrounding countryside, and with the local geology and subsoils. He and another member of FSAG, Sergeant Mick Swindells of the Lancashire Police, then flew to the Falklands in January 1997, where they were hosted by the RFIP.

---

111 Professor John Hunter, OBE, BA, PhD, FSAMI, FAFFSSoc, Professor of Archaeology and Ancient History at the University of Birmingham.

112 The UK definition of forensic archaeology is the application of the principles and methods of the discipline of archaeology to locate and recover buried remains, and associated evidence, but always within the judicial framework.

Their main interest was North Arm Settlement itself, where they spent two days: 5 and 6 January 1997. They paid particular attention to areas in and around the Settlement; several houses, including those occupied by Blake, Clarke, Peck; cowsheds; stables; cemeteries (both human and pets); and the gorse line between the Settlement and the airstrip. They also paid a cursory visit to North Arm House. Following an inspection, they also then stated their opinion that it was unlikely that Addis had fallen off the jetty and drowned.

Their main conclusions were that Addis had been killed in the early hours of 8 August 1980 and that the body had then been concealed somewhere within the Settlement for several hours before being moved to somewhere in the Camp for permanent burial. They also concluded that such was the extent and featureless nature of the Camp that, unless a particular site could be specified, further searches would be a waste of time and effort. Their final conclusion was a side swipe at the Falkland Islands government, commenting that there needed to be a post-mortem of Biggs's exhumed remains, which might throw some light, possibly even only indirectly, on what had happened to Addis.

Forensic Science Advisory Group (FSAG) – Phase Two

The main visit by the FSAG took place in January 1997, when the team consisted of five men and one dog. The team was headed by Professor John Hunter, partnered by Sergeant Mick Swindells, with his cadaver dog, Lee, a Border Collie.[113] The third member was Steve Taylor, a geophysicist from Bradford University, who was responsible for operating the ground penetrating radar (GPR) equipment. Finally, there were two IT specialists from the Metropolitan Police: LPCs 618 Burston and 143 Elliot. These were supported throughout their visit by members of the RFIP. The entire performance was filmed by TV company Lion Films and screened on Channel 4 later in 1998.

The team's aim was to search for a body, which was an implicit acknowledgement that Alan had been killed; whether deliberately or accidentally was not an issue. Thus, the body had to be somewhere in the

---

113 Dog (Lee) had been replaced in UK by new dog. Lee was then left in FI due to UK quarantine rules.

North Arm area. But the body would occupy an area some 6ft 6in by 3ft (2 x 1m) in an area of some 193sq miles (500sq km) – truly, like looking for a needle in a haystack, perhaps even two haystacks.

The team arrived in North Arm on 12 January 1998 and operated every day until 22 January, living in the Settlement, apart from a few nights in 'outside houses'. They searched over fifty locations, using people on foot (the Mark One Eyeball!), the cadaver dog (Mark One Nose!!), GPR, and on the 16th a helicopter. All excavations were carried out according to strict archaeological protocols and standards. Their activities are summarised in the table below.

LOCATION		DATES (January 1998)									
		13	14	15	16	17	18	19	20	21	22
North Arm Settlement	Manager's House			x	x		x		x	x	
	Cemetery					x	x	x			
	North Arm Chapel			x							
	David Clarke's House					x	x	x			
	Cow Paddock									x	x
	Old Dip Paddock				x	x	x	x	x		
	Old Quarry Site						x	x	x		
	Outhouses	x									
	Peck Outhouses					x				x	
North Arm Jetty Area	Shearing Sheds						x	x			
	Sheep Dip			x							
	Sludge				x						
	Stable Area				x						

	Storage Shed at Jetty				x						
	Wool Press						x				
Outside Houses	Congo House		x								
	Danson Harbour House	x				x					
	Mappa House								x	x	x
	Moffatt Harbour House	x				x					
	North West Arm House[114]	x									
	North Arm House						x				
	Peat Banks House		x								
	Wreck House		x	x							
Miscella-neous	Duffins Bridge	x		x						x	
	Garden Point		x					x			
	Hunters Arroyo	x	x	x					x		
	Track Junction		x	x							
	Reservoir						x				
	Sandbeds						x				
Aerial	Helicopter				x						

Table 7. Activities of FSAG 13–22 January 1998

114 This was not the current manager's house.

Not surprisingly, the main concentration was on the Settlement itself, with the properties occupied in 1980 by Tony Blake, Dave Clarke and Bernard Peck coming in for yet more attention. The manager's house was checked on no less than eighteen occasions, which must have tested Mrs Goss's sense of humour (her husband, Eric, formerly of Goose Green, was now the manager) – even the tomato bed in the conservatory was examined. They also searched all the areas around the jetty. The sheep dip was drained on the 15th and the residual sludge examined on the 16th, both unpleasant tasks, helped by men from the Settlement.

Danson Harbour House was a special favourite, together with the vehicle route there, passing over Duffin's Bridge and Track Junction and then through the valley created by Hunter's Arroyo (= stream). The most northerly site visited was Wreck House with Peat Bank House being checked on the way. The most southerly site was Garden Point.

There were two factors of which the FSAG team were not aware at the time. The first was that the killing shed that had been present in 1980 had been totally demolished in about 1983 and, judging by the efficiency with which Tony Blake obliterated Bunkhouse Number Three, no trace would have been left. The second was the bodies that had been discovered in North Arm in 1983, shipped to Stanley and quickly reinterred in an unnamed grave. The existence of these had been revealed by the Pennington enquiry and was then the subject of a police report, which was passed to the Coroner. Professor Hunter was not told about these bodies, which might have affected his plan, and the Coroner, Chief of Police and Attorney-General refused to disclose the report in 2023, which suggests that there is something in it that they do not wish to be published.

The FSAG also commented on Biggs's death, which had obviously been drawn to their attention. As had been recommended in the feasibility study, they suggested that a proper independent post-mortem should be carried out, which, as far as is known, has still never been done. They also commented on the speed with which Bunkhouse Number Three had been demolished.

The conclusions of the FSAG were:
- They were not convinced that Addis had fallen off the jetty – in fact, there was no evidence that he might have done.
- The FSAG's previous experience in Europe and Asia, coupled with

statistical analyses, suggested that the burial site would be well-known to the perpetrator.

- It was unlikely that the body, either as a result of an accident or by ditching by the perpetrators, would have been left in open-air, as some sign would have remained and been found.
- The body was hidden within the Settlement for several hours and then disposed of in a site well-known to the perpetrators, which had good access for a vehicle (almost certainly a Land Rover) and which offered short- and long-term security.

For the future, the FSAG recommended:

a. In view of the vast area to be covered, searches outside the Settlement were unlikely to be productive unless there was good evidence pinpointing a specific location.
b. Areas for future probing within the Settlement included the cavity beneath the disused storage shed; stables; gorse line; manager's house; graveyard.
c. There should be a check on all buildings, structures and other works (e.g., wells) that had been altered in any way since 1980.
d. **Comment**. As far as is known, none of this has been done.

The team also drew attention to the inordinate speed at which Addis's death was handled and the death certificate issued. They also recorded the fact that MV *Forrest's* log and the graveyard record for the relevant period were missing, and, as far as is known, they have never been found.

The FSAG investigation was carefully planned, embraced a wide field of expertise, and was diligently executed. The team managed to clear a number of sites, but, as they themselves admitted, the area outside the Settlement was vast and featureless, and in the absence of specific evidence, there was little point in another general search.

Unfortunately, the Falkland Islands government and the RFIP then became enmeshed in the Bingham affair. The Chief of Police, Superintendent Ken Greenwood, who had supported the FSAG so strongly, resigned on 30 April 1999 and, in October 1999, there was a formal inspection by the Foreign and Commonwealth Office's Police and Criminal Justice Adviser, which led to formal apologies by the Governor and the incoming Chief of

Police (who was later found guilty of perverting the course of justice in an entirely separate case) and Attorney-General. There is no evidence of any similar investigations after the FSAG, so the death of Alan Addis was once again relegated to the 'too difficult' file, where it has remained ever since.

CHAPTER TWELVE

Paranormal

Many families faced with a seemingly insoluble 'missing persons' situation turn to paranormal practitioners for help and Sarah Ann Addis was no exception. But first, let us look at some other examples.

Len Phillips, a businessman living in London, noted in 1970 that he had not heard from his sister, Mrs Doris Symonds, for some time. He conducted a series of personal searches and eventually established that her last confirmed address was in Ipplepen, a small village outside Newton Abbot in Devon. He was told that she had disappeared some years earlier, following which, her husband, an Army officer, divorced her *in absentia* and married another woman. Len therefore contacted the Devon & Cornwall Police and articles appeared in various newspapers, which led to a number of 'mediums' making contact. The first was a Mrs Woodward, who lived in Maidenhead and claimed to have fifty years' experience. She contacted her local police to say that she had seen Doris's picture on TV and had immediately gone into a trance in which it was revealed to her that Doris had suffered a violent death.

Her report was taken sufficiently seriously for the Devon & Cornwall Police to be informed, who passed it on to Len. The latter then attended a séance on 1 March 1973, accompanied by a photographer from the *Evening Mail* newspaper. Mrs Woodward went into a trance and made contact with 'Doris', who told her several facts about her (Doris's) family home, all of which were corroborated by Len. 'Doris' then told Mrs Woodward that she had been killed by two blows to the right side of her head and buried wrapped in a dark car rug in a shallow grave in a violet-covered wood near her home. Len told the paper that he would be visiting Mrs Woodward again the following week, but there were no further reports and, as far as is known, Len had no further meetings with her.[115]

---

115 Source: *Evening Mail*, 2 Mar 73.

Len's second contact came from a Mrs Hancock who lived near St Austell in Cornwall, who sent him three letters.[116] In the first, dated 'May 1973', she wrote [spelling as quoted]: *"Will you send me a small Photo or necktie and I will try my crystal and see if there is going to be anything found in that wood where your sister is supposed to be. Are they still trying to find her there. I ain't seen anything on the papers yet. I don't want anything from you and if you send me Photo or necktie I'll be the experience and return it to you. I just want a try on my crystal. Yours truly, D.A.H."*

The second letter was dated 19 May 1973: *"I wrote asking you for Tie and Photo. Now I don't need it as I've had a go with the crystal and seen what happened in the wood. Its there if it can be found. I dont want to say much about it. I was upset with what I seen. I shall have another look as I want to see more. They were a good way in the wood. The trees are parked like an avenue in rows so far apart this is all I wish to say. I don't want to tell you any more. Hope you will find what you are looking for please destroy my address. Yours truly D.A.H."*

The third was sent after 25 May and was headed by a sketch map:

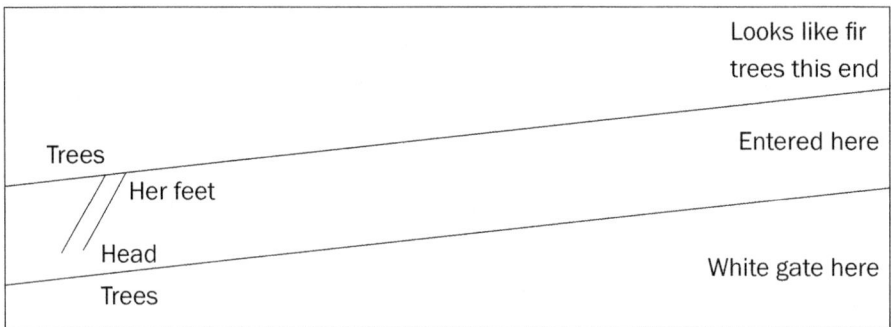

Figure 3

"HE BEHIND HER LAID HER DOWN AS YOU SEE AS HE LIFT THE BODY COUGHT SEE HIS CLOTHS WAS STAINED. WAS SEEN MAKING A TRENCH BEHIND WORKING BEAR-SHOULDERS IF FOUND HIS CLOTHS IS BURIED WITH HER. if there is two [...] the wood they will find it what i seen may 25th.

Do you know if there is an old quarry or gully in this wood as this look like the end trees the last two [...] as they went where she was standing on the right there was young trees and BROUSE (gorse?) growing she is lying on her left side this is what I seen. I may be wrong as I am no first class I'll

leave it with you and with Gods help you will get what you are looking for.
PLEASE BURN"[117]

Although both of these seemed plausible, as far as is known, neither of them were followed up by actual searches on the ground.

Jim Thompson

As described in Chapter Fifteen, Bangkok-based American businessman, Jim Thompson, disappeared in the Malaysian Cameron Highlands in 1967. Major efforts were mounted to find him and several *bomohs*, Malay specialists in the paranormal, were brought in to seek an answer; they did not succeed. In addition, Richard Noone, a British officer with great experience of Malaya and Borneo, arrived, bringing with him a head-hunter from Borneo and an aboriginal *bomoh*, who had successfully helped him with a previous case of a man missing in the jungle. The three spent thirty-six hours in the jungle, both searching and interviewing local *Orang Asli* (aboriginal jungle-dwellers), and then emerged to state positively that Thompson, or his body, were not in the jungle.

Sarah Ann Addis

Like others in a similar position, Sarah Ann Addis believed that she and her son had shared a form of telepathic communication, which led her to become interested in paranormal practices. During her 1995 visit to North Arm, she experienced strong sensations in two places, which suggested that she was close to her son. *"Next we went through the first big storage shed. There was one particular place in here that made me feel very confused, such strange feelings it gave me."* Later: *"We carried on walking through the Settlement and once again I got very distressed. We were in an old chicken coop and once again I got very distressed."*[118]

---

117 Spelling (and misspelling, use of capitals, etc.) as in original. Two words (in square brackets) cannot be deciphered. Obviously, he did not burn the letter.
118 Addis, *Missing on Patrol*; p.46.

Her first contacts were of little help, so she contacted the self-styled 'psychic detective' Nella Jones, a Kent-based, forty-two-year-old Romany gypsy who was well-known at the time for her claims that she had assisted the police in the hunt for the 'Yorkshire Ripper'.

Although Nella's claims were unsubstantiated, both Sarah Ann and the RFIP took her seriously and investigated her visions. An official report states: "*According to Mrs Jones, Addis was killed with a knife in the Settlement and transported to a hiding place by boat. She says that the boat headed straight out from the jetty, and then turned right, and was concealed in a cave, which had a fissure or a blowhole in its roof and had an entrance shaped like an inverted Y, which could only be seen at low tide. With this information, police were able to locate a spot that fitted the description in every detail, and any remaining scepticism about the ability of the medium began to disappear…*" What they found was Devil's Point, several miles South of the North Arm jetty, which not only had an entrance that matched Nella Jones's predictions, but also had a blowhole in the roof. Sarah Ann was with the RFIP when they first visited Devil's Point, but after a fruitless search, they all returned to Stanley. Nevertheless, Devil's Point fitted Nella Jones's predictions so closely that Superintendent Greenland personally led a second reconnaissance for a more detailed search, and the cave was thoroughly examined by both divers and climbers, but no trace of human remains nor, indeed, of any manmade object was found.

Hypnosis

Sarah Ann Addis also tried the use of hypnosis. Sandra Hirtl had written to her early in the latter's research, telling her that she (Sandra) had been at the North Arm party on 8 August 1980 and felt that some of the evidence given to the police was either wrong or incomplete, but without giving specific details. At some time in the early 2000s, Hirtl, by now elderly and ill, was in England and in contact with Sarah Ann, but was unable to recall the details of her allegations. As a result, Sarah Ann arranged for her to see a professional hypnotist, which was recorded on video, but even this lady was unable to extract the details from Sandra's memory.

Comment

Neither the clairvoyants nor the hypnotist were able to add anything significant to the search for Alan Addis's body, but they show how the families of disappeared people are willing to try almost anything in the search for their loved ones. Sadly, in only very few cases, if any, is there a tangible result.

CHAPTER THIRTEEN

Bodie Creek Suspension Bridge

One of the possible fates of Alan Addis's body that is sometimes mentioned is that it was thrown from Bodie Creek Suspension Bridge, which is situated some four miles Southwest of Goose Green. This is such an unusual, indeed, unlikely, structure that its background needs to be described. The names of many geographic features in the Falklands were derived from the name of the man or ship who discovered or which charted them. In this case, some waterways in Lafonia were named in 1842 by Lieutenant Bodie, RN, who commanded the survey brig, HMS *Arrow*.[119] There is a 3 mile (2km) long inland lake linked to Choiseul Sound and thence to the open sea by a 5 mile (3km) meandering tidal estuary known as Bodie Creek.

In 1924, a bridge over this Creek was constructed by Falkland Islanders in what was, by any standard, a substantial engineering achievement. The bridge originated in a Falkland Islands Company (FIC) plan to rationalise its operations on the eastern half of Lafonia by centralising the shearing operation at Goose Green. This meant that sheep from the company-owned farms at Darwin and Walker Creek would need to be herded to Goose Green. The FIC's first action was to authorise the construction of a very large shearing shed, capable of accommodating 5,000 sheep, at Goose Green, and as Darwin was close-by, that was no problem. On the other hand, the landward journey from Walker Creek, although only 13 miles (21km) distant as the crow flies, required an arduous dog-leg path around Orqueta House, a distance of some 28 miles (45km), taking shepherds and their flocks three-to-five days in each direction. There was, however, a solution in that, if the sheep could cross Bodie Creek, the distance would be reduced to 19 miles

---

119 A short distance South, Walker Creek settlement is sited on the shores of Arrow Harbour, named after Brodie's ship.

(30km), with a concomitant reduction in time. The problem then was that, at the most suitable point, the Creek was some 400 yards (366m) wide, 18 feet (5m) deep and tidal.

Following a survey, the FIC authorised the construction of a bridge, but as there was no industrial base on the island, this had to be imported. They ordered the bridge from David Rowell & Co., a long-established engineering company based in Westminster, London, which was well used to designing light suspension bridges for construction by local labour in out-of-the-way places.[120] The components were manufactured in the UK and shipped out in kit form, together with an instruction manual. Construction, however, was entirely a Falklands affair, headed by an engineer directing a crew consisting of a stone mason and some fourteen shepherds, not one of whom had any previous experience of bridge building.[121] The work started in October 1924 and was completed in July 1925, with approach roads taking another three months. This remarkable bridge was fully completed in time for the annual sheep shearing in December 1925.

The bridge consisted of a 40ft (12m) steel tower on each bank connected by two pairs of 2-inch (5cm) diameter steel cables from which was suspended a 400ft (120m) long 8ft (2m) wide deck. The only machines available were a cement mixer and a rock crusher; there were no trucks, and everything was moved in wheelbarrows. An ad hoc crane to hoist the elements of the towers into position was created out of two masts taken from a deserted yacht, while gelignite cartridges were purchased from the FIC to clear the foundations for the towers.[122] When completed, the bridge could obviously take sheep and pedestrian traffic, but could also accept bullocks and vehicles up to Land Rover size, although in the latter case, only one at a time with very little room to spare at the sides.

The bridge was refurbished in the early 1950s, and further maintenance work took place in March 1980, which included descaling rust on the towers, scraping and replacing some of the steelwork, and a thorough paint job. This work was completed by 19 March 1982, but there were further plans by the FIC to replace all of the suspension rods and the iron H-beams, which

---

120 Many Rowell suspension bridges were built in the British Isles, but others were as far away as Chile, Guatemala and New Zealand.
121 It was probably not too difficult for a generation brought up on Meccano.
122 Spruce, *Falklands Rural Heritage*, p.156.

supported the decking, and most of these had reached the Falklands by the end of March 1982. The bridge did not feature in the war of 1982, except that Argentine infantry helped themselves to some of the newly arrived ironwork to provide overhead cover for their trenches.

In later years, however, Walker Creek was given its own sheep-shearing facility and, as a consequence, the bridge fell into disuse and left to quietly rot away. It was eventually closed to both foot and vehicular traffic in 1997. It still stands but is in a sorry condition.

Alan Addis

Reverting now to Alan Addis. One of the curious and seemingly inexplicable episodes in the Addis story was David Clarke's behaviour following Alan Addis's disappearance. Clarke was one of four members of Blake's enforcers in North Arm and is known to have driven a Land Rover from North Arm, arriving at Goose Green at about 1100 on the morning of Friday 8 August 1980.[123]

At Goose Green, he went to see the manager, Eric Goss, and told him that a Marine was missing. In reply to a question by Goss, Clarke said that he had driven via Bodie Creek Bridge and was alone.

Clarke did not explain how or when he had learnt that Addis was missing. To have arrived at Goose Green at about 1100, he would have had to leave North Arm by about 0800. But the first that was known that Addis was missing was aboard MV *Forrest* at about 0700–0730, news of which those aboard were only able to communicate to North Arm via Johnson's Harbour. Further, to have travelled via Bodie Creek Bridge seemed an unnecessary diversion from the more usual route, following the telephone poles via Orqueta House.

The RFIP has periodically reviewed the Addis case and, on two occasions, has considered the possibility that Clarke might have transported Addis's body to Bodie Creek Bridge and thrown it over the side. If weights had been attached, the body would have come to rest in a place and at a depth where it was unlikely to be found, while also getting it away from the inevitable searches in and around North Arm itself. On the first such search, the police employed two of their own staff who were amateur divers – Sergeant Jock

---

123 Eric Goss to this author.

Elliot and Constable Steve Burston – to conduct an underwater survey.[124] They found a lot of debris from the earlier refurbishments of the bridge, including numerous suspension rods. They also found the tides to be harassing. But there was no trace of a body.

Some years later, the RFIP returned to the subject yet again, this time asking an RN specialist diving team stationed at Mount Pleasant to conduct a more detailed search. This team was enthusiastic and, classifying the operation as 'training', they prepared a map of the bottom, which was at a maximum depth of 18ft (5m), showing contours and rubbish accumulations as well as tidal movements. But, despite extensive searches, they found no evidence of a body or body parts.

Assessment

Although Clarke arrived at Goose Green as the sole occupant of the Land Rover, it is possible that he could have been accompanied by one or more men in another vehicle. These men could have assisted in disposing of the body at the bridge but then returned to North Arm without being seen by anyone at Goose Green.

The suggestion that the weighted body lay under Bodie Creek Bridge led to two searches, the second by professional divers, who found no evidence that it had taken place.

An alternative possibility was that the body was thrown over the bridge but without weights, in which case, it would have remained on or just below the surface and, provided the tide was right, floated down to Choiseul Sound and thence to the open sea. Once there, it would most likely have been eaten by patrolling Orcas, who normally fed on sheep carcasses. However, the estuary is tidal and meanders downstream of the bridge and it seems probable that a free-floating body would have been washed up and found on a beach before reaching the sea, which has not happened.

It is assessed that it is certainly feasible that Addis's body could have been transported by Clarke to Bodie Creek Bridge where, either weighted or not, it was thrown into the water below. However, there is no proof of either and they are assessed as unlikely.

---

124 Source: Jock Elliot via Eric Goss.

CHAPTER FOURTEEN

The Royal Falkland Islands Police

The Falkland Islands have always posed an unusual challenge to those responsible for the maintenance of law and order in a population that is both tiny and unevenly spread over a vast area. In 1980, the year of Addis's disappearance, the total population was 1,813, of whom 322 (18%) lived on West Falkland and 1,491 (82%) on East Falkland, but of the latter no less than 1,050 were in the capital, Stanley. The population of Stanley was aligned in a contiguous group of houses along the southern shore of Stanley Harbour, and was composed mainly of government officials, educators and pensioners from the Settlements who had been obliged to leave their houses on reaching the age of sixty. But the 441 in Camp were scattered around the coasts of the islands in some thirty-three Settlements. These Settlements were tight-knit communities, most of them ruled over by the owner or manager whose standing equated in many respects to that of a medieval baron or, in more modern times, a colonial District Officer. Such Settlements tended to be self-policing, and minor transgressions were dealt with quickly and quietly by the owners/managers. Major law-breaking, such as it was, tended to be concentrated in Stanley, which was also the home of the police. The police were, however, called in for the occasional major incidents in Settlements, such as homicide, as was seen in the manslaughter of Kirk in Goose Green as will be described below.

The first Chief Constable, Francis Parry, was appointed in 1846, albeit with a staff consisting only of a gaoler and a night Constable. He could, however, call on a number of special Constables and, if really necessary, soldiers from the Army garrison. The force gradually increased in numbers and, by 1900, comprised seven officers, one of whom was stationed at Fox Bay on West Falkland. By the 1920s, the growth of the whaling industry led

102

to another Constable being posted to what must have been a very lonely posting at Grytviken in South Georgia. A third Constable was sent to Elephant Jason Island to the Northwest of West Falkland, where he lived in a police house and kept watch for seal poachers. These solitary outposts were gradually withdrawn and, by 1980, the entire force was concentrated in Stanley.

The Chief Police Officer (CPO) was appointed by the Governor, who also decided the rank, which varied between Inspector and Superintendent, although three retained their previous UK rank of Chief Superintendent on taking post in Stanley. Traditionally, the police in a colony reported direct to the Governor, who would have spent many years in the Colonial Service before taking up the Falklands post and appreciated his role as representative of the Crown. Sir Rex Hunt was the last of such Governors with colonial experience and understood the relationship between the Crown and police.[125] But he left in 1985 and thereafter the holders have been career diplomats, who may have had extensive experience in diplomatic missions, but none in the governance and administration of a colony. Some of these understood their role concerning the RFIP, but others delegated many of their powers to the Chief Executive, some of whom endeavoured to treat the police as if they were part of the Civil Service and interfered in disciplinary, sometimes even operational matters.

Reverting now to pre-1982, the crime rate was low, so that many miscellaneous civil tasks were loaded onto the Chief Police Officer, including at various times: Chief Immigration Officer, Chief Customs Officer and Government Fire Precautions Officer. He and his staff were also responsible for driving tests and issuing driving licences, together with the registration, inspection and testing of motor vehicles. In addition, and as if that was not enough, the police also issued licences for guns, dogs, trout and salmon fishing, as well as for collecting penguin eggs. There was even a period when the CPO was appointed Inspector of Nuisances, which covered subjects such as crowing cockerels, smelly bins and the like. This latter responsibility was quickly and firmly offloaded by Greenland.

From the earliest days, the only prison was a small annex to the police station in Ross Road, where the CPO was also Chief Prison Officer and

---

125 He had served in Uganda as a District Commissioner from 1951–63 and in North Borneo from 1963–68.

all his police officers were sworn-in as Prison Officers, while a woman served as matron and cook for male prisoners, as well as supervisor of the occasional female prisoners. One incident concerning the prison bears repeating. An Englishman married to a Kelper lady was awarded three months imprisonment for theft, but one night managed to escape over the prison wall, whose barbed wire capping had long since disappeared. The prisoner made his way home where he found his wife in bed with a Royal Marine from Moody Brook. The prisoner immediately returned to the jail, but this time as a complainant, asking the amazed Superintendent what he was going to do about the Marine and his wife? McMillan had no sooner locked his prisoner back in his cell than the man's wife rushed in to complain about her husband being released without her being told and thus catching her *in flagrante*. "*I thought I was safe,*" she told the policeman, which, given the circumstances, was not unreasonable.[126]

Police in 1980

At the time of Addis's disappearance in August 1980, the FIP had seven officers on strength – unchanged from 1900! – comprising the Chief Police Officer, one Sergeant, one Corporal and four full-time Constables, one of whom was a woman. However, the actual numbers of operational police available for duty was usually less than this due to sickness and leave. There were also six reservist police Constables. The situation was exacerbated in 1980 as the Chief Police Officer at the time, Inspector Donald (Toddy) McMillan, CPM, was on long-term sick leave (cancer) and several others were on short-term sick, so when news of Addis's disappearance reached Stanley, only one inexperienced Constable could be sent to North Arm to take statements.[127] Even if all seven were on duty, the force was woefully short of experience and training, as the nearest help or advice was 8,000 miles (13,000km) away in the UK, while sending a staff member on courses in the UK was both time-consuming and expensive.

The FIP had a difficult job. First, they were concentrated in Stanley, only sending an officer to a Settlement when there was a demonstrable need.

---

126 Hunt, p.71.
127 McMillan died in Southampton, England in 1982.

Secondly, they lived cheek-by-jowl with the Falklands government, some of whom sought on occasions to interfere with what were properly police matters. Thirdly, the Constables, with only a few expatriate exceptions, were drawn from the very tight and close-knit community they were mandated to police. Fourthly, they were isolated from the professional command and technical resources that a British county force would take for granted. They could, and did, apply to the UK for help, but in those days, it took time and was expensive, since the Falkland Islands government had to bear the full costs.

The CPO himself was usually an expatriate British policeman, an Inspector or Superintendent with previous service in a UK county force, on a three- or five-year contract. With few exceptions, these men had little or no previous experience of the Falklands, although sometimes a Falklander would take charge after progressing through the ranks.

RANK	NAME	CHIEF OF POLICE		PERSONAL ORIGIN
		FROM	TO	
Supt	Terry Peck, MBE	1966	Jun 1980	Falklander
Insp	Donald (Toddy) McMillan, CPM	Dec 1979	Sep 1981	Falklander
Supt	Ronald (Ronnie) Lamb[128]	Sep 1981	Apr 1982	Strathclyde Police
		Jul 1982	?	
Maj RMP	Anthony J Figg (Provost Marshal)	Jun 1982	Aug 1982	UK Royal Military Police[129]
Chief Supt	Walter (Bill) Richards	Aug 1982	1985	Falklander. Seconded from Met Pol
Supt	Kenneth D Greenland, QPM	1985	Apr 1999	UK Royal Military Police
Insp	Len McGill (Interim)	Oct 2005	Sep 2007	Falklander
Supt	Paul Elliot	Sep 2007	Nov 2009	Lincolnshire Police
Insp	Len McGill (Interim)	Nov 2009	Jan 2010	Falklander

128 It appears that Supt Lamb returned to the Falklands after the war, but how long he remained and when exactly he handed over to Supt Richards cannot now be established.

129 One of Tony Figg's more memorable deeds was to admonish Prince Andrew for being improperly dressed.

RANK	NAME	CHIEF OF POLICE		PERSONAL
		FROM	TO	ORIGIN
Ch Supt	Barry Marsden	Apr 2011	May 2014	Devon & Cornwall Police
Supt	Len McGill	Jun 2014	2017	Falklander
Supt	Jeff McMahon	2017	Jan 2022	Wigan Police
Insp	Gavin Clifton (Interim)	Jan 22	Mar 22	Falklander
Supt	Michael Luke	Mar 2022	Jan 2023	St Helena Police (since 2018)
Insp	Barry Thacker (Interim)	Jan 2023	Jul 2024	Derbyshire Police
Supt	Albert Dann	Jul 2024	–	Kent Police

Table 8. Chief Police Officers 1980–2024

The experiences of the FIP tended to be towards minor violations such as assaults and malicious damage, although the most numerous were road traffic offences, which, prior to the war of 1982, were confined to the Stanley area since there were no roads outside the capital. Their experience with major crimes was very limited. The table shows offences covered in 1970–71 and 1975–76, the most recent figures prior to Addis's disappearance in 1980.

OFFENCES AGAINST:	DETAIL	1970-71		1974-75	
		HEARD	CONVICTED	HEARD	CONVICTED
Persons	Assaults	5	5		
	Intent to murder			2	2
Property	Larceny	13	12	7	6
	Malicious damage	10	8	3	3
Sexual	Indecent assault	2	2	2	2
	Incest	2	2		
Local ordinances	Road traffic	49	49	25	22

	Licensing			28	28
	Firearms			5	4
	Dogs			1	1
Miscellaneous		22	20	8	7

Table 9. Offences Covered in Sample Years
(Sources: Falkland Islands Yearbooks)

The Addis Case

The FIP was involved in the Addis case almost from the start, the first visit to North Arm being by WPC Alice Etheridge, although she did not arrive until some two weeks after the event. She clearly accepted the general view that the disappearance was accidental. That still seems to have been the view in November 1981 when Captain Gallacher of the Army's Special Investigation Branch (SIB) visited, and he and Superintendent Lamb agreed that the FIP would assume responsibility for the inquiry, which was endorsed by the Ministry of Defence and that is the position that remains to this day.

When Gallacher left, Superintendent Lamb was working on a full report on the Addis case. He had completed but not submitted this report when the Argentines invaded. All copies were destroyed, but after the Argentines had been kicked out, he compiled a new version from memory.[130] He ended his report with the clear conclusion that the disappearance was an accident, which was fully endorsed by Rex Hunt, the Civil Commissioner, as shown in the letter on page 75.

Police 1980–2025

During the 1982 war, the Argentine Military Police occupied the FIP HQ in Ross Road and took over all policing duties. Lamb, the CPO, was expelled to the UK, while the Falkland members were sent home, with

---

130 Letter to Civil Commissioner, from Police Headquarters, Stanley, 29 Jul 1982 in National Archives FCO 7/5509.

the exception of one Constable, who was retained and did his best for the civilian community.[131]

Also during the war, the HQ building in Ross Road was hit by a British helicopter-launched missile (12 June 1982), which caused some damage but did not destroy the building. Immediately on the end of the war there was no police force at all, so the Army initially provided Royal Military Police under command of the Provost Marshal of 5 Infantry Brigade, but Superintendent Lamb returned for a short period.[132] Lamb was replaced by Chief Superintendent Bill Richards of the Metropolitan Police, who happened to be a native Falklander. Six Metropolitan Police officers also helped restore civilian policing, and one Sergeant and three Constables were still serving as part of the FIP in 1985, but by this time from disparate county forces, all of whom were rotated regularly, causing an unsettled atmosphere.

As Bill Richards' tour approached its end, he was known to be keen to return to the Metropolitan Police, and the Governor, Rex Hunt, was concerned to replace him and his fellow expatriate policemen and to rebuild the FIP with native Falklanders. Hunt's main problem was that there was no experienced Falklander to take over as chief, so he approached the then Provost Marshal, Major Kenneth (Ken) Greenland, RMP, who agreed to take on the post.[133] Greenland originally hoped to do so on secondment from the British Army, but when this was not permitted, he resigned and took over as Chief Police Officer in 1985, serving for fourteen years until 30 April 1999.

Greenland found a force that was in much the same position as before the war, being both critically understaffed and seriously underfunded, but composed mainly of seconded UK policemen. He fought hard to bring a degree of professionalism and stability to the force, which had been lacking. He gradually increased their numbers from seven to seventeen, and set in hand numerous courses, both at home and back in England. One of the early problems he had to face was that the FIP still concentrated virtually all its efforts on Stanley, while the estate managers ruled their estates and

---

131 He was awarded the Colonial Police Medal for his efforts in what must have been a very difficult period.

132 No documentary record of Lamb's return can be found, but he signed a letter dated Police HQ Stanley on 31 July 1982.

133 Hunt, op. cit. p.343.

still resented, sometimes even prevented, visits by the police, although he gradually overcame this.

Greenland also recognised the need for higher level supervision, advice and administrative support and, having failed to elicit any interest from the Inspector-General of Dependent Territories Police, he managed to establish a formal and very helpful arrangement with the Devon & Cornwall constabulary. He also reopened the Addis inquiry and set up a small team, which started by reinterviewing all those still available in the islands, although they found that in some cases recollections were beginning to fade, while others were simply confused. A few of these interviews led to searches, sometimes of particular spots conducted by the police, or in more general areas by the police with the aid of the military. As in many other cases in the Addis investigation, plenty of theories were put forward, some of which were so improbable that they could be immediately discarded, but, even so, none of those that remained could be substantiated by actual proof.

By now, the belief that Addis had suffered some form of accident, either from exposure or drowning, had lost its credibility, and the presumption became that he had been the victim of a homicide. Curiously, however, this has never been formalised, and his death certificate remains unchanged as an 'accident'.

Searches now switched to possible burial sites, with the ground between North Arm and Danson Harbour being given particular attention. On one occasion, a possible grave was spotted by an Army patrol and the whole area was intensively searched by the police assisted by helpers from the infantry unit at Mount Pleasant Airfield. In other searches, septic tanks were drained and specific sites closely examined, including, for the first time, Cow Park Pond, whose shallow depth made it unlikely, but it was only a short distance inland from North Arm.

An even more unlikely site was Ruggles Island, only a short distance from Danson Harbour House.[134] It was occasionally used for grazing and for picnics and, when the police were informed that someone had found bones there, they felt compelled to have a look. Two Constables[135] were duly sent and quickly found the reported bones, but they belonged to a large seabird.

---

134 Ruggles Island lies across the entrance to Ruggles Bay, located some 16 miles (26km), WNW (283°) of North Arm.

135 PCs Burston and Elliot.

The two men took the opportunity to cover the remainder of the island but found nothing untoward.

The police eventually had four suspects but, despite their intensive investigation, could not find any conclusive proof against any of them. Superintendent Greenland then took advantage of his working arrangement with Devon & Cornwall Police to send the case file to the Chief Constable, with the enquiry: *"Have we missed anything?"* This led to the Pennington enquiry as described in Chapter Ten.

Sarah Ann Addis

Alan's mother got on well with the RFIP, particularly with Superintendent Greenland and Inspector Morris. In 1992, when Sarah Ann, now back in England, was told of a Falkland Islander who boasted in a bar that he had killed a Marine and got away with it, she held a three-way telephone conversation with her informant, a Sergeant who had been with Alan in NP8901 in 1980, and Inspector Morris. This led to another teleconference, this time with Superintendent Greenland.

These discussions led to a second visit by Sarah Ann in February 1995, when she was hosted by the RFIP, who made every effort to help her. She stayed with a police family, the police organised witnesses for her to interview in Stanley, provided a security guard outside the interview room in case of problems, and then arranged a Beaver flight to North Arm where she conducted yet more interviews. Finally, the police organised a search party whose activities extended as far as Devil's Point. As she herself wrote: *"I returned to England feeling very sad, but at least knowing that the police were still working and showing an interest in the case."*[136]

The outcome of the referral to Devon & Cornwall Police was a visit by Detective Chief Inspector Pennington and a team from the Devon & Cornwall Police in August 1995. They conducted a lengthy and very detailed investigation, including many interviews and searches, which culminated in four arrests, but, in the end, like all its predecessors, they were able to add little to what was already known. Indeed, their only significant discovery was that of the radio call from MV *Forrest* to Johnson's Harbour, followed by the

---

136 Addis, op. cit., p.47.

telephone call to North Arm on the morning of 8 August. The next visit was by Professor Hunter and his team who searched and dug up many sites in the North Arm area (Op Lioness II), again with the RFIP accommodating the visitors and providing local knowledge, transport and guides.

The Burgos Case

Although it was rare for the FIP to become involved in investigating crimes in the Settlements, the notorious affray that took place in Goose Green Settlement in the early hours of 2 March 1980 was an exception. Following a prize-giving ceremony, there was, as was customary, a community dance, during which a Chilean shepherd, Francisco Burgos, who normally worked at a distant 'outside house', brushed against the girlfriend of Tony Kirk, a Kelper. Assuming the contact to have been deliberate (which Burgos vehemently denied), Kirk and some comrades assembled in a corridor and waylaid the Chilean with the apparent intention of giving him 'a good hiding'. Kirk punched Burgos in the face, breaking his nose, which must have been a heavy, bare-knuckle blow. In the brawl that followed, the seriously outnumbered and unsupported Chilean drew his shepherd's knife and stabbed Kirk in the stomach.[137] A nurse, who by chance was present, rendered first aid, but help was needed from Stanley and, at dawn, a FIGAS Beaver flew in a doctor, his wife (also a doctor) and the matron of the hospital. Kirk was flown to Stanley but died that afternoon.

Burgos was charged with murder, but Judge Watkin-Williams, who was brought down from England in April, reduced the charge to 'manslaughter with provocation'. Unsurprisingly, Burgos was found guilty by the jury of Falkland Islanders, but the judge sentenced him only to nine months imprisonment. This caused considerable ill-feeling in some elements of the Kelper community, who considered that the death of one of their own at the hands of an outsider had not been properly avenged. Nevertheless, Burgos served his sentence in the cell at Stanley Police Station, following which he was deported back to Chile.[138]

---

137 This was actually an Eskilstuna knife, a high-quality implement, named after the Swedish town where it was manufactured.
138 Hunt, op. cit., pp.17, 48.

The 1983 Bodies Mystery

At the press conference at the end of his 1995 investigation, Detective Chief Inspector Pennington announced that he had discovered that some human remains had been found at North Arm in 1983, which were then transported to Stanley and buried in an unmarked grave. He was clearly suspicious and saw a possible, although probably remote, relationship with the Addis case.

Finding dead bodies was by no means unusual in the Falklands. One of the problems shared by military and civilian communities after the Argentine defeat was that corpses of both Argentine and British servicemen continued to be discovered, some of them many months after the surrender. Further, for many years, bodies had been found on the shore, the remains of people who had died at sea, through either illness or accident. In addition, in the days when travel was difficult, inhabitants who died in the more remote Settlements would be buried in a nearby graveyard; the North Arm cemetery, for example, contains some fifty graves. In other cases, they were buried in some piece of wasteland only to be found years later, usually by sheer chance. In this case, the remains of two adults and a child were discovered in North Arm in 1983 and the remains transferred to Stanley where they were examined by the Coroner and the resident surgeon, who found evidence of diphtheria. Records of the deaths were eventually traced and, since there was no need for a formal inquest, the bodies were buried in Stanley cemetery. This clearly aroused Pennington's suspicions, but further investigation after he had left established the identity of the remains and thus there was no link to Addis.

Some Unfortunate Scandals

The fourteen-year command by Superintendent Greenland gave the RFIP firm and consistent leadership but he retired in 1999 and, unfortunately, the early years of the twenty-first century saw the RFIP suffering a number of setbacks among his successors. In the majority of these cases, the Chief Police Officers concerned took voluntary early retirement in the case of Falklanders, or early termination of a standard contract in the case of expatriates. These events were not related to the Addis case, which remained 'open' throughout, but did mean that the disappearance of Alan Addis may well not have been given the continuing attention it deserved.

In yet another twist to this story, in 2006, a seven-strong team from the Metropolitan Police went to the islands to investigate allegations of police corruption. Conduct of this particular investigation became confused when the head of the police team had a rather obvious love affair with the (female) Attorney-General. This resulted in the latter's rapid departure 'for family reasons'. This team's report has never been released.

As stated earlier, the Chief Police Officer was also the Chief Prison Officer, responsible for the small detention facility attached to the police HQ. In April 2009 it was discovered that the regime was so lax that prisoners were openly taking cocaine, which led to the CPO of the time being reprimanded, whereupon he resigned and left.

In 2009, some new evidence concerning the Addis case was communicated to the RFIP, which led them to request further assistance from the Metropolitan Police. This was given and a MetPol team visited in 2010, but their report has never been released. As far as is known, this was the most recent external investigation, and a suggested follow-up visit by the MetPol never took place.

Since then, while the RFIP maintains that the case is still 'open', little detective work has been done, although they have cooperated with the various TV investigations. An increasing difficulty is that it is now over forty years since the event and not only is there an ever-decreasing number of witnesses, but of those who survive, many find that their memories are increasingly imprecise.

Conclusions

There can be no doubt that, after a shaky start, the RFIP have done their best in trying to solve the mystery of the disappearance of Alan Addis. In the early days, they shared the common belief that Addis had suffered some form of accident, either drowned or lost in Camp, both being by no means unknown in the Falklands. They were neither staffed nor trained for a major investigation and lacked the 'suspicious mind' that is inbred in virtually every UK police officer. But, to place this in perspective, other major police forces have poured huge resources in money and manpower into searches for disappeared persons, many relatively minor, but some newsworthy, such as Lord Lucan, Madeleine McCann and Jim Thompson, and have got nowhere. The Swinscoe disappearance, which is described in Chapter Fifteen, was solved purely by chance and, even then, the prospect of finding the perpetrator (perhaps more than one) seems to be virtually non-existent.

Nor has the RFIP been reluctant to call for help and advice from outside forces from the UK, as shown by the visits from the Devon & Cornwall and Metropolitan forces. But these, too, have been unable to solve the mystery, suggesting that, whatever the reason for failure, it is not the RFIP that can be held to blame.

CHAPTER FIFTEEN

Other Disappearances

Before attempting to analyse Addis's disappearance, it will be helpful to first compare it with similar cases to see whether there might be some common factors. There are many more disappearances than is commonly thought and, even in this modern era, and despite detailed supervision by the state, a profusion of bureaucratic and electronic controls and, in many places, a plethora of closed-circuit TV cameras, people do disappear, either voluntarily, by accident or at the hands of an abductor or murderer.

In the UK in March 2022, some 3,000 adults were classified as long-term (i.e., over one year) missing. In the United States, the National Missing and Unidentified Persons (NAMUS) reported that across the whole of the United States on 30 September 2022, there were 22,018 missing persons and 14,146 unidentified human remains.[139] There is, however, an important caveat in that both the UK and US authorities state that these published figures are almost certainly too low.

Many of these people disappear for only a short period of time and a few are accounted for after a lengthy interval by sheer chance. Some, however, disappear altogether, although whether this is because they have been murdered and their bodies hidden, have suffered an accident in some remote place, or have simply found a new life cannot, by definition, ever be known.

LANDMARK CASES

There are two landmark legal cases relating to charging a person with murder without the fact of murder being proven or a body found, and both have been quoted down the years.

---

139 National Institute of Justice NamUs Fiscal Year 2022 Annual Report.

Mary Eileen Spargo

Thirty-eight-year-old Mary Eileen Jones (née Spargo), always known as Eileen, was a wealthy New Zealand widow, who had the misfortune to meet and become the second wife of George Cecil Horry (1907–81). Born in England, Horry was fourteen years old when he emigrated with his family to New Zealand. But only two years later, he set out on a twenty-seven-year career as a criminal and, by the time of his arrest in 1951, he had no less than sixty-four convictions to his name, with probably many more undetected. He married three times, but it was Eileen, his second wife, who proved to be his undoing. Horry told her that he was a wealthy British industrialist named George Turner and explained that he was currently on clandestine work for the British government. They married in 1942, departing immediately on their honeymoon, as was to be expected. Some six months later (and after he had married wife number three), Horry visited Eileen's parents to tell them that the pair had been en route to England when their ship was torpedoed in mid-Atlantic and, while he had survived, he had been unable to save his bride.

Something made Eileen's parents suspicious from the start and they reported their missing daughter to the police. After a long and painstaking police investigation, Horry was charged and tried for her murder in 1951. The judge took great care to explain the position of a lack of a body to the jury, but there was a strong chain of circumstantial evidence and it took the jury just under three hours to find him guilty, since when the case has been repeatedly cited.[140] He was sentenced to life imprisonment, but in the event, was released in 1967 and died in 1981. He never divulged what had happened to Eileen nor what he had done with her body.

Stanislaw Sykut

Like many Polish ex-Army World War Two veterans, Stanislaw Sykut (fifty-seven) did not return to his homeland in 1946, choosing instead to remain the UK. In March 1953, he entered into a partnership with Michial Onufrejczyk (fifty-eight), a fellow Polish former Army veteran, who was running a rather unsuccessful pig farm in Carmarthenshire in Wales.

---

140 See King v. Horry, New Zealand Law Reports, Vol VIII pp.227–236.

Onufrejczyk proved to be such a bully that Sykut sought to free himself from the contract, but it transpired that Onufrejczyk had insufficient funds for an amicable settlement. At that time, the police were required to visit aliens on a regular basis and, on their next visit, they noted that Sykut was missing. Onufrejczyk claimed that his partner had returned to Poland, but their suspicions were aroused. Not believing him, the police insisted on making a thorough search of the farm. They found nothing untoward, but their suspicions were so strong that they returned some days later, this time accompanied by a forensic team, who found microscopic spots of blood in the kitchen, which Onufrejczyk attributed to skinning rabbits. The police then found another trace, apparently from a human hand, which Onufrejczyk again dismissed, claiming that Sykut had cut his hand on a hay machine. The police conducted two months of meticulous searches with the help of dogs and divers, examining bogs, haystacks and manure heaps, but found not a single trace. Onufrejczyk offered a series of contradictory and unlikely explanations, including that his partner had been kidnapped by the Soviet Union's KGB, but the police did not believe him and eventually charged him with his partner's murder "on or about 14 December 1953."[141]

The trial was held at Carmarthenshire Assizes on 16 November to 1 December 1954, where, despite the lack of a corpse, the circumstantial evidence was so convincing that the jury reached a unanimous verdict of guilty. The example of the Horry case (see above) was frequently quoted. The judge then, in accordance with the law of the time, sentenced Onufrejczyk to death. The condemned man appealed but this was refused, only for the sentence to be commuted to life imprisonment the day before he was due to be hanged. Onufrejczyk was released after ten years but was killed in a traffic accident in Bradford two years later.

Not one trace of Sykut, either alive or dead, has ever been found. The police remained convinced that Onufrejczyk had murdered Sykut in the kitchen, chopped him up, fed the bits to their pigs and ground down the bones, but they had not an iota of proof. Onufrejczyk was the only man who really knew what had happened and he took the secret to his grave.

---

141 See The Law Reports (Queen's Bench Division)[1955] 1 QB 388.

ABDUCTED, NEVER FOUND AND PROBABLY MURDERED

April Fabb

April Fabb was thirteen and lived in the tiny Norfolk hamlet of Metton. On 8 April 1969, she set out on her bicycle to deliver a birthday gift – a packet of ten cigarettes – to her brother-in-law in the nearby village of Roughton – a distance of just over a mile, along a very quiet country road. A witness saw her on her bicycle at about 1406 and only six minutes later two Ordnance Survey surveyors noticed the bicycle lying in a field, although they left it there. At about 1500 a passing motorist also saw the bicycle but, not suspecting anything untoward, picked it up and took it to the village police station. It was not until 2200 when April's mother contacted the police to say that her daughter was missing that the Constable realised that the bicycle handed in earlier might be April's.

Her disappearance quickly led to the biggest police search operation the UK had seen up to that time, with the police conducting hundreds of interviews, as well as searching some four hundred houses. Later searches included the use of then novel thermal imaging cameras, as well as the excavation of a well, but all failed to produce a single fresh lead. There were several suspects, including two serial killers, but there was never any firm evidence of a link. April was described by all who knew her as a happy girl, with no known reason to abscond, so the presumption must be that she was abducted and murdered, but no body has ever been found nor has any killer confessed. Her case remains 'open'.

Genette Tate

Genette Tate, thirteen, lived in the Devonshire village of Aylsebeare with her father, stepmother and stepsister. She had undertaken to deliver the local *Express & Echo* newspaper in place of the regular delivery boy, who was on holiday, and on the afternoon of 19 August 1978, she set out to deliver the round. She was pushing her bicycle up a hill when she met two friends. They chatted briefly and Genette handed them a newspaper, which contained an article of interest. The friends paused to read the paper, while Genette mounted her bicycle and rode off. Just seven minutes later, the two friends found Genette's bicycle lying on the road, together with her handbag and a purse containing the money collected from newspaper customers. There were also some copies of the newspaper scattered around. The friends took the bicycle to Genette's home where they asked her parents if she was at home, only to discover that she was not.

Her father immediately organised a local search with family, friends and neighbours, and when this found nothing, he reported her disappearance to the local Devon & Cornwall Police (DCP). The police showed commendable energy and, by the next day, there were some fifty detectives and seventy police from DCP, some with search dogs, plus mounted officers from Avon and Somerset Police, as well as diving teams, who searched local ponds. The searches involved thousands of volunteers, and the police eventually held over 20,000 index cards.

Various possibilities were quickly ruled out. A hit-and-run traffic accident was discounted as there were no tyre marks, the bicycle was undamaged and no car had passed the two girls following the same narrow country lane. It seemed improbable that she was running away from home, as she only had the clothes she was wearing for the delivery round, while her saved holiday money was still in her room. Some eyewitnesses reported seeing a car on that road at the time of Genette's disappearance and the police issued a photofit picture of the driver, but without known success.

There was one serious suspect, Robert Black from Grangemouth in Scotland, a convicted serial killer of young girls. His job involved him driving all over the UK and Northwest Europe delivering film posters. He was found guilty of numerous murders of other girls with a *modus operandi* strikingly similar to the disappearance of Genette Tate. Although the police were never able to link him positively to Genette's disappearance, they were on the verge of charging him when he died in prison and the charges had to be dropped. Genette's father died in 2020, his final wish to give his daughter a proper burial unfulfilled. To this day, her disappearance remains unexplained, and her case remains 'open'.

The Beaumont Children

The sudden and total disappearance of three children, Jane (nine), Anna (eight) and Grant (five), in Australia on 26 January 1966 remains unsolved almost sixty years later. Their parents were Jim, a taxi driver, and Nancy, a housewife, and the family lived on the outskirts of Adelaide, the capital of South Australia. It was a particularly hot day, and the three children took the 0845 bus for the five-minute ride to nearby Glenelg beach. It was not unusual in Australia at that time for young children to roam around unescorted and the children knew the beach well, so their parents assumed they would be safe.

But the children did not return home on the 1200 bus as promised, nor were they on the 1400 bus. So, when Jim came home at 1500 and learnt of his wife's concerns, he immediately set off to search the beach. Having drawn a blank there, he returned home and collected his wife. They drove around the neighbourhood and, when they still could find no trace of their children, they reported to the police at about 1730.

Over the next few days, the police found some witnesses who reported having seen the children, sometimes in the company of a tall man with light-brown hair and a suntanned complexion, who appeared to be in his mid-thirties. One confirmed sighting was that the eldest girl had gone to a bakery where she purchased a meat pie. This was odd because not only were none of the children known to particularly like meat pies, but Jane had paid for it with a one-pound note, whereas her mother knew that she had had no more than six shillings when she'd left the house.

Despite several known child abuse suspects, not a single clue has been found. In 2018, the South Australia government offered a one-million Australian dollar reward for information; it remains unclaimed.

Madeleine McCann

Perhaps the highest profile of recent cases is that of Madeleine McCann (three), who disappeared on the evening of 3 May 2007 from a holiday apartment in Praia da Luz, Portugal. Her father, Gerry, and mother, Kate, were only some 55 yards (50m) away, having dinner with friends, while

Madeleine and two younger siblings were in a bedroom on the ground-floor apartment. The parents took it in turns to make regular checks on their children, but at 2200, Kate discovered that Madeleine was missing and immediately raised the alarm. Despite intense efforts by her parents, the continuing involvement of numerous provincial and at least three national police forces, intense media activity and rewards reputed to be in the region of £2,500,000, Madeleine's disappearance remains unsolved.

Claudia Lawrence

Claudia Elizabeth Lawrence (thirty-five), the daughter of an English solicitor, disappeared on 19 March 2009 and, despite rigorous searches, not a single trace has ever been found. She had remained single, but was very sociable and known to have had a number of short-term relationships with men, some of them married. She had also spent several holidays in Cyprus and was reported to have been investigating job opportunities there.

Claudia worked as a chef at a college in York and completed her final shift there at 1400 on 18 March 2009. She spoke to her parents by telephone that evening, but she failed to report for work at 0600 the following morning. On the evening of the 19th, she also failed to turn up for a prearranged meeting with a friend at her 'local', The Nag's Head. That friend, having failed to reach Claudia by telephone, spoke first to mutual friends, then the manager of The Nag's Head and finally to Claudia's father. None of those had had any contact with her, so her father went to Claudia's house, which he found to be neat and tidy, but no daughter. He also found her handbag, which contained a small amount of money, her bank cards and her passport, but no mobile phone. It appeared that she had breakfasted on the 19th and then left the house at about 0500, but she never reached the college.

Her father contacted the North Yorkshire Police at about 1400 and met them later that day. The initial police view was that there was no obvious reason for Claudia to go missing and that, as in many other cases, she would soon turn up in a few days. But, after five weeks without a reappearance, they took it more seriously and considered various possibilities, such as absconding with one of her many lovers, or that she had suffered an accident, but both were quickly dismissed. Another theory was that she might have accidentally bumped into a serial killer on the prowl, but this, too, was eventually rejected. Her mobile telephone, which might have provided a clue, was never found.

There were numerous public appeals for help in finding Claudia, some of them including generous financial rewards, but although there were many responses, none helped solve the case. Several men were arrested and then released without charge. Frustrated in their local investigation, the police turned their attention to Claudia's contacts in Cyprus and a team from York were sent to conduct interviews, again to no avail. The police have returned to this case several times, but without success, their eventual conclusion being that she was murdered by a person known to her and that her personal life held the clue to her disappearance. But that is as much as they have managed, and the case remains 'open unsolved'.

MURDERED AND DISAPPEARED BUT FOUND BY CHANCE

Carol Ann Park

Carol Park (thirty), a teacher, lived in Leece, a village on the Furness Peninsula in Cumbria, England. In early August 1976, her husband, Gordon (fifty-one), told her solicitor and family that she was missing and that he had not seen her since 17 July. He claimed that the six weeks delay had been because he thought that she had left him for another man, which she had done twice before, but had come home on both occasions, and it was only when she failed to return for the start of the new school term that he concluded that she must be missing. The police recorded this as a straightforward missing person case and, after extensive searches had failed to locate either her or her body, they ended their involvement.

However, in 1997, some amateur divers were operating in Coniston Water in the English Lake District when they chanced on a body lying on an underwater ledge at a depth of some 75ft (23m). The body was weighted down with rocks and lead piping, all bound together with rope. The body was identified as that of Carol Park and the police opened a murder enquiry, which resulted in the husband being convicted and sentenced to life imprisonment. The divers told the police that had Park dropped the body just a few metres further from the shore, it would have fallen into much deeper water – the lake is 184ft (56m) deep in places – and would almost certainly never have been discovered. Park lost an appeal and committed suicide in 2010.

Shafilea Iftikhar Ahmed

Shafilea Iftikhar Ahmed (seventeen) was the eldest daughter of immigrant parents. Born and brought up in Warrington, West Yorkshire, she was a popular young woman with an excellent school record, who intended to become a solicitor. She wished to lead a British-orientated life, but when she was sixteen, her parents determined that she should marry a cousin in Pakistan. Shafilea refused such an arranged marriage and sought to avoid it by swallowing bleach in an apparent suicide attempt. The attempt failed but left her with a seriously damaged throat, which required regular medical treatment.

The family returned to the UK, but on 18 September 2003, her school informed the police that she had been missing lessons since 11 September. The hospital also became alarmed when she failed to turn up for regular treatment on her damaged throat. A major national search was mounted, although the police suspected, but at that time could not prove, a so-called 'honour killing'.

Five months later, particularly heavy rain caused extensive flooding in the Lake District and a set of dismembered remains were revealed on the banks of the River Kent, some seventy miles (100km) from Shafilea's family home. These remains had been deliberately hidden and were in an advanced state of decomposition but were identified using DNA and dental records as those of Shafilea. Her parents were found guilty of murder and awarded long custodial sentences.

Roger Dale Parham

Roger Dale Parham (fifty-three) was an American man living in Fort George, Kansas. He was described by the FBI as "particularly charming", which was offset by his long criminal record. In November 1998, he was charged with raping a minor. He was bailed but failed to attend his next court appearance, so a warrant was issued for his arrest. He was never seen again, although there were unsubstantiated rumours that he had fled to Mexico.

In May 1999, two fishermen chanced upon a body on the bottom of nearby Lake Barkley, a 58,000-acre (230km^2) reservoir in the state of Kentucky. The body was encased in tyre chains, with a weighty hydraulic jack serving as an anchor. The Kentucky police used the best methods available at the time but were unable to identify the remains, other than that they were of a white male. The body was exhumed and re-examined in 2016, but again without result.

In 2023, the police reopened the case yet again, this time enlisting the help of a private laboratory specialising in forensic geology, which resulted in the remains being identified as those of the missing Roger Parham. The cause of death could not be determined, but as Parham could scarcely have wrapped himself in chains and attached a heavy weight, it was a crystal-clear case of murder, although how, when, why and who was responsible have never been established.

Alfred Swinscoe

Alfred Swinscoe (fifty-four) lived in the village Pinxton, on the Derbyshire/Nottinghamshire border, 2 miles (3km) Southwest of Sutton-in-Ashfield. The only industry in the village was the Pinxton mine, one of three forming the Langton colliery, where Swinscoe had worked for forty years and, at the time of his disappearance, was responsible for operating a coal-cutting machine. He was well-known and popular in his village, where, like many miners, his hobby was pigeon fancying, in which he won many championships. Also, like the vast majority of miners, he was fit and physically strong. He was married with six children.

One evening in January 1967, he went for a drink at his local pub, the Miner's Arms, accompanied by his son and some friends. At about 2230, he handed his son a ten-shilling note to buy the next round of drinks and, saying that he was going to the outside toilet, left the bar. He never returned and there was not the slightest hint of how or why he had disappeared.

His family alerted the police and, when they failed to find any leads, turned to the missing person's department of the Salvation Army. The latter carried out their own investigation, which also proved fruitless and, assuming that Alfred was still alive, they told his son, *"Trust that your father will decide to contact you direct at some point in the future."* There the matter rested with the generally accepted belief that he had absconded to start a new life, although there had been not the slightest indication of any intention to desert his family.

All that changed in April 2023 when a local farmer was digging a drain along the edge of a field off Coxmoor Road, just outside Sutton-in-Ashfield and some 4 miles (6km) from Pinxton. This man stumbled on human remains buried some 4–6 feet (1–2m) deep and conclusive evidence showed that the victim had been killed with a series of blows, so it was an obvious case of murder. As a result of a media appeal, the body was identified using DNA as that of the missing Alfred Swinscoe, although the police investigation was hampered by the fact that the pit had closed in 1969 and many of the miners and their families had moved away, some of them abroad. Despite hard work by the police and repeated media appeals for witnesses, nothing has ever been established. Alfred Swinscoe, missing for fifty-six years, was murdered, but by whom and why is still not known. It is also clear that when his remains were found only four miles away, it was not as a result of painstaking detective work, but by pure chance.

DISAPPEARED AND NEVER FOUND

Simon Parkes

Women and young girls are not the only people to disappear without trace. Simon Parkes (eighteen) was a Royal Navy radio operator serving aboard the aircraft carrier HMS *Illustrious* when it called at Gibraltar on 12 December 1986 on its way home from a round-the-world voyage. Naturally, most of the crew went on a 'run ashore' that evening and Simon was initially with a group of shipmates, leaving his passport and Christmas presents for his family in his bunk. He stayed with his chums in the Horseshoe Bar but then left, saying that he was going to find something to eat. This was the last positive sighting of the young sailor and, when he failed to report for duty the following morning, there was a massive search over the small colony, but it failed to find any trace of him. The naval authorities originally thought that he had, either intentionally or unintentionally, gone absent without leave, and he would have been by no means the first sailor to have missed his ship.

Gibraltar is a small place, less than 3 miles^2 (7km^2) in area, with sea on three sides and the Spanish border on the fourth, but repeated searches have failed to find any trace. Apart from those by the Royal Gibraltar Police, searches have also been conducted by the Hampshire Constabulary in 2003 and again in 2024, and there have been several TV programmes devoted to the subject.

The one seemingly relevant lead was that Petty Officer Alan Grimson was convicted in 2002 of murdering two young men in England, one a serving sailor, the other who had been in the RN. Their deaths were known to have been on 12 December 1997 and 12 December 1998, possibly marking some form of anniversary for Grimson, although its nature has never been discovered. But Grimson had also been one of HMS *Illustrious'* crew at the same time as Parkes, and as Simon disappeared on 12 December 1986, there seemed to be a possibility that Grimson could have murdered him, too. Although he admitted to the 1997 and 1998 murders, Grimson denied murdering Parkes and it has never been proved. The case remains open, but, despite repeated searches of the tiny colony, Parkes's body has never been found.

Ray Gricar

Ray Gricar (fifty-nine) was a District Attorney, working and living in Bellefonte, the county seat of Centre County in the Commonwealth of Pennsylvania in the USA. He was a popular, hard-working and clean-living lawyer, who was due to retire in December 2005. On 15 April that year, he used his mobile telephone at 1130 to tell his partner that he was driving his Mini Cooper towards neighbouring Lewisburg. But that was the last she heard from him, and, at 2330, she reported him missing to the police. He was an important figure in local government, so extensive searches were made, but he has never been seen nor heard of again.

The police found his abandoned car the next day at Lewisburg, some forty-five miles from his home. The car was locked and undamaged, with the cell phone and a water-bottle lying on a seat, the only suspicious element being that the cabin smelt of cigarette smoke, which was strange as he was known to be a dedicated non-smoker. His bank accounts and credit cards had not been used, nor was there any trace of suspicious emails or telephone calls. The police examined his prosecution cases but found that he had received no threats of retribution, while his county financial accounts were clean. His laptop computer was later found in a river; it was undamaged except that the hard drive had been removed. The hard drive was also later found, but it was so damaged that it could not be read.

One of the odd features was that Gricar's brother had drowned in May 1996, in what was declared to have been suicide. The police thought that this might have affected Ray, causing him such distress that he took his own life, but there was no evidence of depression or any mood swings. There were also reports of possible sightings, but most were considered lacking in credibility. No body was ever found, nor was any reason for his disappearance established, and he was declared legally dead in July 2011.

Patricia, Jonathan, Victoria Allen

An Englishwoman, Patricia Walker (thirty) had the misfortune to fall in love with a smooth-talking confidence trickster named Tony Allen (thirty-four), who seems to have totally lacked any form of moral compass. Recently divorced, Patricia married Allen in January 1968, although, unknown to her, he was still married to his first wife, by whom he had had two children. Struggling with debts, he had abandoned all three, feigned suicide and fled to Manchester.[142]

Allen was frequently caught out by sheer bad luck, as in this case when he was walking down a street in Manchester and met a man who not only knew him from their childhood days but was also acquainted with his purported widow and family. This man said: "*You are supposed to be dead!*" and promptly reported him to the authorities. He was charged with several offences, including bigamy. He was found guilty, although Patricia made such a tearful

---

142 He had been born Anthony John Angel, but he changed his surname to Anthony John Allen after his supposed suicide.

plea that, when the judge sentenced Allen to two years, he suspended them for two years. His first wife then divorced Allen, enabling him to marry Patricia legally in 1971. The couple had two children: Jonathan, born in 1970, and Victoria in 1972.

Allen then committed further offences, but was, as usual, caught out and sentenced to three years imprisonment, of which, due to good behaviour, he only served a year. On his release, the family moved to Salcombe, where Allen talked his way into a restaurant manager's job. He also started an affair with Eunice, the owner of a neighbouring restaurant, and seems to have been besotted with her. On 26 May 1975, Patricia disappeared, leaving Tony with the two children, but on 31 May, they, too, disappeared.

A few months later, Patricia's brother came looking for her and, when he could not find her, he went to the police, who then carried out extensive searches. These included Allen's small motorboat and dinghy, as it was thought that he might have taken the bodies out to sea, weighted them, and dumped them. Police divers were brought in, but nothing was found. The case was referred to the Director of Public Prosecutions in 1977, who ruled that there was insufficient evidence for a prosecution and Tony was released.

Allen and Eunice then moved to London, where he eventually made the foolish mistake of ditching her, whereupon she published a book making it clear that she suspected him of killing Patricia and the children. Meanwhile, the Devon & Cornwall Police had carried out a 'cold case review' resulting in him being arrested in October 2001 and charged with the murder of Patricia and the two children. The trial opened on 27 November 2002 in Exeter Crown Court where at the end of the prosecution case defence counsel submitted 'no case to answer' due to the lack of bodies and the very long time – twenty-seven years – since the alleged offences had been committed. But the judge did not agree and instructed the defence to present its case. The twelve-day trial ended on 16 December 2002 with the jury spending nine hours in deliberation, at the end of which, they unanimously found a verdict of guilty.

Allen was imprisoned, where several appeals were rejected. He died, still a prisoner, on 8 Aug 2015 of natural causes; he was seventy-two years old, always denying any responsibility for the disappearance of his wife and children. There are two local suspicions about the bodies. One is that they were concealed in a nearby rubbish tip outside the village of Malborough, the other that they were weighted down and dumped in the sea, but the inescapable fact is that they have never been found.

Lord Lucan

One disappearance has held a secure place in the interests of both journalists and the general public for over fifty years. This is partly due to the brutality of the murder, but also because the perpetrator was a lord – the Seventh Earl of Lucan (thirty-nine). He was married to Veronica (née Duncan, thirty-six), but they were estranged and living apart. They had three children who lived with their mother, but were looked after by a nanny, Sandra Rivett (twenty-nine).

On the night of 7 November 1974, Lady Lucan rushed into a nearby pub, covered in blood and in a hysterical state. She told all who would listen that her husband had murdered Rivett and then tried to murder her, but she had escaped. The police were called and, on entering the house, found Sandra Rivett's body in a mail bag in the cellar, but Lord Lucan had vanished. It was later established that he had contacted his mother and then visited a friend before dumping his blood-soaked car in Newhaven, East Sussex, near the ferry terminal. He has never knowingly been seen again.

There have been many theories. Lady Lucan claimed that her husband had committed suicide by jumping off a ferry en route from Newhaven to France, although what evidence she had for this has never been established. Spotting the missing earl became a global pastime with 'sightings' in Australia, France, Hong Kong, India, Macau, Mozambique, New Zealand, Paraguay, Rhodesia and South Africa. Some of these theories were plausible, as was the suggestion that he had undergone plastic surgery to alter his appearance, but others were on the wild side. One such was that he had been captured and held to ransom by the IRA, another that he had committed suicide with a request that his body be fed to the lions at Howlett's Wild Animal Park in Kent, whose owner, John Aspinall, was a friend.

A warrant for Lucan's arrest was issued by the police, but could not be served, and in June 1975, an inquest jury named him as the killer. Lucan was declared legally dead in 1999 and a death certificate issued in 2016. The fact remains that Lucan's fate is totally unknown and, if anyone knows what happened to him, they have successfully kept very quiet.

James Thompson

James (Jim) Thompson (sixty-one), a very successful and wealthy American businessman based in Bangkok, disappeared without trace on 26 March 1967, while on holiday in the Cameron Highlands in West Malaysia. This area, first explored in 1885, was jungle-covered, but boasted a temperate Europe-like climate, leading to its development as a 'hill station' for British colonial administrators and troops, and increasingly after World War Two, with civilian tourists, for all of whom it offered a revitalising 'change of air' from the humidity of the tropical lowlands.

Thompson and a companion arrived on Friday 24 March 1967 to stay with two friends. On Sunday 26 March (Easter Sunday), all four went to church. The service ended at about 1200, following which, they went back to the host's house for a picnic lunch. Then, at about 1330, Thompson set out on his own for an 'afternoon stroll', seemingly in good spirits, waving a cheerful goodbye to the two ladies in the party as he went. He left his cigarettes, driving licence, medications, money, passport and wallet in his room, thus giving every indication that he intended to return.

At about 1800, the others realised that he had not returned and contacted the police. The usual sudden tropical sunset just before 1930 meant that no search was possible that evening, but as Thompson was a man of some consequence, a full-scale search began early the following morning. Over the next eleven days, some five hundred people took part, including the Malaysian Army and Police Field Force, Gurkhas, British servicemen from the nearby British Military Hospital, as well as many civilians living in the area. There were also outsiders such as other tourists and, as the word spread, fortune hunters. Notable participants were local *Orang Asli*, aboriginal jungle-dwellers, who were renowned for their tracking capabilities. Three cadaver dogs were also involved. The terrain was very rugged and jungle-covered, making the searches very difficult and exhausting. After eleven days, no body had been found nor had the searchers come across a single clue, so the operation was called off, although further searches have been mounted from time to time, usually in response to some new theory.

The disappearance of an internationally important and wealthy person in such exotic circumstances was quickly seized upon by media around the world and speculation on his fate was rife. Theories included that he had:

- simply got lost and either suffered an accident or was exhausted;
- had walked along a road and been killed by a car, whose driver then buried the body;
- been murdered by business rivals or communist terrorists;
- been kidnapped;
- deliberately engineered his own disappearance to enable him to set up a new life somewhere else;
- been spirited away by a US agency to undertake secret work associated with the Vietnam war;
- been attacked and eaten by a tiger known to be in the area;
- been bitten by a poisonous snake.

There was not a shred of evidence to support any of these theories, nor has any been found since. As seems usual in such cases, a well-known psychic detective, Peter Hurkos (1911–88), was one of many paranormal practitioners to become involved, although not one of them contributed anything to a successful outcome. There was even a possible sighting by a friend in Tahiti, but nothing came of that, either.

Dr Llewellyn 'Lew' Toulmin, PhD has conducted very extensive and deep research into Thompson's disappearance and published a detailed outcome of his researches. He has found some new evidence and has some criticisms of the way the searches were conducted, but he seems to be no closer to finding the body than anyone else, although he concludes that the probability (albeit not the certainty) is that the remains are somewhere in the Cameron Highlands.

UNIDENTIFIED HUMAN REMAINS

Human remains are sometimes found, which, despite major efforts, the police are unable to identify. Just two examples among many, two women's bodies were washed ashore on the South Devon coast in late 1963. The first was found on the beach at Dawlish on 4 November 1963 and the post-mortem indicated death by drowning some four-to-five weeks earlier, i.e., late September/early October 1963. The clothing had French markings, but there were no clues to her identity. A second female body was found on St Mary's Beach, Brixham, exactly one month later (i.e., 4 December 1963). A post-mortem examination established that this woman was between fifty and sixty years old, approximately 5ft 6in (167cm) tall and of 'heavy build'. It was assessed that she had died by drowning, probably some six-to-eight weeks previously, i.e., late October 1963. Neither of these bodies was ever positively identified, although from their clothing, UK police suspected that they were both French and, in view of the proximity of the dates, the similar causes and the closeness of the places the bodies were found, they felt, but could not prove, that the deaths may have been somehow linked. The British police obtained French help, but neither body was ever linked to a missing person in France, so their identities and the circumstances of their deaths remain unknown.

LOST AND FOUND

There is, however, another side to this coin which needs to be mentioned. There are a number of examples of people who disappeared and, after extensive searches, were considered dead, only for them to turn up very much alive many years later. Usually, they have been found by pure chance, without which it must be assumed they would have continued in their new role and surroundings for the rest of their lives.

Willam Harrison[143]

The 'Campden Wonder', as it became known, happened some 340 years ago but the story is repeatedly retold as a dreadful warning of the danger of condemning without a body, since the three supposed perpetrators were hanged, only for the missing man to reappear, alive and well, several years

---

143 *The Campden Wonder*; Clark, Sir George (ed.); Oxford University Press, London, 1959.

later. The location was Chipping Campden, a small Gloucestershire market town, where the most important landowner was Lady Campden, whose steward for the previous twenty years had been William Harrison (seventy), who lived with his wife, younger son, Edward, and manservant, John Perry, near the church.

On 16 August 1660, William Harrison walked to the village of Charringworth to collect rents, a journey he had undertaken many times before. When he had not returned by nightfall, his wife became concerned and sent the manservant to find him. Perry searched as best he could, but when it became too dark, he slept under a hedge. In the morning, he reached Charringworth, where he quickly established that his master had been seen the previous afternoon but had then left. On his way back to Campden, Perry met Edward, his master's son, who had been despatched by his now very worried mother. The two continued their search, but on their way back to Campden, they chanced upon a woman who told them she had found a hat and comb in the road, together with a blood-stained collar. Perry and young Harrison searched the area, but, discovering nothing further, returned to Campden to inform Mrs Harrison.

That lady promptly accused Perry of killing and robbing his master. Perry was arrested and did not help matters when he concocted a series of unlikely tales, the most damning of which was that the murder had been committed by his mother in collaboration with his brother and himself. The three were charged with murder and tried twice, being found not guilty the first time and guilty (under a different judge and jury) the second. They were condemned to death and hanged a few days later.

Two years later, and to general astonishment, Harrison returned to Campden. He told a complicated story of having been kidnapped, sold to Arabs as a slave, and then escaping back to England. He was reintegrated into Campden life, but his wife, for reasons never explained, committed suicide. Meanwhile, Mrs Perry and her two sons had been hanged, so there was no exoneration for them and this case was frequently quoted over the following three centuries when a disappearance might lead to a charge of murder and then, as was the law in those days, to a hanging, only for the purported victim to reappear.

Lucy Ann Johnson

The Johnson family lived in Surrey in British Columbia, Canada, and consisted of husband, Marvin; wife, Lucy Ann; daughter, Linda; and son, Daniel. Marvin was abusive, a heavy drinker and had multiple affairs, so, in 1961, Lucy Ann threatened to leave with the children. When he refused to let them go, she just walked out and disappeared. Marvin did not report her disappearance until 1965 and, after such a long delay, the police suspected that he had murdered her; they even dug up the back yard in their search for a body. But they did not find any evidence, so the police were eventually compelled to let the case turn cold.

But some fifty-two years later, the daughter Linda, now in her sixties, placed notices in several newspapers, asking for any information about her missing mother. The notices included a photograph and someone replied, saying that she recognised her own mother. It turned out that Lucy Ann had moved to Alaska, married and raised a new family, and that the person who answered the notice was, in fact, Linda's half-sister. Lucy Ann said that she had tried to leave and take the children, but her husband would not let her, so she had just left and started a new life.

Petra Pazsitka

In 1984, a German woman, Petra Pazsitka (twenty-four), was studying computer science at a college in Braunschweig when she failed to return from a visit to the dentist. She disappeared without any warning or explanation and the police could find no trace of her. The situation was complicated in 1985 when a convicted rapist/murderer confessed to raping and killing her, although he later retracted both. No body was ever found, and she was declared dead.

Then in 2015, in the German city of Düsseldorf, a woman reported a burglary and, when the police asked her for proof of identity, she was forced to admit that she was the missing Petra Pazsitka. She had survived for thirty-one years without a bank account, driver's licence or social security card, but did retain her old identity card, which she then used to prove her identity. She had had various jobs, which were always paid in cash, moved several times, changed her name, paid all bills in cash, and had survived until then 'under the radar'.

Having identified herself, she was adamant that, while her family had not been the cause of her disappearance, she wanted nothing to do with them. The police said that there was no question of a prosecution as she had never presented false papers because, until the burglary, she had avoided any situation in which she would have been asked to produce them.

ASSESSMENT

This brief survey shows that disappearances may be rather more common than is usually perceived, but, except in a few cases such as those of Madeleine McCann, Jim Thompson and Lord Lucan, public attention is usually short-lived. On the other hand, the families have to live with the inexplicable absence of a loved one for the rest of their lives.

The abductions of the two teenage girls who went missing – April Fabb and Genette Tate – were almost certainly unplanned. But it would seem that the perpetrator had a well-tried *modus operandi*, so that when a target of opportunity unexpectedly presented itself, as in these cases of lone teenage girls on a deserted country lane, he could take immediate action and make off before being detected. It must now be assumed that the two girls are dead, but where their bodies lie and who was responsible remain total mysteries. The third girl to go missing – Madeleine McCann – was almost certainly the victim of a carefully planned operation, preceded by surreptitious and carefully conducted reconnaissance, although it is also possible that a thief chanced upon the open window and took the opportunity to seize the sleeping child. But that, too (as of May 2025), remains unsolved.

Unlike the teenagers April Fabb and Genette Tate and the even younger Madeleine McCann, Claudia Lawrence was a mature woman. She had a steady job and was financially independent, with her own house and car. She lived in a large city, albeit with moors and extensive woods not far away. The only unusual aspect was her very active social life, with a succession of lovers, although the police were unable to link any of them to her disappearance. Like those three much younger girls, it seems certain that she must have been murdered, but when, where, by whom and what happened to the corpse remain complete mysteries.

The bodies of Carol Park and Roger Parham were disposed of in lakes. Their bodies were found later but only by pure chance – divers in the case of Park and anglers in the case of Parham. Both bodies were heavily weighted and had remained fully submerged and undisturbed until being discovered. Shafilea Ahmed's remains were found in a river, also weighted but not so efficiently as Park and Parham, and they were revealed by unexpected flooding. These examples suggest that securely weighting a body and planting it in water at a sufficient depth is probably one of the most effective means of disposing of a victim. Using inland lakes and rivers in this way is open to discovery by chance, either by divers or anglers, or by unexpected changes in water levels. The sea is much more secure. This also begs the question of how many more weighted bodies have been successfully submerged, particularly at sea, never to be found?

Alfred Swinscoe's remains were found by pure chance and his disappearance remains a total mystery. He left the bar to visit the toilet never to return and his battered body was found many years later but only four miles (7km) away and the other side of a hedge from a regularly used road. Who killed him, why, and how was the body transported to the burial site? Only the perpetrator knows the answers.

Simon Parkes and Stanislaw Sykut are almost bigger mysteries. Assuming that they are dead, their bodies must have been disposed of in a very small area: the tiny colony of Gibraltar in the case of Parkes and the pig farm in the case of Sykut. But repeated and very thorough searches using the most sophisticated modern techniques have failed to find a single trace of either.

Gricar, Johnson, Pazsitka were responsible for their own disappearances, and in the cases of the two women, their disappearances were eventually solved, although more by good luck than any startling discovery by the police.

Where Gricar, Thompson and Lucan are concerned, no body has ever been found, so whether they committed suicide, suffered an accident, were murdered or went off to start a new life elsewhere is unlikely ever to be known.

The two female corpses found in Devon were wearing ordinary clothes, had both drowned and almost certainly came from France. When they drowned, their unfettered bodies would have sunk to the seabed, but risen to the surface some weeks later and then been carried by currents across the English Channel. But despite extensive searches on both sides of the Channel, they remain unidentified and the reason, if any, for their demise unsolved.

These examples show that the disappearance of Alan Addis is by no means unique, nor is the lack of a body. Curiously, Thompson's disappearance in Malaysia bears some similarities to that of Addis on the Falklands. On initial inspection, nothing can seem so dissimilar as the dense, hilly jungle of the Cameron Highlands and the treeless, low-lying, rolling landscape surrounding North Arm. But both areas pose very similar problems. First, there were very few tracks and, once off a beaten path, it is very easy for someone on foot to become disorientated and head off in completely the wrong direction, particularly if they are not carrying maps or other navigation aids. Similarly, a body in either terrain, whether buried deliberately or fallen by accident or exhaustion, is extremely difficult to find without either very precise information or by sheer chance.

However, it is the setting in a remote Settlement in the Falkland Islands that makes Addis a special case.

CHAPTER SIXTEEN

Precedents – Disappearances in the Falkland Islands

At the time of his disappearance, an early theory, which was strongly supported by the Royal Marines Board of Inquiry and the Falkland Islands government, was that Alan Addis had become disorientated and wandered into Camp, where he died of exposure after either being injured or getting lost – or both! This was not as far-fetched as it appears at first sight because there are a number of examples where people have disappeared in the Falkland Islands, a selection of which are listed below (in alphabetical order by surname).

Ned Casey[144]

In late June 1890, Ned Casey, a shepherd, was despatched from Saunders Island to Hill Cove to summon a doctor to treat a sick fellow worker. Ned was an experienced man, who knew the area well, so it was not considered necessary to send someone else with him. He successfully rowed across Byron Sound, a distance of some nine miles, and landed at Shallow Bay, where he drew his boat above the high water mark and then set out to walk to the nearest house, which was some twenty minutes' walk away. But there was a dense fog at the time and Casey simply disappeared. Several days later, another man was sent from Saunders Island to discover why the doctor had not arrived, only to discover that was because Casey had never delivered his message.

Casey's boat was found, proving that he had reached the mainland, and

---

144 Spruce, *Falklands Rural Heritage*, p.81.

parties of men, many on horseback, searched the area for a week, but when they did not find a single trace, the search had to be abandoned. Then, on 30 November 1913, some twenty-three years later, Casey's skeleton was found on the West side of Darry Valley, ten miles away and in totally the wrong direction from his intended destination. Crossing Byron Sound was probably considered more hazardous than the subsequent short walk, but once ashore, he seems to have become completely disorientated and wandered off until he collapsed from exhaustion and died what must have been a very lonely death.

Dr Jameson[145]

Dr Jameson, the resident doctor in Darwin, went missing when riding home from Hill Head on 8 March 1906. A search on 9 March proved fruitless but, when it was resumed the next day, the body was found at about 1100 in the high ground near Ceritos. He had no provisions and appeared to have dismounted for some reason, but there was no injury or indication of cause of death. His two horses were unharmed and waiting patiently nearby.

W A Johnston[146]

On 25 June 1904, Johnston was on his way home to Findlay Harbour House from North Arm when he got lost in a fog.[147] He was found the next day and taken to Darwin, but died there on the Monday.

Oscar Kibery[148]

In July 1892, Kibery was the newly arrived cook at Douglas Station, and disappeared after a few days. Search parties were sent out, but his body was not found until ten days later, on the South bank of the San Carlos River.

---

145 Spruce, op. cit., p.95.
146 Spruce, op. cit., p.193.
147 Findlay Harbour House is now Wreck House.
148 Spruce, op. cit., p.62. *Falkland Islands Magazine*, September 1900.

His clothing was found on the North bank. There was no explanation as to the cause of death, nor, indeed, as to why he was naked.

John Mackintosh[149]

John Mackintosh was travelling alone from Teal Inlet to Estancia in the 1840s. The distance was some fifteen miles along a well-worn track, but he drowned in a river, just North of the rocky outcrops known as The Gorge, in unknown circumstances.

Evander Morrison[150]

On 18 July 1901, and while living at Horn Hill House, Morrison went to collect a horse from Mappa Island. When he did not return, a fellow shepherd searched for him and, when he could not be found, went to North Arm to raise the alarm. Morrison's body was discovered the next day lying on the ground, without the horse but with his dogs. He was within sight of Mappa House, which was a considerable distance from both Mappa Island and Horn Hill House, so how he got there is a mystery. He had no apparent injuries, and the cause of death was given as "exposure and exhaustion."

Rendle[151]

Rendle was riding from Teal Inlet to Douglas Station on an unspecified date but described as "some years ago" in a report dated July 1892. The horse had become bogged, so that Rendle dismounted and removed the saddle, which was broken, and placed it, together with the bridle, in a hole and covered them with diddle-dee (*Empetrum rubrum*, also known as red crowberry). It appears that he then walked to find help. The ground was very swampy. The horse seems to have struggled free after its rider left and was recovered, but Rendle's body was never found.

---

149 Spruce, op. cit., p.98.
150 Spruce, op. cit., p.197.
151 Spruce, op. cit., p.62. *Falkland Islands Magazine*, July 1892, p.4.

Guardsman Philip Williams[152]

Williams (eighteen) was a stretcher-bearer in 2nd Battalion Scots Guards during the Falklands War. The battalion attacked Mount Tumbledown on the night of 13 June 1982, in the course of which, Williams was knocked out by an exploding mortar bomb. In the excitement and bad weather, he was left for dead when the battalion advanced on Stanley. On recovering consciousness and finding himself alone, Williams sheltered on high ground for three days and nights, surviving on an Army twenty-four-hour ration pack he happened to possess. He hid from patrols and helicopters believing them to be Argentine and had no way of knowing that the Argentines had surrendered. Possessing neither map nor compass, he then blundered down to the shore at Port Harriet where he found a Falklands' shepherds' 'outside house', which was empty apart, very fortunately, from a stash of abandoned Argentine Army twenty-four-hour ration packs. On 1 August, he managed to reach a farmhouse at Bluff Cove, some ten miles from where he had started, where he was given food and shelter and then helicoptered to Stanley. There are various explanations for his experience, and there is no doubt that the chance discovery of Argentine rations helped him enormously, but in the final analysis, he survived totally alone for forty-eight days.

Tony McClelland

Tony McClelland (thirty-six) was the assistant engineer aboard a tug, MV *Indomitable*, which was under contract to the Ministry of Defence to provide tugboat services in the East Cove Military Port (ECMP) in the Falkland Islands. On the night of 25 November 2005, he went to a party at the military-run Harbour Lights Bar, which was within the port area, and when his fellow crewmen returned to their ship at about 2300, he remained, sitting on his own. He is believed to have left the bar shortly after midnight, but that is the last that was ever seen of him, and he simply disappeared. Not a single trace of him or his clothing has ever been found, no witness has come forward, nor has any rational explanation of his disappearance ever been offered. There were repeated searches at the time and both the

---

152 *Penguin News* 66 August 1982, pp.1–2. UPI, 2 August 1982

Services Police and the Royal Falkland Islands Police conducted lengthy investigations but without any success.

McClelland's disappearance bears what appears at first sight to be a remarkable resemblance with that of Alan Addis. Both were on their own in a crowded bar and dressed for a casual night out, only to walk out of the bar and disappear without trace. There were, however, significant differences. The disappearances were some twenty-five years apart and the location in McClelland's case was a military bar on Ministry of Defence property as opposed to the civilian bar at North Arm. Further, the people involved in the Harbour Lights Bar were almost entirely British military, while at North Arm they were, the six Marines apart, all local civilians. Thus, there are no evidential links and any resemblance between the two events appears to be fortuitous. But, as with Alan Addis, the disappearance of Tony McClelland remains a complete mystery.

Assessment

There were probably more cases across the Falkland Islands where men, perhaps also a few women, were lost for one or two days, but then found alive, which would, of course, not have been considered worth recording.

All of the above examples, with the exceptions of Kibery, McClelland and Williams, were men who knew their locality well and were at least reasonably, if not fully, fit, and yet they seem to have become totally disorientated.

Fog was definitely a factor in some of these cases, but it may also have been an unrecorded factor in others. The Falklands are particularly susceptible to fogs, which can be very dense, with visibility reduced to as little as ten yards. It was also a factor in the 1982 war, when a thick fog around Mount Kent, only twelve miles from Stanley, slowed the arrival of ammunition and supplies needed for the final offensive. According to Falkland residents, fogs of the type which hampered British operations sometimes lasted for a week at that time of year.

Even in clear daylight, it is very easy to become disorientated, especially if one does not have a map or a compass – and why would a local shepherd or doctor need those? The landscape, particularly in Lafonia, is flat and featureless.

Another factor, but one which is difficult to quantify, is the silence when away from the Settlements. Falklands' silence is absolute, perhaps mitigated slightly if the lone man is accompanied by animals, but its effect, particularly when combined with a dense fog, must be quite terrifying.

Could Addis have wandered into the Camp and survived, as did Guardsman Williams? He might have survived for a few days eating diddle-dee when his hunger would have overcome the slightly sour taste, but not for long. However, this would have depended upon eventually being found or giving himself up, which did not happen. Could he have wandered into Camp, become totally disorientated and died of a mixture of exhaustion and hunger, as did Casey, Morrison and others? This is certainly a possibility, and he could have been a considerable distance from North Arm by the time he collapsed and died.

CHAPTER SEVENTEEN

Sudden Deaths

The general opinion among Falklanders is that there was a fight at North Arm, a not unusual conclusion to a weekend party. That said, it seems highly unlikely that Addis's attackers intended anything more than inflicting a few bruises and cuts in order to 'teach him a lesson'; death had never been part of their plan. This had been the original intention in the Burgos affair at Goose Green some months earlier and, like that fatal event, the fight at North Arm had an unintended outcome. Alan Addis undoubtedly died that night, and it seems most probable that this was not deliberate, but happened during the fight, the most likely cause being either a sudden cardiac death, or a sudden cardiac arrest. These will now be examined in more detail.

SUDDEN CARDIAC DEATH[153]

Sudden cardiac death (SCD) occurs when all heart activity suddenly stops without prior warning, with the result that the person loses consciousness and dies within seconds.[154] It is more common in older people, but can occur in those under thirty-five, even though they seem otherwise to be healthy. There are few, if any, warnings. It is not necessarily associated with physical activity and there is no known cure. Such cases are usually reported as 'found dead, but not in suspicious circumstances'; for example, when a person living alone is found sitting lifeless at his or her dining table. It seems highly unlikely that this happened to Alan Addis.

---

153 The correct medical term is 'Sudden Arrhythmic Death Syndrome' (SADS).

154 This differs from a heart attack in which the supply of blood to the heart is suddenly blocked, usually by a blood clot, and whose onset can be indicated by chest pains and shortness of breath.

SUDDEN CARDIAC ARREST (SCA)

Sudden cardiac arrest (SCA) is different from sudden cardiac death and is the precipitate loss of heart activity due to an irregular heart rhythm. Unlike SCD, survival from SCA is possible provided that fast and proper medical attention, together with the necessary equipment, are available. This is known as cardio-pulmonary resuscitation (CPR).

Although not common, it is by no means unknown for a fistfight (i.e., without a firearm, dagger or other weapon) to result in a fatality for one of the participants, in what is generally designated formally as a 'one-punch death' and colloquially as a 'sucker punch'. It should be noted that farmhands in the Falklands Settlements were tough and strong and used to lifting heavy weights and relished scraps of this nature. As described earlier, in the fight at Goose Green, the Kelper, Kirk, broke the Chilean Burgos's nose with a single blow to his face. There is even a charity on the subject.[155] Three possibilities are suggested.

Blow to the Head

Punching someone in the head can be just as lethal as an attack with a weapon and does not need to be particularly powerful. But, if the victim is not expecting such an attack and the blow impacts the right spot on the head, with sufficient force and at the necessary angle, it can cause the brain to shift and collide with the internal wall of the skull, suffering irreparable damage as it does so. Alternatively, the blow can twist the top end of the spinal column, thus also causing instantaneous damage to the brain.

Dean Skillin (twenty) was killed in a one-punch assault in Bangor, Gwynedd, North Wales. On 19 September 2020, Skillin and his cousin, Taylor Lock, went out together for some drinks to celebrate the lifting of lockdown restrictions. They were standing outside the Waverley Hotel when they became the victims of an unprovoked attack by Brandon Sillence (twenty-five), who was described in court as a boxing fan with an "aggressive and confrontational" character. Sillence landed several blows on his two victims, but a fatal punch to Skillin's head caused the latter's skull to rotate

---

155 https://onepunch.org.uk/

on his spine, causing immediate and catastrophic subarachnoid bleeding.[156] This brain injury resulted in immediate death and, according to the post-mortem, he was actually dead before he hit the ground. Sillence appeared before Caernarfon Crown Court in December 2021, charged with murder, to which the jury found him 'not guilty', but he had already admitted both the manslaughter of Skillen and assault occasioning actual bodily harm on Lock. He was sentenced to ten years imprisonment for the manslaughter charge and a further one year on the assault charge.

Head Hits the Ground

Wayne Sheppard (forty-four) met Darren John Fell (forty-one) at about 2000 on 2 July 2022, on New Park Street, Devizes, Wiltshire. They did not know each other, but for an unknown reason, after exchanging a few words, Fell, without warning, suddenly launched a single punch, hitting Sheppard on his jaw. Sheppard collapsed to the ground, hitting his head on the pavement as he did so, whereupon Fell left him there and went into a nearby pub where he boasted that he had just knocked someone out. Sheppard was found unconscious by others and rushed to Swindon Great Western Hospital but never regained consciousness and died six days later. Fell appeared at Winchester Crown Court in October 2023 where he pleaded not guilty to the charge of manslaughter, claiming that, while he did not deny punching the victim, he had done so because he felt threatened and was acting in self-defence. The jury did not believe him, and he was sentenced to nine years imprisonment.

Gediminas Vaitkus (forty-three), a married man of Lithuanian origin, was living in Boston, Lincolnshire, when on 28 July 2020, he suffered serious head injuries from a single punch to his head in an incident on Red Lion Street. The quarrel started in an off-licence shop where Vaitkus sought to buy a bottle of alcohol but for some reason the seller, Hikmet Maez (nineteen) refused to serve him. Vaitkus left that shop, presumably to find another off-licence that would serve him, but Maez followed him and, while both

---

156 A subarachnoid haemorrhage is caused by bleeding on the surface of the brain. It's a very serious condition and can be fatal.

were on the pavement, shoved him in the back. When Vaitkus retaliated, Maez picked up a bottle and threw it at him, but Vaitkus managed to block it and continued to walk along the street. Maez continued to follow him and then kicked him on the leg before punching him straight in the face. At this, Vaitkus fell to the ground, hitting his head on the pavement, causing the serious injury from which he died. Maez fled the scene, but the fatally injured Vaitkus was discovered lying in the street and rushed to hospital where he died five days later. The attacker, Maez, was quickly tracked down by the police and arrested only two hours later. He appeared at Lincoln Crown Court on 24 September, where he pleaded guilty to the charge of manslaughter, and was subsequently sentenced to three years imprisonment on 21 December.

Blow to Chest

A rare cause of death in a fight is where the victim is struck on the chest in the precordial area, near the centre of the heart's left ventricle[157] at an exact moment during a heartbeat, with neither a bruise nor any outward indication of a serious blow. This is known as *commotio cordis*. Typically, the victim falls to the ground and is unresponsive and with no detectable heartbeats. It is essential that immediate first-aid treatment is given, which involves placing the injured person in the recovery position and defibrillation using an automated external defibrillator. Without such treatment, the patient will die.

No Third Party

It is also possible for SCA to take place without the direct involvement of a third party. In such cases, the heart stops pumping blood, leading to unconsciousness and death unless treatment is given within minutes.[158]

Christian Eriksen, then aged twenty-eight, was a Danish professional

---

157 The left ventricle is the lower left chamber of the heart.
158 SCA is different from heart attack. See https://www.mayoclinic.org/diseases-conditions/sudden-cardiac-arrest/symptoms-causes/syc-20350634

footballer. On 12 June 2021, during a UEFA Euro 2020 match in Copenhagen, he was playing for his country against Finland and, in the forty-second minute, was standing on his own, positioning himself to receive a throw-in from touch when, without any warning, he collapsed and fell to the ground. Very fortunately for Eriksen, his teammate, Simon Kjaer, responded instantly and placed him in the recovery position. Urgent medical attention was immediately given by the doctor and paramedics who were in attendance for the match. They performed CPR and defibrillation where he had fallen. He was then taken to hospital, where his condition was stabilised. After further treatment, he made a full recovery and returned to international football on 26 March 2022, representing his country against The Netherlands and scoring just two minutes after coming on.

Fabrice Muamba, then aged twenty-four, was another professional footballer. On 17 March 2012, he was playing for Bolton against Tottenham Hotspur, where, during the first half, he suddenly suffered a cardiac arrest and collapsed. He was given immediate and lengthy treatment on the pitch, including from a consultant cardiologist who happened to be present as a spectator. He was then taken to the specialist coronary care unit at the London Chest Hospital. Like Eriksen, he was fitted with an implantable cardioverter-defibrillator and was discharged on 16 April, although in his case, he was unable to return to professional football as a player.

ASSESSMENT

The first three examples of SCA all occurred during a fight. Skillen was a prime example of a single blow to the head causing such catastrophic damage that he died where he stood. Shepherd and Viatkus were both knocked out and fell to the ground where their heads impacted with such force that their deaths followed in a few days. Most importantly, there were no trained medics present, nor equipment, such as defibrillators, immediately available and thus no timely help that might have saved them.

The other two were victims of SCA while taking part in high-level football matches; Eriksen in an international, Muamba an English First Division match. No third party was involved, but both were taking part in a physically demanding game. They would both have been subject to regular and strict medical examinations and would have been declared fit to play in these matches. Presumably, also, neither had exhibited any preliminary symptoms. But when the trauma occurred, both were very fortunate in that their teammates were close at hand, one of whom administered essential first aid, and fully trained medical help was quickly available in the stadium. Without all of that, they would almost definitely have died.

There is no direct evidence that any of these occurred with Alan Addis but are suggested as possible explanations of how he might have died in a fight. If one of these did occur, his opponents had none of the necessary training to recognise what had happened, nor did they have the correct equipment. Lyn Blake, the manager's wife, was a trained children's nurse and, like many other managers' wives, is known to have given treatment for minor illnesses and injuries. However, it does not seem that she was summoned on this occasion, and, in any case, there was no defibrillator in the Settlement.

Had his attackers decided to own up to what had happened, they might have sent an urgent message to Stanley for professional medical help from the hospital, but, at best, that would have taken several hours to arrive and would almost certainly have been too late. It would also have alerted the police, who would then have had no choice but to become involved.

CHAPTER EIGHTEEN

Allan Addis Death: Previous Inquiries

Alan Addis's death and the subsequent disposal of his body are two distinct issues, which require separate analyses. This chapter deals with only the first of those, i.e., how, when, where and by whom was he killed? First in the field was the Royal Marine Board of Inquiry, which sat in September 1980 and managed to reach two seemingly contradictory conclusions:

> "... *Addis was drowned. As his body has not been found near the jetty or along the shore, it would be wrong to rule out the possibility that he may have been disorientated on leaving the Social Club and wandered off into Camp and died of exposure.*"[159]

This was endorsed by Alan's death certificate, which states the cause of death was: "... *that he drowned or died of exposure in the hinterland.*"

His mother, Sarah Ann Addis, visited the Falklands in 1995. She interviewed numerous people in the strict privacy of one-to-one interviews and was given a host of suggestions:

> "... *some said Alan had been stabbed and his body was under a peat stack. Others said he was buried in an old sheep dip, some said in the cavity of the Social Club walls. Yet others said he had been put in the furnace at the 'Big House', this being the North Arm manager's house. It was also said he had been taken to the sheep-shearing shed by two men and beaten to death. Another story said he was deliberately run over with a Land Rover. One lady I talked to indicated he was in Cow Park Pond...*"[160]

---

159 Board of Inquiry, October 1980, para. 17.
160 Addis, op. cit., p.44. Cow Park Pond was about half a mile to the West (inland) of the Settlement.

During that 1995 visit, Sarah Ann Addis also interviewed the man who had been manager of North Arm estate in 1980, Tony Blake, and secretly recorded him saying: "*My opinion obviously at the time was that something had happened around the jetty…*"

DCI Pennington of the Devon & Cornwall Police conducted an investigation later in 1995 and concluded that:

"*Despite the many enquiries made following the disappearance of Royal Marine Alan ADDIS over the 15 years since August 1980, there has been no explanation to suggest how he met his death. His body has not been recovered. There is no evidence to connect any person with his death. In the absence of evidence, there is no more support for a foul play explanation than there is an accident theory, which must remain a possibility.*"

Prof John Hunter, the renowned forensic archaeologist, spent three weeks in the Falklands in 1998. He, too, did not find a grave, but said that:

"*… there is a general consensus among a lot of people now that Alan Addis died there as an accident, not as part of a particular plan, a duffing over that went too far.*"[161]

CONFIRMED EVENTS LEADING UP TO THE DISAPPEARANCE

Background

On 7 August 1980, Alan Addis had been in the Royal Marines for over two years. He was trained in handling small arms, such as rifles and light machine guns; minor tactics; self-defence; map reading and land navigation; unarmed combat; and survival. He was twenty years old, 6ft 2in (1.88m) tall, weighed 12 stone (76kg) and was physically fit, with no known health or mental problems. He was also a good swimmer and canoeist. He appears to have had a pleasant personality, and as far as is known, there was no reason for his fellow Marines to dislike him.

In late July 1980, while serving with NP8901 in the Falkland Islands,

---

161 *Missing in the Falklands*, TV programme. Episode 4. <Minutes 1.09 et seq.

Alan heard about an undertaking to give members of the Falkland Islands Defence Force in two Settlements some on-the-spot training in weapon handling and fieldcraft. He was not among those initially selected for the task, but persuaded one of those who were to exchange duties. There is no reason to believe that his was anything more than a wish for a change from the stultifying repetition of barrack duties in Moody Brook. In his last letter to his mother, he told her: "*... only tomorrow to crack and I'm off sailing to Fitzroy. It should be a laugh. Will write again in two weeks when I get back.*"[162]

With two fellow Marines (Corporal Roger Davis and Marine Chris Johnson), Alan sailed from Stanley on the morning of 7 August 1980 aboard MV *Forrest*. According to the later Royal Marine Board of Inquiry (BoI), the three men did not get their pre-booked early call that morning and had to leave Moody Brook barracks in a hurry and without eating breakfast. During the twelve-hour voyage to North Arm, *Forrest* rolled severely and Alan, who was known not to be a good sailor, remained in his bunk in the forward hold all day. It is not known whether he was actually seasick or not, but he did not get up for the midday meal nor did he have any hot drinks.

MV *Forrest* moored alongside the jetty at North Arm as dark was falling and, although none of the three Marines had been to the Settlement before, they were told that there was to be a party that night in the Social Club, to which they were invited. They had supper aboard the *Forrest,* which would have been Alan's first hot meal that day.

The Party

After supper aboard *Forrest*, the three Marines (Corporal Davis, and Marines Johnson and Addis) walked to the Social Club, arriving at about 2000. This walk from the ship to the party was short and straightforward; 100 yards (91m) along the pier to the shore, then turn right and follow the only track to the Settlement, with the Social Club one of the first buildings. About ¼ mile (400m) and ten-to-fifteen minutes in all. At this time of the evening, the generator would have been running, so there were no navigation problems,

---

162 Letter from Alan to Sarah Ann Addis, 5 August 1980 in Addis, op. cit., p.24.

all they had to do was to head for the lighted and noisy building.[163] None of the three men had a map or compass, nor did they need them.

At the risk of stating the obvious, this was their first visit to North Arm, so the three Marines knew none of the Falklanders, nor did the latter know these particular Marines. The numbers at the party probably fluctuated during the evening but one of those present estimated that some fifty Settlers were present, plus the six Marines; this suggests a total of between fifty and sixty. The three Marines in Alan's group were dressed in civilian clothes and Alan's appearance, as reconstructed by the RFIP, is shown in Figure 1, page 51.[164] In essence, he was dressed casually in jeans and open-necked shirt, with a jacket and torch, which he deposited at the bar on arrival.

Leaving the Party

The Board of Inquiry and subsequent investigations did their best to reconstruct the events at the party, but, as with most parties (and by no means only in the Falklands), the drink flowed freely, with most of those attending becoming inebriated, and maybe in some cases drunk, so that memories were somewhat confused and contradictory. Nevertheless, Mr Blake, the manager of the estate and organiser of the party, reported afterwards that he had never felt it necessary to assert his authority to restore order. He also told the Board of Inquiry that he and his wife had chatted to Addis, but without noticing anything unusual.

The Board of Inquiry records that:

> *"Addis appears to have been in good spirits throughout the evening and held conversations with a number of people, who report him to have been acting normally but more drunkenly as the evening went on, but that at no time had he drunk so much that he was incapable."*

The two other Royal Marines in Addis's group (i.e., Corporal Roger Davis and Marine Chris Johnson) left at about 2315 and appear to have invited

---

163 At this time, most Settlements had small generators. They operated after dark, but there was no TV on the islands, so the gennies tended to be closed down at about 2200–2300. The close-down time for the North Arm generator is not known, but it may have been kept going for the party.

164 Addis, op. cit., p.45. Reproduction of police sketch with added manuscript comments by Sarah Ann.

Addis to go with them, but he declined. They felt no anxiety as to his behaviour or that he might be incapable of making his own way back later. These two made their way back to the ship and to their bunks without any apparent difficulty.

At some point, someone suggested to Addis that he should spend the night in a nearby Bunkhouse, and rejoin the ship in the morning, but Addis made no known attempt to take up this offer. The most reliable report is that he left the Social Club building at about 0130 – apparently peacefully and alone, as there are no reports of shouting, shoving or fisticuffs. It is presumed that he collected his torch and civilian parka as he left, because neither is listed among the effects collected after his disappearance.

There are two other reports about his departure. One witness claimed to the Board of Inquiry that Addis left at 0230, but this witness proved unreliable in other respects, so his statement was disregarded by the Board. The other witness was a twelve-year-old boy who told Sarah Ann that he saw Addis leave carrying a crate/box of beer. This cannot be proved or disproved. (As an aside, Governor Hunt also remarked on young children attending such late-night parties, but there can have been little other entertainment for them.)[165]

Thus, the situation as Alan left the Club at about 0130 on 8 August 1980 was:

- It was very cold – about freezing. There was no reported snow, but the ground was frosted, suggesting that footprints would have shown up.
- He had been drinking but was not incapable.
- He was a physically fit and well-trained Royal Marine.
- He was a good swimmer.
- He was dressed as shown in the police sketch, which was suitable for the intended short walk from the ship to the party and back again.
- He was not carrying a map, whistle or compass.
- He was carrying a torch.
- Outside the Social Club, it would have been totally silent apart, perhaps, from some subdued noise from the party.
- There were electrical light installations at either end of the jetty, although whether they were on or not is not known.
- He had never visited North Arm before, had not seen it in daylight and

---

165 Addis, op. cit., p.32.

probably had little or no idea of the layout of houses and tracks.

- As far as is known, he had not met any of the inhabitants of North Arm before about 2000 on 8 August 1980.
- Immediately on leaving the light and noise of the party, it is safe to assume that Alan closed the door and found himself in a silent and very dark environment with few electrical lights.
- He did not intend to return to the Social Club party.
- The other two members of Team B had returned to MV *Forrest* without any reported difficulty.

THE DISAPPEARANCE

MV *Forrest* sailed at about 0720 on 8 August 1980. Aboard were Captain Sollis and his crew; Sergeant Howden and his two Marines; plus, Corporal Davis and Marine Johnson, as well as, it was initially assumed, Marine Addis. But, at about 0730–0740 on 8 August 1980, when MV *Forrest* was about twenty-to-thirty minutes outward bound from North Arm, the two Marines from Sergeant Howden's party took their kit down to the hold and saw that Addis's bunk had not been slept in. They immediately conducted a search of the ship, found no trace of him, and reported to Sergeant Howden. Thus, by about 0740–0750, the ship had been thoroughly searched from stem-to-stern and it had been established that he was not aboard.[166] There are a number of possible explanations, which will now be examined in turn. It is important to note here that the two Marines who went down to the hold noticed not only that Addis was missing from his bunk, but also that the bunk had not been occupied at all.

Had Alan Addis decided to return to MV *Forrest*, he should have retraced the route he had covered only a few hours earlier. In other words, he had to walk with the sea on his left until he reached the unmistakeable bulk of the shearing shed and then turned left onto the jetty and traversed its full length until he reached the *Forrest*. He was also an experienced swimmer.

Assessment. It was high tide and the bottom shelves gently from the high water mark, so that had he kept straying from his path and entered the sea, the level would have steadily risen above his feet, then his ankles, then

---

166 Why there was no headcount before sailing has never been explained.

his shins, and so on. The water was also very cold – at or just below freezing – which, even if he was drunk, should have alarmed him before it was too late. Thus, it seems improbable that he could have walked into the gradually shelving and very cold sea until he drowned.

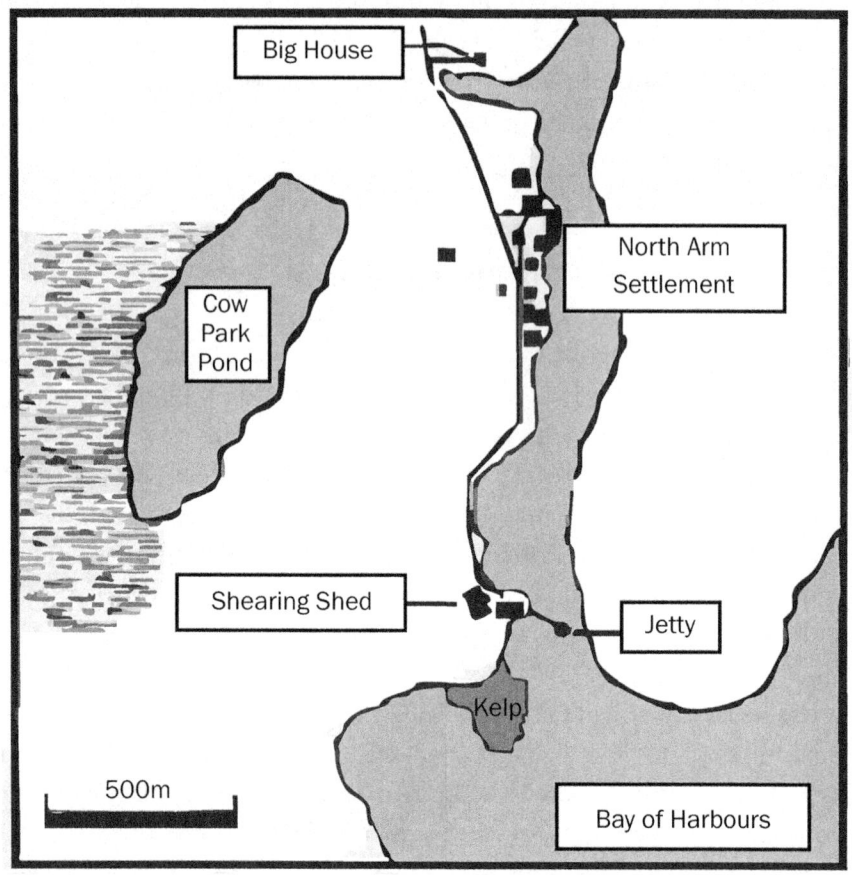

North Arm Settlement in 1980.
Alan Addis walked from Jetty to Social Club at about 2000 and should have walked the exact opposite at 0130 the next morning. (Note: Map is to scale but buildings are indicative and not exact as to scale or location.)

POSSIBILITY A. HE FOLLOWED THE CORRECT ROUTE TO REBOARD MV FORREST, BUT AT SOME POINT ALONG THE WAY, AND BEFORE REACHING THE JETTY, STRAYED INTO THE SEA AND DROWNED

Had Alan Addis decided to return to MV *Forrest*, he should have retraced the route he had covered only a few hours earlier. In other words, he had to walk with the sea on his left until he reached the unmistakeable bulk of the shearing shed and then turned left onto the jetty and traversed its full length until he reached the *Forrest*. He was also an experienced swimmer.

Assessment. It was high tide and the bottom shelves gently from the high water mark, so that had he kept straying from his path and entered the sea, the level would have steadily risen above his feet, then his ankles, then his shins, and so on. The water was also very cold – at or just below freezing – which, even if he was drunk, should have alarmed him before it was too late. Thus, it seems improbable that he could have walked into the gradually shelving and very cold sea until he drowned.

POSSIBILITY B. HE FOLLOWED THE CORRECT ROUTE TO REBOARD MV FORREST, BUT AT SOME POINT WHILE WALKING ALONG THE JETTY, FELL INTO THE SEA AND DROWNED

The jetty at North Arm in 1975. The black building at the landward end of the jetty is the shearing shed, the Settlement is off picture to the right. There are low wire fences either side of the walkway. Note the light standards on the pierhead.
(Courtesy Philip Davis)

The picture shows the jetty in 1975. The jetty was some 100 yards (91m) long, with a wide walkway of substantial wooden planks and a low three-strand wire fence on either side. There were two parallel rails for a wheeled carriage running the full length of the jetty to carry bales of wool from the sheds to the pierhead for loading into a ship. There were three electric lights on poles, one at the landward end of the jetty, two at the pierhead, but whether these were lit or not is not known.

Assessment. If he was really unsteady on his feet, he might have tripped over the rails, staggered to the edge and fallen over the fence into the water. The sea was very cold – about 0° – and the shock might have knocked him out, leading to drowning. In such a case, the expert divers considered that his body would have remained at or very close to the jetty, which it did not. The other two Marines of Team B appear to have found their way back to MV *Forrest* at about 2300 and the three of Team A at 0630 the following morning, all in darkness, and without difficulty. This possibility is considered to be not impossible but very unlikely.

POSSIBILITY C. HE FOLLOWED THE CORRECT ROUTE ALONG THE JETTY TO BOARD MV FORREST, BUT AS HE TRIED TO BOARD THE SHIP, FELL BETWEEN THE TWO, BECAME TRAPPED UNDERWATER AND DROWNED

It was a neap tide, so transferring from the jetty to board *Forrest* should have been easy, but such accidents are known to happen. An added potential complication was the suggestion that, having fallen into the water and becoming unconscious, his body might have been sucked under *Forrest,* caught on some underwater protrusion on the hull, dragged out to sea and released at some distant point. Several divers examined the bottom of *Forrest* but could find no protrusion that might have dragged the body out to sea. Such accidents have happened elsewhere. In this case, it was possible, but there was no proof.

POSSIBILITY D. HE BOARDED MV FORREST, BUT SHORTLY AFTER SAILING, HE JUMPED OR WAS PUSHED/THROWN OVERBOARD

It is possible that, having left the Social Club at ≈0130, Alan did reach and board MV *Forrest* and fell asleep somewhere, albeit not in his designated bunk in the hold. The two Marines of Team A reported that they had found Alan Addis's bed unslept in and then, after searching the ship, told Sergeant Holden that Addis was missing. This took place some ten-to-twenty minutes after *Forrest* had sailed and at a time when *Forrest* was not very far from the shore:

- **Possibility D1.** He fell overboard. MV Forrest's weather deck was completely surrounded by a bulwark some 2ft (60cm) high. The upper (bridge level) deck was completely surrounded by a three-strand rail. It would have been difficult, albeit not impossible, for Addis to have fallen overboard, perhaps when being seasick?
- **Possibility D2.** He jumped overboard deliberately. See 'suicide' below.
- **Possibility D3.** He was either pushed or thrown overboard by a person/ persons unknown.

Assessment. Addis was a fit young man and an experienced swimmer, so it is not impossible that he could have jumped overboard with the intention of swimming to the shore. If he had, the distance was not great and, being a strong swimmer, he should have made it to the shore. But, he would have arrived soaking wet and bitterly cold (temperature was around 0^0C). He did not have a map nor would he (as far as is known) have had any food or drinkable water. Thus, the chances that, having reached the shore, he would have survived are very slim and, if he perished in the open, his body should have been found by now. The people aboard MV *Forrest* were Captain Sollis and his crew and the five other Royal Marines. It is difficult to see how or why any of those, either alone or in combination, could have pitched Alan overboard without being seen by others. Nor, indeed, would they have had any known reason to do so. This is not impossible, but it is difficult to guess why this should have happened.

OVERALL ASSESSMENT – DROWNING

From the start of the searches, one of the two leading possibilities was that he had drowned. This was carefully considered. Boats surveyed the surface, some of which had glass-bottomed boxes to examine the area immediately beneath the boat. Trained military divers also conducted extensive underwater searches, including a detailed examination under the jetty and the bottom of MV *Forrest*. The first of these searches was on 9–11 August 1980, the second on 15–18 August 1997, but neither found any trace of Addis. Beaches and kelp reefs out to a distance of 10 miles (16km) were repeatedly checked. Detailed plans of underwater profiles and currents were prepared and analysed.

The possible behaviour of an unweighted corpse, dressed as Addis had been, was considered and it was agreed by the professional divers that experience had shown that gases would have brought the corpse to the surface, probably about three weeks later, following which, it would almost certainly have been washed ashore. Not only was no body found, but nor was a single trace discovered, such as torn clothing or the torch he was known to be carrying.

The Board of Inquiry found that: *"As it is assumed from the evidence that Addis was capable of returning to MV Forrest (and there is no evidence to indicate that he would do otherwise as he did not sleep ashore) the Board conclude that Addis was drowned."*[167] This was endorsed by Governor Hunt, who wrote to Sarah Ann stating that: *"We live in hope that the sea will deliver up that which it appears to have taken away."*[168] It is not impossible that he drowned, but, in view of the careful consideration, repeated searches, including by separate groups of professional divers, coupled with a total lack of any evidence, it is concluded to be unlikely and that the Board of Inquiry was mistaken.

POSSIBILITY E. HE REACHED THE JETTY, STOLE ONE OF THE DINGHIES LYING THERE AND MADE OFF WITH IT

There were several small boats in the Settlement, which are mentioned as taking part in the searches and can be seen in contemporary photographs. These were dinghies with oars, perhaps some with a small outboard motor. As a teenager, Alan had become an experienced canoeist and, during his Marine service, short as it was, would have trained in the use of small boats. It is, therefore, possible that he could have taken one, although quite what he would have intended thereafter is impossible to tell. But, there were no reports that any boat was missing, while the oars and rudders were secured in

167 Board of Inquiry, Sep 1980, para 17.
168 Addis, op. cit., p.14.

a locked shed. Further, none of the repeated searches of the shoreline found an abandoned boat of any description. This possibility can be dismissed.

POSSIBILITY F. HE TOOK THE WRONG DIRECTION IMMEDIATELY ON LEAVING THE SOCIAL CLUB (i.e., away from Forrest) AND THEN KEPT WALKING INTO THE HINTERLAND (CAMP) UNTIL HE EITHER SUFFERED AN ACCIDENT OR BECAME EXHAUSTED AND DIED FROM EXPOSURE

It is possible that Alan Addis, although intending to return to MV *Forrest* (i.e., to his South), became disorientated and headed in the wrong direction, obviously neither realising nor intending that he was doing so, and then becoming totally disorientated. As described in Chapter Sixteen, there were many historical precedents. Had he headed West, he would have soon encountered a dense gorse hedge and, even if he succeeded in fighting his way through that, would soon have come up against Cow Park Pond. In any event, as he had not encountered any gorse hedges during the walk to the Social Club, he would surely have realised that this was a mistake? Had he headed East, he would have reached the long northern inlet of the sea (known locally as 'the Creek').

So, had Alan headed in the wrong direction, it is considered most likely that he would have headed North. After leaving the Social Club and heading up the track, he would quickly have encountered a Y-junction with the right fork leading to the main part of the Settlement, while the left fork led northwards, passing the Settlement to his right, and into the Camp.

It is important to remember at this point that it was pitch dark, completely silent, and he was in surroundings of which he had no previous knowledge. He was dressed for a short walk, not a long trek in wintry conditions, and had neither map nor compass. In fact, the only navigation aid he had was his Ever-Ready torch, which was probably not particularly powerful, its only real use being signalling or to illuminate the ground up to about 12 feet (4m) ahead.

He would have become increasingly anxious, not only about where he was, but also about the possibility of failing to reach MV *Forrest* before it sailed, thus committing not only a military disciplinary offence for which he would undoubtedly be punished, but also letting down his mates, a serious consideration for a professional British Royal Marine. He was also, probably for the first time in his life, totally on his own, with nobody else at all to provide support, advice or help.

If he suffered an accident or reached a state of exhaustion from which he died, his body would have lain exposed on open ground. In such a case, the vultures would have quickly located the body and started to circle above it. This was a phenomenon well-known to Falkland Islanders and, if Alan's body had been lying in the open, it should have quickly been found.

On the assumptions that he remained on the vehicle track, it is estimated that his rate of advance would have been about 2–3 miles (3–5km) in the hour, and that had he started at about 0130, he would have kept going – and always hoping that the jetty lay just out of sight. By this reckoning, by first light at about 0730, he could have been as much as 5–7 miles (8–11km) North of the Settlement. Because of the flatness of the terrain, the Settlement would have been out of sight to his South and there would have been no obvious landmarks.

It has already been noted that a Settler (David Clarke) drove a Land Rover from North Arm via Bodie Suspension Bridge to Goose Green on the morning of 8 August. If Addis's body had been on that particular track, it seems safe to assume that Clarke would have seen it.

Sphagnum are a series of mosses associated with peat that can store large quantities of water inside their cells. They tend to congregate in discrete areas forming a roughly circular area of varying diameters and up to 20 feet (6m) in depth. They have an effect similar to quicksand, with the victim being sucked down and eventually disappearing altogether. Sheep on Dartmoor in England occasionally disappear without trace, their loss being attributed by local farmers to straying into sphagnum bogs. Such areas are known to exist in the Falkland Islands and when horses are described as 'bogged down' this is almost certainly due to sphagnum moss. The areas are very difficult to detect and are by no means well-mapped.

Assessment. Becoming lost and perishing in the Camp was considered one of the two most likely courses by the early investigations and remains a possibility, but as with the other outcomes, there is not a single shred of evidence that it either did or did not happen. Falling into a sphagnum bog has not been considered by previous investigations, but it would explain both the disappearance and the lack of any evidence. It is considered a remote possibility, but it is impossible to prove.

POSSIBILITY G. HE USED HIS DISAPPEARANCE
AS A MEANS OF ESCAPING

It has been suggested that one possibility was that he wanted to escape from the Royal Marines and did so by feigning an inexplicable disappearance, while actually following a preconceived plan. As a person subject to military law, short-term absence followed by a return (either compulsory or voluntary) would have been 'absence without leave', while a desire never to return to the Royal Marines would have amounted to 'desertion'. Addis would have known this.

Had he tried to escape via another Settlement or via Stanley, he would almost certainly have been recognised and reported. Thus, any escape from the Falklands would have been frustrated. But, some foreign ships were known to send parties ashore to deserted beaches; for example, to collect penguin eggs without a licence to do so. Thus, it was theoretically possible for Addis to have escaped from the Falklands aboard a foreign ship.

Assessment. It is not clear how he would have set this up, as it would have required previous liaison with the ship concerned. He would have burnt his bridges not only with the Royal Marines, but also with his beloved mother and her family. It is concluded that this was a very unlikely course.

POSSIBILITY H. HE DELIBERATELY TOOK HIS OWN LIFE

Suicide is not totally impossible, but:
- Alan had shown no signs of depression to his comrades.
- His letters to his mother were consistently cheerful and upbeat, and if he made minor criticisms of the food at Moody Brook, that is normal for the vast majority of soldiers and Marines wherever they might be.[169]
- He had no known health or mental problems that might limit either his lifespan or a full career in the Royal Marines. If he did have such problems, they would have been reported on by at least one of the inquiries/investigations, which they were not.
- He had a regular career, which he appeared to enjoy, and if the pay was not great, he had his adoring, well-off and always generous mother to fall back on.

---

169 Addis, op. cit., pp.22–24.

- It is not known whether he had any romantic problems with one or more girlfriends in the UK sending him a 'Dear John' letter. He is reported to have had a photograph of a cousin (presumably female) in his wallet. 'Dear Johns' happened a lot in the lengthy overseas unaccompanied postings of that era and the great majority of recipients just shrugged them off.

There was, however, one factor which *might* have been preying on his mind, in that he never knew his father; indeed, he may not even have known who his father was, except that it could not have been Keith Addis, whose surname he bore. There is no evidence one way or the other, so it is impossible to tell whether this lack of a father could have led Alan to be suicidal. None of the various official investigations have recorded considering suicide, so presumably such a possibility was never suggested by any of their many witnesses.

Assessment. There is no known reason for him to have taken his own life and had he done so it seems unlikely that he would have taken steps to ensure that his body could not be found. It is concluded that, while suicide cannot be totally excluded, it is unlikely.

POSSIBILITY J. HE WAS THE VICTIM OF AN ATTACK BY ONE OR MORE ASSAILANTS

It has been reported by former Marine Philip Davis, who was a member of the NP8901 (1974–75) detachment, that there was ill feeling in North Arm against the Marines, although he never discovered why. When his concert party visited the North Arm Settlement in July 1975, a Kelper named Titch Jaffray tried very hard to pick a fight with him for no discernible reason, although, in the event, no fight actually took place. See Annex D.

As Addis had never visited North Arm before and had come to the party straight from the newly arrived MV *Forrest*, there can have been no previous cause of friction attributable to him as an individual, i.e. *'let's get Addis'*. In other words, whatever the reason for the attack, it must have arisen either at the party or in some confrontation immediately after he had left. One witness at the Royal Marine Board of Inquiry reported raised voices at the party, but this was dismissed as unreliable. There is no other report of any serious altercations at the party, and Addis seems to have been unaccompanied as he left, i.e. he was neither ordered nor escorted out.

By about midnight, all other Marines had left, so that Addis was on his own and unlikely to receive support in an affray from other locals. This also means that all witnesses as to Alan's departure were locals, some of whom may not have been entirely truthful to subsequent inquiries.

It seems possible that Titch Jaffray may have deliberately picked a fight with Alan Addis, as he had tried to do with Philip Davis in 1974. In a TV interview, Jaffray said: "... *I like a punch-up – any trouble, I'm there. They're like a magnet to me.*"[170] But, it should be stressed that Jaffray denied taking part in any assault on Addis and there is no reason to suggest that he was involved in any affray, although he was one of those arrested and questioned in the Pennington Inquiry. In any case, Robin Goodwin states that Titch normally got very drunk at parties and was usually rolled up in a carpet to immobilise him and keep him out of trouble.

Although a confrontation may have been for no particular reason other than to start a fight for the sake of it, it could also have been over a woman; for example, if one of the Kelpers thought that Addis was 'chatting up' or even touching his wife or girlfriend, as had allegedly happened with Burgos at Goose Green.

Addis was a tall, strong and physical fit young man and, if attacked by one man, the attack could only have succeeded if he was taken by surprise, but it seems more likely that at least two attackers would have been involved.

The manager, Blake, is known to have carried a 0.22in revolver on at least two occasions.[171] He is also reported to have carried a 0.41in revolver, although this could have been intended to despatch sheep or rats. Most of the farmhands had shotguns, but there is no suggestion that any carried pistols. The attacker/s may have found wooden staves, metal bars or tools such as shovels or hammers, which would have been lying around any farming site. In addition, most workers in the Settlements, particularly shepherds and general labourers, carried a short but very sharp shepherd's knife, which was used to despatch any sick or injured sheep encountered during the working day.[172]

---

170 Lion TV *Bodyhunters*.

171 These occasions were (a) the arrest of the crazed Chilean aboard *Ilen* and (b) the apprehension of the Argentine pilot.

172 This was confirmed with a professional shepherd in the UK.

This is considered a strong possibility, with the proviso that, except in the case of a knife, Alan's death was not the intended outcome.

POSSIBILITY K. THAT HE HAD AN ASSIGNATION WITH A WOMAN, WAS CAUGHT, ASSAULTED AND KILLED

One suggestion from a number of sources is that, during the party, Alan arranged an assignation with a married woman, that he left the party to meet her, and that the couple had been caught *in flagrante delicto* by her husband or boyfriend who then attacked (in Prof Hunter's words, 'duffed him over') and accidentally killed him. There are even some discretely veiled hints that the woman concerned may have been the manager's wife, Lyn Blake, who is known to have been interviewed by the FIP, but her husband later refused to allow her to be interviewed by Sarah Ann. According to reports from people who knew them both, Lyn was a devoted wife and mother, and very unlikely to have made such an assignation. But that is not to say that there might have been another woman at the party, one, in particular, being a well-known flirt.

Despite the rumours at the time, it seems improbable that Lyn Blake was the woman involved. It is, however, possible that another woman was involved, but there is no proof.

POSSIBILITY L. THAT HE DIED FROM A STILL UNKNOWN CAUSE

Having discussed all the circumstances above, there is still the possibility of a hitherto unconsidered cause. As described by Donald Rumsfeld, *"There are known knowns; there are things we know we know. We also know there are known unknowns; that is to say we know there are some things we do not know. But there are also unknown unknowns – the ones we don't know we don't know."* [173]

For example, Malaysian Airlines Flight MH370 on 8 March 2014 and Germanwings Flight 9525 on 24 March 2015 were lost to unpredictable (and in the former case, still unexplained) causes. These events, and many like them, are mentioned here because they could not have been foreseen and, although something similar may be included in national or corporate

---

173 Internet. *"Defense.gov News Transcript: DoD News Briefing – Secretary Rumsfeld and Gen. Myers, United States Department of Defense"*. February 12, 2002.

contingency plans, when and where they will happen and their precise nature is simply unknown.

The point here is that while it has been possible to envisage the possibilities described in the paragraphs above, Alan Addis's disappearance may still have been due to a currently unconsidered cause.

HYPOTHESIS

Having examined all those possibilities, the following is suggested as a *possible* sequence of events:

- At some point during the party, Addis upset/annoyed one or more of those Settlers present, possibly by showing an interest in a wife/girlfriend.
- This encouraged a group of young Settlers who were spoiling for a fight, which was a frequent outcome of a Falklands party.
- Addis was an outsider and the only Royal Marine to remain at the party, so was an easy target, although, as he was obviously large and strong, more than one assailant was needed, i.e., safety in numbers.
- Knowing that Addis must return to MV *Forrest*, the small group of assailants assembled in the shelter of, or perhaps inside, the shearing shed.
- Addis departed the party at approximately 0130 and walked towards the jetty.
- Addis was decoyed into the shearing shed.
- Assailants attacked Addis – probably two, three or four men.
- Addis fell to the floor, either:
  - As a result of a blow that unexpectedly caused a medical termination.
  - Or, in falling, his head struck a sharp object.
- On examination, he was found to be dead.
- His assailants were astonished by this unintended outcome. Nonplussed and not knowing what to do, they sent for Blake, who made all the major decisions in the Settlement, and clearly had to be consulted on this one.

CHAPTER NINETEEN

What Happened to the Corpse?

It is an inescapable conclusion that Alan Addis died at some time between 0130 and dawn on 8 August 1980, somewhere in the area of North Arm Settlement. It is also clear that something must have happened to his corpse, which has ensured that it has remained totally undiscovered for forty-five years. As discussed in Chapter Eighteen, how and precisely where he died and who else, if anyone, was involved remain totally unknown, but with the one exception, which will be addressed later, there must have been a corpse. There have been numerous attempts to locate the body, both on the ground and through research, but not one has achieved a scintilla of success. Indeed, every suggestion simply gives rise to a plethora of reasons why it could not have happened that way. But the truth must lie somewhere. The possibility that he died in some form of accident will first be considered, followed by foul play.

Accidental Death – Drowned

In the days immediately following Alan's disappearance, one of the two possibilities considered by the investigators was that he had drowned. For example, the Royal Marine Board of Inquiry found that: *"As it is assumed from the evidence that Addis was capable of returning to MV Forrest (and there is no evidence to indicate that he would do otherwise, as he did not sleep ashore) the Board conclude that Addis was drowned."* This was endorsed by Governor Hunt who wrote to Sarah Ann stating that *"We live in hope that the sea will deliver up that which it appears to have taken away,"* although Hunt seems to have been hedging his bets as the word *'appears'* seems to not totally exclude other possibilities.

Numerous searches were made of North Arm inlet (the Creek), some of them employing glass-bottomed boxes to examine the area immediately below the boat. Trained divers were also brought in to conduct extensive underwater searches. The first of these searches was on 9–11 August 1980 by Royal Marine divers from NP8901 at Moody Brook, the second on 15–18 Aug 1997 by divers from the garrison at Mount Pleasant Airfield, but neither found any trace. These underwater searches included a detailed underwater examination of the jetty and its surroundings, but when it was suggested that the body might have snagged on some protrusion on the bottom of MV *Forrest* and been carried out to sea, a careful underwater examination of the hull showed that was not possible.

The behaviour of a submerged unweighted corpse, dressed as Alan had been, was considered and it was agreed by the practical experience of professional divers that gases would have brought the corpse to the surface, probably about three weeks later, following which, it would almost certainly have been washed ashore. Not only has no body ever been found, but neither has a single trace been discovered.

The RFIP, under Superintendent Greenland, carried out tests with a floating dummy equal in size and weight to Alan Addis. They found that the dummy never left the confines of the Creek, and whenever the 'body' reached the kelp barrier at the mouth of the Creek, it was prevented from exiting to the open sea and sent back up the Creek by a countervailing current. The RFIP admits that this was not a truly scientific test conducted by professionals but believe that it gave a good indication.

Apart from these underwater searches, beaches out to a distance of ten miles (16km) from the Settlement were repeatedly checked, and detailed plans of underwater profiles and currents were prepared and analysed. Kelp forests were also examined, although even the skilled divers admitted that they could not penetrate too deeply for fear of getting trapped themselves. Nevertheless, it is difficult to imagine how a large human corpse could be carried into such a maze of fronds.

It is not considered impossible that Alan Addis could have met his death through accidental drowning but, in view of the careful consideration, repeated searches, including by professional divers, coupled with a total lack of any evidence, it is considered unlikely. Thus, the Board of Inquiry and the Governor were mistaken in reaching this conclusion.

Accidental Death – Land

As described earlier, Alan could have become disorientated and headed inland in the wrong direction, eventually becoming either lost and exhausted or suffered an accident, for which there were plenty of precedents in the Falkland Islands. Thus, immobilised, he would almost certainly have frozen to death, in which case his fully dressed body would have remained on the surface in the open. There were no roads as such in 1980, but frequently travelled routes such as those from North Arm to Danson Harbour or other 'outside' elements of the North Arm Settlement would have been relatively easy to follow. The track to Goose Green would have been even easier to follow as it was marked by telephone poles. Had Alan frozen to death on or near one of these tracks, his body should have been found either within days by one of the search teams or in the succeeding forty-five years by chance. Alternatively, if he had wandered off the track he was trying to follow, he could have collapsed on open ground, whereupon his body would soon have been found by vultures, which, in turn, should have been spotted by Settlers. On the other hand, had the body not been spotted, but had lain on open ground and picked clean by vultures, the area is so vast that the chances of what few remains were left could only have been found by chance.

Homicide – Burial on Land

If Alan was killed – almost certainly by accident – within the Settlement, and his assailants, for whatever reason, decided that they could not report it, they would have been faced with the totally unexpected problem of disposing of a sizeable corpse, plus whatever property he had on his person at the time. What is more, the disposal had to be total, i.e., not a single trace could be left. The time being about 0200 in the morning and, knowing that dawn was at about 0830, they had some six-and-a-half hours in which to dispose of the body and to eliminate all traces – and all without alerting the other inhabitants of the Settlement.[174]

---

174 According to government statistics in August, the average length of the day in North Arm is nine hours and forty-nine minutes. On 1 August, sunrise is at 0832 and sunset at 1732; both times would be marginally different one week later.

The most probable course for his adversaries was to bury the body, although any site within the Settlement itself was impossible, except perhaps as a very temporary expedient. However, there is a vast area of Camp. Numerous searches for a grave have been conducted over the years, but nothing has been found. Rocky areas can clearly be discounted but this still leaves a very large area. Professor Hunter, a professional and highly respected forensic archaeologist, who has extensive experience on the ground in Lafonia where he conducted Operation Lioness II, has pointed out that, without a specific clue, the chances of finding the body are extremely remote.

Homicide – Burial at Sea

As recorded in Chapter Seven, the divers who searched under and around the North Arm jetty remarked that an unfettered body will lie on the bottom for a period and then rise to the surface. However, the cases of Park and Parham whose bodies were weighted suggest the possibility that a similar fate might have befallen Addis, except that his body would have been dumped at sea. Further, if it had been dumped far enough from the shore, the chances of it being snagged by an angler or a trawler would have been very remote.

There is a curious link with Nella Jones, the clairvoyant consulted by Sarah Ann Addis. Nella, who had never been to North Arm, 'saw' the body in a boat, which turned right from the jetty and then arrived at a cavern with an entrance that was only visible at low tide and had a blowhole in the roof. If Alan's body had been moved as she described, that boat would, indeed, have turned right to go out to sea and, as confirmed by the police, her description of the cavern exactly matched the real-life cave at Devil's Point, albeit they found no human traces there. But it is possible that, having been killed in the area of the jetty, Alan's body was taken immediately to Devil's Point, which was well away from the Settlement and unlikely to be searched in the short term. This would have given those involved the opportunity to assemble ropes, weights, etc., in the Settlement, affix them to the body, and then transport it well out into the Bay of Harbours before dumping it in deep waters.

Homicide – Burial in Rivers/Lakes

As discussed in Chapter Fifteen, murderers frequently dispose of their victims' bodies in rivers or lakes, often (but not always) by attaching heavy weights to ensure that the body does not return to the surface. There is an inherent danger in that the corpse, while remaining at the bottom, might be discovered by chance by divers, or 'caught' by anglers. There is also a danger that inland waters might dry out.

One of those interviewed by Sarah Ann suggested the body might be in Cow Park Pond and she commented that it had never been searched. This stretch of water is half-a-mile due West of North Arm and was well-known to all in the Settlement. The maximum depth is 6ft (2m), but in many places much less, and frequent southerly gales generate large waves, which wash over the retaining bank, thus reducing the depth of water in the pond yet further. On balance, dumping a weighted body here would almost certainly have been discovered and can be rejected.

Homicide – Bodie Creek Suspension Bridge

A particular case is that of disposal over the side of the Bodie Creek Suspension Bridge. This could have been done by David Clarke during his journey to Goose Green, either with or without help from other conspirators. The RFIP clearly considered this possibility since they sent two separate teams of divers to examine the riverbed under the bridge, which was done with great thoroughness, but neither found any trace of human remains. Nevertheless, the possibility of Addis's weighted body being disposed of in this way is not impossible.

An alternative possibility is that the body had no attached weights and was simply pitched over the railings and into the Creek. However, the chances of the body reaching the open sea without running aground and being discovered en route seem remote.

Homicide – Dismemberment

Another way of disposing of a body is by dismembering it and scattering the parts over a wide area. There are numerous examples of dismemberment, but since it is a somewhat macabre subject, just one example, albeit not a very successful one, will suffice here. Stephen Marshall (thirty-eight), a nightclub doorman, and girlfriend Sarah Bush (twenty-one), a sex worker, lived in a flat in Southgate, North London, which they shared with the landlord, Jeffrey Howe (thirty-nine), a kitchen salesman. Howe asked his two lodgers to leave, which they refused to do, so on the night of 8–9 March 2009, Marshall stabbed him twice in the back with a four-inch blade, assisted by Bush. Following that, he cut up the body and the parts were later dumped around the local countryside, only to be found by unfortunate and unsuspecting members of the public (listed in chronological order):

- 22 March 2009. The left leg and foot in a lay-by inside a green holdall.
- 29 March 2009. The left forearm, dismembered at the elbow and wrist, on a grass verge.
- 31 March 2009. The head by a farmer in a field.
- 7 April 2009. The right leg in a holdall.
- 11 April 2009. The torso, right arm, dismembered at the wrist, and upper left arm in a ditch inside a green suitcase.
- Only the hands were never found, probably, the murderers may have thought, to ensure that fingerprints could not be used to identify the corpse.

The press nicknamed the victim 'The Jigsaw Man', as the police assembled the various parts in order to identify him, which actually did not take too long. The trial of this inept couple was held at St Albans Crown Court, starting on 12 January 2010, but on 29 January, Marshall changed his plea to guilty. He was then sentenced to thirty-six years imprisonment on 1 February, upon which he formally admitted to dismembering four other bodies between 1995 and 1998 and scattering them in Epping Forest.[175]

In the Falkland Islands, if the assailants decided to dismember Alan's body, it would not have been difficult. The killing shed was nearby where cattle and sheep carcasses were routinely cut up prior to issue to the Settlers for cooking. It thus had a sturdy operating platform, together with an array of tools, such as axes, saws and knives. There was also good drainage and washdown facilities. Once the body had been dismembered, it would have

---

175 They were victims of a gang war in Central London. Marshall was unable to identify them, and they have never been found.

been relatively simple to dispose of the parts – certainly easier than disposing of a 6ft 2in (1.88m), 12 stone (76kg) body. Alan's clothing would also have had to be discarded, probably burnt in one of the many small furnaces, although it might have been tempting for one of the gang to have quietly pocketed his wallet and Rolex watch. The killing shed in use in 1980 was totally dismantled some two years later and the site hosed down.

Homicide – Burning

Another way of getting rid of a corpse is by burning and this was suggested by several of those interviewed by Sarah Ann in 1993: "... *Yet others said he had been put in the furnace at the 'Big House', this being the North Arm manager's house*"[176] It was certainly correct that there was a peat-fired furnace in Blake's house, as, indeed, there was one in every Settler's house to provide hot water and heating. But the firebox hole was only some 15 inches (38cm) square and the grate some 30 inches (76cm) long, so the body would have had to be cut up to fit in. In addition, human flesh gives off a very characteristic smell when burning, which would have permeated the entire house. It is, therefore, considered that this was not correct.

Conclusion

None of the above can be supported by forensic evidence, witness statements or deathbed confessions, but it is clear that Alan's body must have been disposed of somehow and that it would have required at least two, perhaps as many as four, participants. Whoever they were, they have remained remarkably quiet for forty-five years and not even Sarah Ann's heartfelt pleas for closure were able to break through that wall of silence.

---

176 Addis, op. cit., p.44.

CHAPTER TWENTY

The Falklands Factor

There can be little doubt that one or, more probably, several people in North Arm must have been involved in the affray that led to Alan Addis's death, or, in its aftermath, transporting the corpse and its interment. But, as already explained, it would seem that this outcome was almost certainly the unintended consequence of a so-called 'teach him a lesson' that went wrong.

All over the world, small, isolated communities, particularly on islands, tend to resent, resist and, in many cases, actually oppose what they see as interference by outsiders, which might be termed 'community solidarity'. Thus, it appears that in North Arm, while those who actually took part in the affray would naturally have wanted to maintain silence, so, too, would those who did not take part but had strong suspicions as to who had; for example, through family connections or overhearing a chance remark. Beyond that, there must also have been a few people who knew or suspected that *something* had happened to cause Alan Addis to disappear, but who just did not want to be involved, either through community solidarity or because they were too frightened. Finally, there would inevitably have been others, almost certainly the great majority, who genuinely had no knowledge of the affair, apart from the fact that a Marine was missing, and they had to take part in searches for him.

While it is doubtful that he took part in the actual affray, the manager, Tony Blake, was known to keep a tight grip on the Settlement and its people, thus controlling all events within his domain. It is, therefore, reasonable to assume that he would have become involved very shortly after Addis's death and was then the decision-maker over what needed to be done and how to do it.

More difficult to explain are the reactions of senior officials in the

Falklands government at the time, i.e., the then Governor and Colonial Secretary. These men failed to regard the deaths of Alan Addis and Jimmy Biggs as requiring some sort of further and formal explanation, even though both occurred in suspicious circumstances, within a fortnight of each other and at the same tiny Settlement. Instead, they appear to have allowed themselves to be fobbed off by a brief report from the manager in which Blake described both Addis's disappearance and Biggs's death as 'accidental' – which he must have known to be untrue. They also accepted without question the Royal Marines Board of Inquiry, although it was quickly seen by others to be inept. Despite these reservations, when Superintendent Lamb reviewed the case in 1982, he still concluded that it had been an accident, an opinion which was heartily endorsed by the then Civil Commissioner.

The one person who kept the issue alive was Alan's mother: memories of the case live on. In 1992, some twelve years after her son's disappearance, Sarah Ann Addis wrote: "… (I) received information regarding a Sergeant who had been a young Marine in the Falkland Islands at the same time as Alan. The Sergeant reported that he had heard a disquieting story about Alan in a pub in Plymouth recently. He was not sure what to do with the information, so went to see a Lieutenant Colonel RM and repeated the conversation he had heard. It transpired that he had been talking to an ex-policeman who had served in the Falkland Island Police after the Falklands War. He reported that there was a Falkland Islander, still living in the islands, who was boasting that he had murdered a Marine and had got away with it. It would appear that this individual and Alan, both worse for wear from drink, had a violent disagreement over the man's girlfriend. The story went on that he had either asked Alan outside or had followed him outside and had killed him. The ex-policeman, who could be traced, confirmed that during the war all records concerning the incident had been destroyed."[177]

There can equally be no doubt that the majority of people in North Arm had no knowledge whatsoever of these events and wished that they would be resolved and thus remove what they regard as a serious slur on the reputation of the Falkland Islands in general and North Arm in particular. As recently as 2021, Helen and David Jeffrey, two English tourists, visited North Arm and recorded that: "The Settlement has a somewhat sinister reputation due to the disappearance here of a nineteen-year-old Marine called Alan Addis in August 1980, while on a routine exercise. He arrived in North Arm by sea with two colleagues to collect some equipment/stores to deliver to Fitzroy Settlement. Their work for the day

---

177 Addis, op. cit., pp.41–42.

done, the Marines all went to the social for some refreshment. His colleagues returned to their boat shortly after 11pm, assuming he would follow later. They set off the following morning, before discovering he wasn't on board and never saw him again. No body has ever been found and the local residents were unable or unwilling to explain what happened to him. No body has ever been found despite the involvement of the Devon & Cornwall Police and, later, the Met, who sent sniffer dogs and a forensic archaeologist.[178] Four men were arrested some years later, but no one has ever been charged in connection with the disappearance. It seems equally possible that he fell off the gangplank in a state of intoxication or that he was fatally injured in a bar brawl that went too far, and his assailants hid the body and covered it all, but essentially there is no evidence at all."[179]

---

178 This is marginally incorrect as the forensic archaeologist (Professor Hunter) and sniffer dog were not part of the Met's involvement.

179 *https://helenanddavidinthesouthatlantic.wordpress.com/2021/08/21/north-arm/*

CHAPTER TWENTY-ONE

Conclusion

The inescapable fact is that not a single trace of Alan Addis has been found since he was last seen leaving the North Arm Social Club at about 0130 on 8 August 1980. This makes it certain that he must be dead, which in turn gives rise to three questions: how did he die; who, if anyone, was responsible; and what happened to the body?

North Arm Settlement and its immediate environs have been repeatedly searched, including, as far as is known, all byres, buildings, chicken coops, gardens, graveyards, kennels, outside houses, peat piles, rubbish dumps, stables, stores, vegetable patches and the void under the sheep-shearing shed, as well as several other potential burial sites.

The 'Big House' (i.e., the manager's residence) and its surrounding gardens were searched repeatedly and in great detail by the Operation Lioness II team. The jetty area has been searched by two separate groups of professional divers, as has the riverbed underneath Bodie Creek Suspension Bridge. The North Arm Creek, sea and shoreline have been searched on numerous occasions. In addition to these official searches, the whole area has been travelled over for forty-five years by locals who would have recognised and reported anything suspicious, such as a skeleton, a human bone, a grave, a scrap of clothing, disturbed ground or circling vultures.

As far as can be ascertained, all five Marines who were at North Arm on 7/8 August 1980 have been interviewed on numerous occasions, as were many Marines who were at Moody Brook, not members of the North Arm group, but who had served alongside Alan. So, too, have all the Falklanders who were at North Arm on that fateful night. Such interviews have been conducted by:

• The Royal Marines Board of Inquiry; 23–24 August 1980.

- Sarah Ann Addis; March 1981 and February 1995.
- The Army's Special Investigation Branch (SIB) and Superintendent Lamb; June to November 1981.[180]
- Detective Chief Inspector Pennington's team, August to October 1995.
- Superintendent Greenland and the Royal Falklands Islands Police on several occasions over the years.

On the assumption that his body might be buried outside the Settlement, particular areas of the hinterland ('Camp'), such as Danson Harbour House, Mappa House and Wreck House have been searched and declared clear. But a detailed search of such a vast area of open and relatively featureless countryside is clearly impossible – akin, it has been suggested, to searching for a very small needle in at least two haystacks.

There was a remote possibility that Alan Addis might have deliberately engineered his own disappearance, which would have been classified as a military offence contrary to Section 37 of the Army Act, 1955, dealt with as a domestic matter by the Royal Marines. In the event of his returning to duty after a few days, he would have been charged with Absence Without Leave (AWOL), but if he disappeared without any obvious intention of returning to duty, the charge would have been Desertion. In either case, it would have entailed him making it to another Settlement, but a living Alan Addis never showed up in any and these were all so small that his presence would have been immediately noticed and reported. An even more unlikely destination was Stanley, since he would soon have been found by his fellow Marines. Even if he had somehow evaded those, the only practicable point of exit from the Falklands at that time was by civilian ship or aircraft from Stanley, but these were monitored and there were no reports that he had done so. There was an even more remote possibility that he might have boarded a foreign vessel, but it seems very unlikely that he did and, even had he done so, it would probably have been reported. Further, so close were the ties between Alan and his mother that it seems highly unlikely that, had he somehow escaped from the Falklands, he would never have contacted her,

---

180 The only three he was unable to interview were a Chilean and a Colombian, both of whom had returned to their native countries. The third was a British yachtsman, temporarily employed in the crew of MV *Forrest*, who had disappeared without trace in his yacht after leaving the Falklands. None of these three was thought to have had any possible link with Addis's disappearance.

in which case her relentless – if eventually fruitless – pursuit of her son's fate would not have been necessary.

Physical searches have been carried out by: Army Special Investigation Branch, Devon & Cornwall Constabulary, the Forensic Science Advisory Group, Metropolitan Police, North Arm Settlement inhabitants, Royal Falklands Islands Police, Royal Marines and Sarah Ann Addis, as well as several investigative TV programmes. Not one of those has found even the slightest trace of either the body or its clothing, nor, despite some suspicions, have they identified a single credible witness.

It would have been impossible to hide a living Addis in North Arm Settlement after daybreak on 8 August, so it follows that he must have died between about 0145 and 0700, at which point there must have been a corpse, as well as the clothing he was known to have been wearing, such as the unusual jacket and the few possessions he was carrying that night, including his wallet, identity card and very expensive watch. It also seems reasonable to assume that when going to the party at North Arm, he would have had a small amount of cash to pay for drinks, but no more. Not a single item has ever been found, so where did they all go?

Why Did He Die?

There is no reason to believe that Alan might have been the specific victim of some long-standing personal feud, i.e., 'Let's get Addis.' As far as is known, he was not unpopular among his fellow Royal Marines – certainly not to the point of murdering him – and as he had never set foot in North Arm Settlement before that night, it is very unlikely that one of its inhabitants would have been harbouring a grudge against him as an individual, although there may well have been some ill feeling towards Royal Marines in general concerning their attractiveness for local girls.

There were allegations that Alan Addis was seen 'chatting up' one or more women at the party, which is not surprising as he was a fit, well-spoken and good-looking young man. This may well have caused some jealousy among the male Falklanders, especially husbands or boyfriends, but whether any of the women considered taking it further than just chatting is not known.

Aboard MV *Forrest*

One of the allegations is that Addis did actually return to MV *Forrest* after leaving the Social Club in the early hours of 8 August and was on board her when she sailed, only to be killed shortly thereafter and his body pitched over the side. Only then, according to this allegation, was his absence noted and reported to Sergeant Howden. This could only be feasible if the murder was committed by either one of his fellow Royal Marines or by a member of the crew of MV *Forrest*. This was Addis's first voyage aboard the ship and he had spent most of the voyage from Stanley to North Arm in his bunk, either asleep or being seasick, so his contact with any member of the ship's crew could have been minimal at best, and he was not known to be rude or overbearing. So, it seems highly improbable that any member of the crew could have harboured homicidal intentions towards a Royal Marine he can have scarcely known. An alternative version of this theory is that it was carried out by a Royal Marine. This is not impossible but seems scarcely credible as Addis was not unpopular and, in any case, the perpetrator would very likely soon have been identified and caught.

In either of these cases, had he been killed and the body thrown into the water, there would have been no time to add weights, so it would soon have been washed up on a nearby beach and found – which never happened.

The Manager

In the pre-1982 Falklands, managers exercised an almost medieval control over their Settlement, its people and their lives. Thus, in addition to organising and controlling the farming activities, the manager also ran the daily lives of those in the Settlement, which meant that he not only knew everything that went on, but also that no decision of any importance was, indeed could be, made without him being involved.

One theory about Alan Addis's disappearance that featured in Falklands' gossip was that, at the end of the party, Blake had gone home to the Big House, where he found Addis in bed with his wife, Lyn. According to this theory, the husband, who was known to be very quick-tempered, became so angry that he fought and killed the imposter, although perhaps not on purpose. However, this never got beyond gossip and there is not a shred of evidence to support it; indeed, most reports state that Lyn was a devoted wife. It should also be noted that Sergeant Holden and another Marine were sleeping in the Big House on the night of 7/8 August and should have heard the noise of any altercation.

On the other hand, even if Blake himself was not involved in the actual affray, his long-standing control over the Settlers' lives makes it seem impossible he could not have become involved after the event, i.e. '... *What shall we do now, boss?*' Further, he subsequently ordered the complete demolition of the Bunkhouse where Biggs was killed and, a few months later, a similar destruction of the killing shed. In both cases, the structures were totally demolished and the sites then washed down with high-pressure hoses, thus, if that was what was intended, removing any lingering evidence.

On the morning of 8 August, David Clarke drove to Goose Green, and it is almost certain that he could not have done so without permission from Blake. However, this aspect does not seem to have been pursued by the various investigations, or, if it was, it was never recorded. Blake also signed a report to his superiors in Stanley that Addis's disappearance was an accident and did not involve foul play. But, if Blake was consulted *at any point* by the perpetrators, or *knowingly signed a document he knew to be false,* under UK law, he became 'an accessory to an indictable offence' under Section 8 of the Accessories and Abettors Act 1861 (as amended), which meant that he would have been treated in the same way as if he had committed the offence:

> "*Whosoever shall aid, abet, counsel, or procure the commission of any indictable offence, whether the same be an offence at common law or by virtue of any Act passed or to be passed, shall be liable to be tried, indicted, and punished as a principal offender.*"[181]

It is presumed that similar provision was included in the various Falkland Islands government Ordinances of the time.

---

181 Section 8 of the Accessories and Abettors Act 1861 (24 & 25 Vict. c. 94).

DAVID CLARKE

The only other person against whom specific allegations have been made is David Clarke, a farmhand at North Arm. A tall, strong and fit man, he was one of the three members of Tony Blake's enforcer gang, the others being Louis Morrison and Bernard Peck, with Titch Jaffray as a hanger-on. Clarke made the journey to Goose Green on the morning of 8 August, which remains difficult to explain, as described below. He was one of the four arrested by DCI Pennington in 1991 (the others being Tony Blake, Bernard Peck and Titch Jaffray), although it must be emphasised that all four were subsequently released without charge. Clarke's wife, Gwyn, was a known 'maneater' and had a reputation for flings with other men. Clarke died in Stanley in 2023 without revealing what he knew, if anything, about the death of Alan Addis and the disappearance of the body.

UNEXPLAINED EVENTS

There are several events which simply cannot be explained at this remove in time.

The Roll Call Aboard MV *Forrest*

An oft repeated question is why was there no proper head count before MV *Forrest* sailed from North Arm on 8 August 1980? After all, there were only six Marines to be accounted for and MV *Forrest* was a small ship, so a physical check would have been neither difficult nor time-consuming. Five of the Royal Marines were on the upper deck at the time, but either Sergeant Howden or Corporal Davis appear to have assumed that the sixth man, Marine Addis, must be in his bunk in the hold, without someone actually going below to confirm it. Had they done so, and reported that Addis was missing, Sergeant Howden might have persuaded Captain Sollis to delay sailing, and the five Marines could have joined the search. Nevertheless, with the benefit of hindsight, it is clear that while the failure to call the roll before sailing was remiss, it is very unlikely that it would have made any contribution to finding the missing Marine.

News in North Arm That a Marine Was Missing

There has been some mystification over the fact that the workers at North Arm were told at 0900 that a Marine was missing, but that this could not have been communicated from *Forrest* until 1500, when it arrived at Fitzroy. It is correct that those on board MV *Forrest* did not realise that Addis was missing until some fifteen to twenty minutes after the ship had sailed and, by all reports, they were unable to communicate this direct back to North Arm using the 2m radio. However, DCI Pennington's investigation revealed that *Forrest* was able to speak to the Settlement at Johnson's Harbour and to request that they pass the information by the landline telephone to North Arm that Marine Addis was not on board the ship and was believed still to be somewhere in the Settlement. This message was received at North Arm by Lyn Blake, who immediately told her husband, who used the routine 'turn-to' at 0900 to organise search parties.[182]

David Clarke, who left North Arm at about 0800–0830 on 8 August, also knew about the missing Marine when he met Eric Goss, the manager, at Goose Green at about 1100.[183] He may already have known prior to leaving North Arm; indeed, he may have been one of the participants in the homicide, although it is not impossible that he came by this information while listening to the 2m radio set in his vehicle.

Proposal that Addis Should Walk from North Arm to Fitzroy

Why did Sergeant Howden and Captain Sollis decide that Addis, whom, at this point they assumed to be still alive, should make his own way from North Arm to Fitzroy? This would have involved a forty-mile (64km) trek to Goose Green followed by a further forty miles (64km) to Fitzroy. He could have walked, although making his way on foot, even on a vehicle track, and in winter, would have been hazardous. Further, Sergeant Howden would have known that Addis had neither foul-weather clothing nor a map.

---

182 It was previously thought that the first news of Addis's disappearance was passed by telephone from Fitzroy at about 1500. However, information about this contact with Johnson's Harbour was discovered by DCI Pennington in 1995 and explains why the early searches came about. It also explains how David Clarke knew. Information from DCI Pennington via Supt Ken Greenland.

183 Goss email 24 August 2023.

The best that could be expected was that Addis might 'thumb a lift' from a passing vehicle. But a much more sensible alternative would have been to instruct him to wait at North Arm for the next available spare place on a visiting ship or FIGAS Beaver. This was a curious decision, which is often queried, but, in the event, irrelevant to Alan's disappearance.

Gold Chain

In her Will, Sarah Ann stated: "*7. (b). I GIVE free of tax my said son Alan Addis's gold chain, which is currently held by the Falkland Island Police force, to my brother RALPH LONGTHORP of 29, Mount Crescent, STONE, Staffordshire absolutely.*" This Will was dated 8 October 2001 and, as Sarah Ann had visited the Falklands in 1995 where she had been in close contact with the RFIP, this establishes that the gold chain was in the possession of the RFIP then and, when she signed her Will in 2001, she would have had good reason to believe that it was still there. It was suspected that the chain had been recovered from Addis's possessions and taken to police HQ where it had somehow survived the Argentine invasion. However, Superintendent Greenland has confirmed that the chain had been found by Sarah Ann Addis in her son's room at home in Wharmby, and after wearing it for some time herself, she passed it to LPC Burston of the RFIP, as she thought that it would somehow help the latter find her son's remains. Its current whereabouts are unknown.

Unexplained Skeletons

DCI Pennington's investigation in 1995 revealed that a number of skeletons had been discovered in North Arm at an unspecified date in 1983, sent to Stanley and buried in an unregistered and unmarked grave. There had been no inquest. Having been brought to their attention by the Pennington report, the RFIP conducted an investigation in 1995 and submitted a report to the Coroner.

A request from this author to release this report was refused by both the RFIP and the Coroner and was referred to the Attorney-General, who also refused to release it. A further request to the Attorney-General by Professor Hunter was also refused.[184] It appears at first sight that there would be no harm in releasing the report if the skeletons were nothing to do with Addis, so the refusal to release it suggests that there could be some relevance. However, further research by the author reveals that the skeletons were of two adults and one infant, with signs that they had all suffered from diphtheria. Their deaths had been officially recorded, but for some reason, they had not been given a proper burial. What is certain is that they had nothing to do with Addis, but why the Attorney-General should choose to hide such a mundane explanation cannot be explained.

The Death of Jimmy Biggs

It is often suggested that Jimmy Biggs's death was somehow linked to the disappearance of Alan Addis because he might have seen or heard something about the events on 8 August that was so dangerous to the perpetrators that they considered it necessary to eliminate him. Danson Harbour House had neither a telephone nor a radio at this time, so that he could not have received any news between leaving North Arm on 8 August and returning there a week later.

But, he had been present in North Arm on 7–8 August collecting supplies and, presumably, he attended the party because there would have been nothing else to do. Afterwards and probably the worse for drink, he would then have slept in his allocated room for a few hours in Bunkhouse Number Three, before setting out back to Danson Harbour House with his supplies. It is thus possible that he either saw, or heard something unusual, and others, realising that he had done so, decided to eliminate him, but there is no proof.

BE SUSPICIOUS: THINK MURDER

The guidance issued by the UK's Association of Chief Police Officers in 2005 is quite clear, stating that: "*One of the fundamental facts to be determined in*

---

184 Email Simon Young to John Hunter 2 August 2023.

a missing person investigation is the reason why the subject has disappeared. In cases where the circumstances are suspicious or are unexplained, use the maxim: IF IN DOUBT, THINK MURDER."[185] Although issued some twenty-five years after Addis disappeared, this was based on previous guidance and there can be no doubt that the RFIP did not consider the possibility of a violent death until many months after the event.

It is also clear that all those not directly involved in Addis's disappearance assumed at the start that there were just two possibilities. The first was that he had walked off into the Camp where he had suffered an accident and been unable to obtain help, for which, as explained in Chapter Sixteen, there were plenty of precedents. The alternative was that he had drowned, although there were minor variations in the theories as to how this might have come about.

Either of those assumptions was not unreasonable; after all, NP8901 was in the Falklands to defend their people from Argentina and the Marines who had gone to North Arm had done so as friends and to train them how to defend themselves. There might even have been a degree of wishful thinking at government level to avoid any suggestion that his death had been due to one or more indigenous Falklanders and thus harmful to the colony's international reputation.

These theories still held good in November 1981 when Captain Gallacher of the SIB visited and, presumably, he and the then Chief Police Officer, Superintendent Ronnie Lamb, were in agreement. Gallacher's report states that: "*… Nothing came to light following conversations with the local populace to suggest either the cause of his presumed demise or support the theory that he was subjected to foul play.*"[186] This suggests that the possibility of foul play had, at least, been considered, even though it was then rejected. Lamb carried on with the investigation after Gallacher had left and was preparing a comprehensive report when the Argentines invaded in April 1982. Lamb was deported by the Argentines and reported after his return that all records had either been destroyed by Falklands police before the enemy arrived or had been destroyed during the war. Lamb reinvestigated the case after his return to the Falklands and concluded that Addis's disappearance was the

---

185 Capital letters as in original, which were also in red ink.
186 HQ Western Region SIB RMP UKLF letter 27 November 1981, para 7.

result of some form of accident. This conclusion was formally endorsed by Rex Hunt, the then Civil Commissioner.

Finally, why was Tony Blake's written report accepted in which he stated that both Addis and Biggs had died as a result of accidents and that there was no question of foul play in either case? Further, the total dismantling of the Bunkhouse immediately following the fire on 21 August 1980 and of the killing shed in 1982 should have raised some suspicions in Stanley. Possible explanations are that:

- Blake was an influential man in the Falklands.
- He was the manager of one of the largest farms and his superior in the Falkland Islands Company was Brooke Hardcastle, a close personal friend from their New Zealand days.
- He was also a member of both the Legislature and the Legislative Committee.

The Chief Police Officer was terminally ill, and several of his Constables were also sick, leaving only three available for duty. At that time there was no Attorney-General to offer legal advice. As a result, advice from the authorities in Stanley on the situation in North Arm seems to have been virtually non-existent and Blake's written statement that the deaths were accidents appears to have gone unchallenged by all levels of the Falkland Islands government. This, despite that fact that both deaths fell within the accepted legal definition of a suspicious death, i.e., a death which appeared to result from suspicious circumstances or unknown cause and was not due to an identifiable natural cause. Inspector 'Toddy' McMillen, the Chief Police Officer at the time, was very ill and his force seriously understaffed, so the responsibility lay with the then Coroner. There had been no reluctance to investigate the death of Kirk and to prosecute Burgos only ten months previously, so it seems very remiss that the police should have failed in this case.

What Happened to the Body?

As the self-burying corpse has yet to be invented, it is self-evident that the outcome of a death is a body, which must be disposed of. In this case, it was about 0200 on a frosty morning with only a few hours of darkness remaining.

The perpetrator/s must also have realised that, once it was known that a Royal Marine was missing, there would inevitably be search parties formed by Settlers and, almost certainly, reinforced by other Marines from Moody Brook, as well as police from Stanley. So, on the assumption that Addis died by accident in a fight, Blake and the perpetrator/s were faced with seven major possible courses of action:

- **Admit what had happened, call the police and face the consequences**. This was the only legal, responsible and moral course, but, even if it was considered, it was clearly rejected. However, that it did not happen indicates that there was something about his death that the perpetrators felt needed to be hidden.

- **Hide the body in a temporary site somewhere within the Settlement**. Although the quickest short-term solution, this would have been very risky, with a high possibility of discovery and, in any case, the body would have had to be moved clandestinely to a more permanent site within days.

- **Hide the body in a temporary location outside the Settlement**. This would have needed to be within reach before dawn and unlikely to be found by the inevitable search parties. This could be done either to a land site by Land Rover, or by boat. The body would be left there until the initial hue-and-cry was over. This might explain the clairvoyant's belief that the body was in Devil's Point, which she described with considerable accuracy, although no trace of Addis was found by the police searchers in 1995. However, it seems possible that the body could have been secreted there in the early hours of 8 August 1980 but later moved to a permanent site.

- **Hide the body in the void beneath the shearing shed**. The floor of the shearing shed was formed by wooden slats with gaps, so that sheep droppings would go straight down into a large rectangular pit – the 'void'. This was of slightly less area than the shearing shed and about 3ft (1m) deep. It was cleaned out at the end of every shearing season. It might have been used as a temporary hiding place for the corpse, but it would have had to be removed before the annual clean-out.

- **Move the body to the hinterland (Camp) that night and bury it in a permanent grave**. This was the course considered most likely by both Operation Lioness investigations (i.e., Pennington and Hunter), as well as the numerous police searches. However, the area is so vast and featureless that, without a specific clue, it is impossible to cover it effectively and none of the investigations achieved even the slightest degree of success.

- **Weight it down and dump it in the sea**. The body, together with weights, could have been taken well out to sea in one the Settlement's boats, and dumped overboard. As described in Chapter Fifteen, in other cases, some such bodies have become detached from their weights and floated to the surface, while others have been found by pure chance by anglers or sub-aqua divers. An unknown number presumably remain submerged and undetected. In this case, the boat would have had to be back in its original position by daybreak to avoid suspicion and is certainly feasible.

- **Dismember the body**. There are plenty of precedents for killers to dismember their victim's body. Tools for dismemberment were readily to hand in the killing shed, and it is likely that at least one of the perpetrators would have been skilled in the routine dismembering of animal carcasses. In this case, Addis's body could have been divided into six to ten parts, which would then have been much more easily dispersed.

- **Feed the parts to the pigs and/or birds**. Some, at least, of the dismembered parts could have been fed to the pigs, others dumped in Camp and disposed of by vultures.

- **Dump the body over Bodie Creek Suspension Bridge**.
  - ○ This was possible as David Clarke made no secret of the fact that he had driven from North Arm to Goose Green via the suspension bridge on the morning of 8 August 1980.
  - ○ The bridge was only marginally wider than a Land Rover, which would have made it virtually impossible for Clarke to dismount from the vehicle, and there were also guard rails, which would have made it difficult to manhandle the body and drop it into the water. Further, while it was unlikely that any casual observer was on hand to see Clarke on the bridge, it was by no means impossible.
  - ○ Alternatively, Clarke could have crossed the bridge to the North end, which was mounted on a small cliff, where it would have been much easier to tip the body into the water.

○ Further, he could have been accompanied as far as the bridge by one or more collaborators in another vehicle, who, having helped him toss the body into the water, then returned to North Arm, again unseen by anyone in Goose Green.

○ That the RFIP had their suspicions was demonstrated by twice deploying divers to search the Creek's bed under the bridge. Nothing suspicious was found and, as no floating body had been washed up along the long reach to the sea, it seems unlikely, although still not impossible, that this happened.

HYPOTHESES[187]

Having examined all those factors, the two following suggestions are offered as *possible* sequences of events culminating in the death of Alan Addis and disposal of his body. The first is:

- At some point during the party, Addis upset or annoyed one or more of those Settlers present, possibly by showing an interest in a wife or girlfriend.
- This encouraged a group of young Settlers who were spoiling for a fight, which was a frequent outcome of many Falkland Islands party events.
- Addis was an outsider and the only Royal Marine to remain at the party after about 2330, so was an easy target, although, as he was obviously tall and strong, more than one assailant would be required, i.e., they needed safety in numbers.
- Knowing that Addis must return to MV *Forrest*, a small group of assailants assembled in the shelter of, or perhaps, inside the shearing shed.
- Addis departed the party at approximately 0130 and walked towards the jetty in order to rejoin his ship and, as he passed the shearing shed, was decoyed inside.
- As with Burgos at Goose Green, the assailants confronted and attacked Addis – probably not fewer than two and not more than four men with the aim of 'teaching him a lesson'.
- A blow either led to a sudden cardiac arrest, or caused Addis to fall to the

187 A hypothesis is a proposed explanation made on the basis of limited evidence as a starting point for further investigation.

floor, his head striking a sharp object as he did so. In either case, Addis's death was a totally unintended outcome.

- The use of a knife by one of his assailants is considered highly unlikely.
- On examination, he was found to be dead.
- His assailants were dismayed by this unintended outcome. Nonplussed and not knowing what to do, they sent for the manager, Blake, who routinely made all the major decisions in the Settlement.
- Blake had not been involved in the affray, but arrived quickly, assessed the situation, decided not to be open about what had happened, and made and implemented a plan, which involved the total disappearance of the body, together with all its clothing and impedimenta.
- All those directly involved were sworn to secrecy.
- Word was circulated around the Settlement that nobody was to admit knowing anything or having suspicions about the event.

The second suggestion is:
- At some point in the party, Addis paid particular attention to Gwyn Clarke, the wife of David Clarke, who was on duty as barman. Clarke was a large, tough man with a short temper and sensitive where his wife, a known flirt, was concerned. Clarke observed that both Addis and his wife had left the building but was unable to do so himself, as he was on barman duty.
- On completing his duties, Clarke returned home, where he found Addis and his wife.
- Clarke flew into a violent temper and sought to 'teach the Marine a lesson', but in doing so, accidentally killed him.
- Clarke's immediate reaction was to seek the help of the manager, with whom he was on very good terms.
- Clarke and Blake loaded Addis's body in the back of Clarke's Land Rover and covered it with a tarpaulin.
- Clarke left North Arm before anyone else was around. He drove towards Goose Green, via Bodie Creek Suspension Bridge.
- Clarke halted at the northern end of the bridge, unloaded the body, added weights, and dropped it into the deep water.
- Clarke then drove on to Goose Green, arriving at about 1100.

CONCLUSIONS

The original Royal Marine and Royal Falkland Islands Police investigations identified two possible causes: Addis had either drowned in the nearby North Arm Creek or walked into the Camp and died there. In other words, they assumed that he was the unintentional cause of his own death and there was no involvement by any third parties. They had not a single piece of evidence to support either of these propositions and, while neither was totally impossible, it is now concluded that they were very unlikely.

It is clear that, at some point, probably in the early nineties, the possibility of third-party involvement became the more likely explanation. The investigations by DCI Pennington in 1995 and Professor Hunter in 1997–98 show that, by then, homicide was considered most probable, and the searches had become aimed at finding a grave and one or more of the perpetrators.

As discussed above, it seems reasonable to assume that Addis died within the geographical limits of North Arm Settlement and, that being so, his attacker/s were landed with the body. The first option, which, if it was even considered, was rejected, was to declare what had happened and face the consequences. The only alternative was to dispose of it. In the event, this was achieved in such an effective way that, despite numerous further investigations over some forty-five years, it has not been found, nor, indeed, has a single evidential trace come to light. Various ways of disposing of a corpse have been considered in this book and, while some are more likely than others, no evidence has been found that has led to the discovery of the body.

Some observers have suggested that another Marine might have been involved. As with so many other possibilities, that cannot be entirely ruled out, but it seems unlikely that one Marine would murder another, particularly in the tight-knit situation of NP8901. In any case, had one done so, it does not seem possible that a third Marine would not have raised the possibility at some time in the ensuing forty-five years.

Having ruled out all other possibilities and people, it is clear that the perpetrator/s could only have been Falkland Islanders, specifically members of the North Arm community. This does not mean that responsibility lies with all Falkland Islanders, nor even with all members of the North Arm community, but with a very tiny number. Apart from those perpetrators involved in the fight or disposal of the body, there must also have been a further very small number who either knew or strongly suspected what had happened and where responsibility lay, but who, for reasons of misguided loyalty or fear of the consequences, have declined to come forward.

It seems doubtful that the manager, Tony Blake, was involved in the affray itself, but in view of his dominance over every aspect of life in the Settlement, it would be surprising if he was not dragged into the affair very soon after Addis had died. Thereafter, it was he who planned and organised the disposal of the body, and who submitted a certificate of 'accidental death', which made him an accessory after the fact.

ENVOI

One of the surprising omissions that is never mentioned is the lack of an offer of a financial reward for information. In other countries, such rewards are sometimes offered by the police, sometimes by associations with a link to the missing person, occasionally by a newspaper, and a few by well-meaning philanthropists. The sum concerned has to be meaningful, perhaps as little as several thousand pounds, but often much more. The 1967 reward for information on Jim Thompson, for example, was $US10,000 ($94,000 (£73,000) at today's prices), while that currently on offer for Madeleine McCann from a variety of sources comes to well over £2,600,000. In the Addis case, the possible informants were all in North Arm and not particularly well-off, so a sizeable reward could have proved attractive, but it was never even tried.

The disappearance of Alan Addis is one of those mysteries that, like those of Lord Lucan in England, Madeleine McCann in Portugal and Jim Thompson in Malaysia, will just not go away. It is still discussed by Falklanders, while tourists visiting North Arm are soon made aware of the story. Books, magazine articles, TV programmes and websites will continue to be published until his death is properly explained. Nobody suggests that this was a massive conspiracy, and the main suspects may well all be dead, but there must be some in the Falklands who, even though they were not involved directly, know what happened and either choose or are forced to keep their mouths shut. The bottom line is that a very small group of farmers and labourers, within a known, clearly defined population, concocted and carried out a plan at zero notice, which has baffled several very sophisticated police forces.

But Alan Addis was a Royal Marine, one of forty-three men stationed in the Falklands at that time to defend its people against a predatory Argentina. Indeed, twenty-seven Marines would die in the Falklands War two years later and, since then, the UK has spent billions on defending the islands – is it too much to expect that, in return for all those sacrifices, the death and disappearance of one Royal Marine could not be explained? Those who know or suspect what happened to Alan Addis but remain silent should be thoroughly ashamed. The time for lying and obfuscation is past, and it is high time that Alan's death is explained and his body recovered, so that it can be brought home to be buried with his mother, as she had so desperately wanted.

SOURCES

Addis, Sarah Ann. *Missing on Patrol,* Arthur H Stockwell, Ilfracombe, Devon, 2003

Clark, Sir George (ed). *The Campden Wonder*, Oxford University Press, London, 1959

Godwin, G.M. (ed). *Criminal Psychology and Forensic Technology, A Collaborative Approach to Effective Profiling*, CRC Press, London, New York, Washington, D.C., 2001

Hunt, Sir Rex. *My Falkland Days*, Politico's Publishing, London, 2002

Spruce, Joan and Smith, Natalie. *Falkland Rural Heritage,* Stefan Falkland Heijtz, Fox Bay, Falkland Islands, 2018

Tatham, David. *Dictionary of Falklands Biography, including South Georgia.* Stanley Services, Ltd, Stanley, Falkland Islands, 2008

TV Documentaries

Equinox: Bodyhunters, Lion TV, Camden, England, 1997

Falklands, Islands of Secrets, TrueVision, London, 2022

Web Articles

Lange, Katie, *With Dignity and Care: Inside the Process of Bringing Our Overseas Fallen Home.* US DoD News, Jan. 10, 2024 [Source: https://www.defense.gov/news/Feature-Stories/Story/Article/3586998/]

Peters, Stephen, *Bodie Creek Suspension Bridge, built 1925.* [Source: https://bodiecreekbridge.com/index.html]

GOVERNORS OF THE FALKLAND ISLANDS 1977–2025

FROM	TO	NAME
1977	1980	James Roland Walter Parker CMG OBE
1980	1985	Sir Rex Masterman Hunt CMG[188]
1985	1988	Sir Gordon Wesley Jewkes KCMG
1988	1992	William Hugh Fullerton CMG
1992	1996	David Everard Tatham CMG
1996	1999	Richard Peter Ralph CMG CVO
1999	2002	Donald Alexander Lamont
2002	2006	Howard John Stredder Pearce CMG
2006	2010	Alan Edden Huckle
2010	2014	Nigel Robert Haywood CVO
2014	2017	Colin Roberts CVO
2017	2022	Nigel James Phillips CBE
2022	Incumbent	Alison Mary Blake CMG

---

188 Civil Commissioner of the Falkland Islands at Stanley 25 June 1982 – 16 October 1985.

The Death of James Keith Biggs (Jimmy)

INTRODUCTION

Jimmy Biggs, a shepherd based at Danson Harbour House, died in a fire in North Arm Settlement only days after Alan Addis disappeared. The circumstances of the fire were suspicious, and several people have suggested that he knew 'something' about the disappearance of Alan Addis and that he travelled to North Arm Settlement on 20 August 1980 specifically to pass this on to a visiting police Constable. One example is Sarah Ann Addis, who recorded that: "*It has been alleged that Mr Biggs was going to talk to the police regarding Alan's disappearance.*"[189] Another comment came in the commentary on the Lion TV programme, where it was said that: "*… He (Biggs) rode in unexpectedly to give evidence to the police inquiry…*"

JIMMY BIGGS

James Keith Biggs (always known as Jimmy) was born at Roy Cove Settlement[190] on 28 January 1924. His father was William James Biggs (1879–1944), a labourer/shepherd, and his mother, Mary (nee Goodwin) (1880–1966). He had one brother and two sisters. He married Dorothy Stella Lindsay, a divorcee, at Stanley on 25 March 1950, but they had no children and were divorced in 1964. He was physically fit, strong and well used to an

---

189 Addis, *Missing on Patrol*, p.36.

190 Roy Cove is a small Settlement on the western shore of West Falkland, some forty miles (64km) due west of Port Howard.

'outdoor life', having spent his entire working life as either a seaman or as a shepherd. He was in the latter employment when he died, aged fifty-six, at North Arm Settlement in the early hours of 21 August 1980. He was buried in Stanley Cemetery on 25 August 1980.[191]

SITUATION IN 1980

In August 1980, Biggs and a fellow shepherd, Hector Tellez, a Chilean, were living and working at Danson Harbour House, an 'outside house' some distance from North Arm Settlement (see frontispiece map).[192]

They were responsible for the Northwestern sector of the North Arm estate. They had several horses, and it was their practice to take it in turn for weekly visits to collect supplies from the North Arm Settlement shop. They would ride one, with the other horse/s carrying the supplies on the return journey. These visits also enabled them to catch up with the news and gossip, and to be briefed by the manager or foreman on forthcoming farming requirements and other business matters. Such visits were also an opportunity for socialising in the Social Club as well as chatting to friends, particularly Robin Goodwin, who records: "*He (Jimmy) would often come to my place for a chat with Mandy and I.*"[193]

Among others living in North Arm were Bernard Peck and his wife Evelyn. Evelyn was known to have a 'roving eye' and there were well-founded rumours that she had had a relationship in the past with Jimmy Biggs, which gave rise to considerable ill feeling on Mr Peck's part.

Danson Harbour House was a large, two-storey, prefabricated building, with basic domestic facilities and furniture, sited adjacent to a small rise in the otherwise bleak and featureless Lafonia landscape. At this time, as with most other 'outside houses', Danson Harbour House had no radio or landline telephone communications with the Settlement at North Arm.[194]

There was a vehicle track from North Arm Settlement, which was not very well defined, but usable by Land Rovers, the total distance being some

---

191 Grave U1812.
192 Actual location: Map. Falkland Islands 1:25,000 Sheet 25 Location 59⁰ 43' W 52⁰ 07'N.
193 Email Goodwin/Miller 5 March 2023.
194 Email Goodwin/Miller 5 March 2023.

12 miles (19km). It is almost certain, however, that Biggs and Telez would have taken a more direct cross-country route, using local knowledge to take advantage of gates and breaks in the fences.

Biggs was at the party on the night that Addis disappeared, as recorded by Captain Gallacher of the SIB in his report dated 30 June 1981: "*It is now understood that Mr Biggs had been present at the Social Club during the night of 7/8 Aug 80.*"[195] Biggs's presence on 7 August is also confirmed by Robin Goodwin.[196]

There is no record of any episode at the party involving Jimmy Biggs and it seems safe to assume that his intention would have been to snatch a short sleep in Bunkhouse 3, then to return to Danson Harbour House early on 8 August, at which time it is very unlikely that he would have been aware that Marine Addis was missing. However, some of the search parties deployed on 9–11 August are believed to have reached Danson Harbour House, in which case, Biggs might have been told of Addis's disappearance.

VEHICLE TO DANSON HARBOUR: NIGHT 7 AUGUST 1980

It is reported that someone in Speedwell Island Settlement saw moving vehicle headlights on the mainland in the vicinity of Danson Harbour House in the early hours of 8 August. Speedwell Island Settlement lies on the southern shore of Halfway Cove at 59^0 41' W. 52^0 13' S. There is a clear line of sight across the sea in the direction of Danson Harbour House at a bearing of $\approx 46^0$ and distance of ≈ 5.6 miles (9km). Danson Harbour House was, in fact, erected on the site of the former semaphore signal used to communicate with Speedwell Island. This consisted of a long pole topped by a white-painted arm, which, when raised to the horizontal, indicated to those on Speedwell that they should send a boat to collect mail. Thus, the top floor of Danson Harbour House must have been visible from Speedwell and, in the blackness of the Falkland night, vehicle headlights might well have been seen, particularly if the vehicle was moving and there was reflection from a low cloud-base.

---

195 Source: SIB Special Investigation Report 01281/1 dated 30 June 1981, which was released in response to an FoI request by an unknown person on 22 June 2017.
196 Email Goodwin/Miller 5 March 2023.

THE BUNKHOUSE

On his visits to North Arm, Jimmy Biggs had a room allocated to him in Bunkhouse No 3. This was one of a number of such structures purchased in the early 1960s by the Falkland Islands Company. These prefabricated structures were marketed from 1958 by Coseley Buildings Ltd, of Lanesfield, a suburb of Wolverhampton. They were specifically intended for the export market, the concept being for customers to use the variety of components in the Coseley catalogue to design a structure to meet their needs. A plan view of Bunkhouse 3 is on the next page.

The outer structure was standard, but purchasers were offered a variety of doors, windows, internal walls and fittings to choose from. Coseley then assembled the component parts into a kit, which, together with tools and instructions, was shipped to the user, who was responsible for laying the plinth and constructing the building. All such buildings in the Falklands had an attached outhouse for a peat-burning boiler, although they were widely regarded as particularly cold to live in.[197] In 1980, there were eight of these structures in North Arm, four of which were designed, outfitted and occupied as family homes. The other four were completed as bunkhouses for unmarried shepherds and labourers:

- Bunkhouses Numbers 1 and 2. Unmarried Settlement navvies who lived and worked on the farm.
- Number 3. 'Outside' shepherds, who came in from outside houses for short visits.
- Number 4. Hired help on a casual basis.[198]

On the night of 20 August 1980, there were two inhabitants of Bunkhouse Number 3. One of these was Chilian shepherd José Ruiz, who occupied Room 3. The second was Jimmy Biggs, whose accommodation was in Room 1. Rooms 2 and 4 were normally occupied, but on this particular night, the men concerned were away (see Figure 4).

---

197 R Goodwin, Esq.
198 This was furthest from the main Settlement and closest to the Shearing Shed and was later converted to a new Killing House for Settlement mutton and beef.

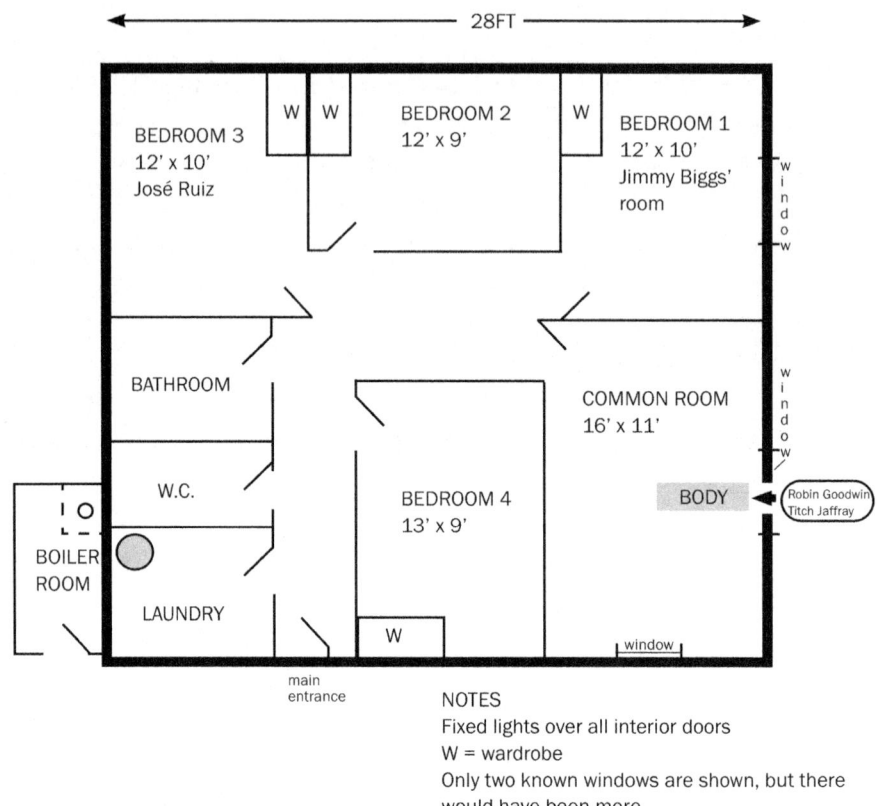

Figure 4. Bunkhouse 3 Plan

FIRE

Fire was an ever-present hazard in the Falkland Islands for three main reasons:

- **Peat**. Spontaneous fires could erupt within the peat beds, usually as a result of lightning strikes. Known as 'zombie fires', these were often deep underground, generated great heat, and tended to come to the surface in unexpected places. It was impossible to fight such fires and people were left with no option but to allow the fire to burn itself out, although it was necessary to watch progress and, if necessary, evacuate people whose houses appeared to be under threat.

- **Aircraft**. The Falkland Islands government and FIGAS were well aware of the danger to aircraft when taking off and landing. There was a permanent fire detachment at Stanley Airfield, while Settlements such as North Arm with facilities for fixed-wing aircraft were required to man a government-provided bowser during aircraft movements in case of accidents.[199]

- **Buildings**. These could catch fire for the usual reasons (burning fat, cigarette end down back of sofa, electrical short circuit, lightning strike, etc.), but in the Falklands, for unknown reasons, they tended to burn very quickly. However, the fact that most buildings were well spaced meant that there was limited danger of the fire spreading to engulf an entire community. Examples are:

  o King Edward VII Memorial Hospital, Stanley, the only hospital in the Falkland Islands, was destroyed by fire in 1984. Built in 1915, it offered fifty beds and had a staff of four doctors, nurses and auxiliaries. It was of wooden construction, which would have been common at the time it was built, but was reported to be in a poor state of repair and some fire hoses and pumps were known to be unserviceable. Fire broke out in the early hours of 10 April 1984. The destruction was total.[200] Most patients and staff were rescued but among the seven dead was Barbara Chick, who ignored orders to keep out of the burning hospital and stayed with her patients until she was overcome by smoke.[201] It is of interest that the entire site was levelled by bulldozers within forty-eight hours, thus preventing any forensic analysis.

  o An example of the rapidity with which a typical Falklands Settlement structure could be overwhelmed by fire was the total destruction of Harps Farm on West Falkland on 10 October 1995. The fire was believed (but not confirmed) to have started with a spark in the eaves, but despite efforts by neighbours using a foam appliance and a water pump, it quickly consumed the house and adjacent barn, which were both totally destroyed.[202]

  o There had been a previous fire at North Arm in 1973, destroying an entire Bunkhouse. It happened one evening when the occupants had all gone down to the jetty to help load the auxiliary ketch, *Penelope*.

---

199 Info from Robin Goodwin.
200 An Army medic, LCpl Shorters, was later tried for arson, but was acquitted.
201 She was later awarded a posthumous QGM.
202 *Penguin News*, 11 October 1995.

The cause was attributed to the wind blowing a curtain into contact with a candle, which had been left alight, and the building was well ablaze before anyone noticed.[203]

Settlements were widely separated and, in 1980, the routes outside Stanley were poor or non-existent, so there was no question of the Stanley Fire Brigade (such as it was) going to the aid of the Settlements. Most buildings in Settlements were equipped with a handpump, water bucket and fire blanket. In addition, there was a Settlement fire section of four men, who were trained in the use of a petrol-driven pump and hoses to project water from the nearby sea against the fire. Such equipment may have been sufficient to deal with a small fire at an early stage but was insufficient to deal with a major fire that had obtained a hold.

THE NIGHT OF 20 AUGUST 1980

On the night of 20 August, Bunkhouse 3 allocation of rooms was:
- Room 1. Jimmy Biggs (present).
- Room 2. Sydney (Charlie Stinker) Smith of North West Arm house (absent).
- Room 3. José Ruiz (present).
- Room 4. Jimmy Miller. Wreck Farm House (absent).

Biggs was allocated Room 1 and could have been asleep there, although it is also possible that he may have returned the worse for drink and fallen asleep in the common room.

Ruiz detected the fire at about 0430 and was singed as he ran out of the building, shouting the alarm. The fire had started in Room 2, which was unoccupied at the time, although how it started and why it took such a strong hold so quickly is a mystery to this day. The events are described by Robin Goodwin, who was there:

"That fire started in an unoccupied room that was used by another outside shepherd. The building was for all outlying shepherds to use when in the Settlement. The whole incident is marred with events that simply did not add

---

203 Email Goss-Miller 15 September 2023

up. First that the fire started in an unoccupied room. That we firefighters were refused entry into the building and that one person went around breaking the windows fanning the fire. That was not in our fire training. You are supposed to starve the fire of oxygen. The fact that the water pump could not be started by someone, which could have given us much-needed water from the Creek to douse the flames. The fact that, even though we could see Jimmy slumped in the common room by a radiator under a window, we were told not to go in to get him out. I saw red and together my late uncle Robin (Titch) Jaffray and I ignored the manager and climbed in through the window and lifted Jimmy out."[204]

Robin Goodwin continues:

"I still can't understand why two people went around breaking the windows fanning the fire. I still don't understand why the water pump failed to start. Two people operated that pump on that day: David Clarke and Bernard Peck, the same two that broke the windows. I don't think that fire was designed to kill Jimmy, but it may very well have had something to do with Alan's disappearance. We may never know because, as I have said before, that site was cleaned bare of everything just hours after it burnt out. That water pump started very easily, and I was one who hosed the cement slab down that the building was on."[205]

The names David Clarke and Bernard Peck appear regularly in this saga as suspects and were two of the four arrested in 1995 by DCI Pennington. Robin says that: *"There was animosity between him (Biggs) and Bernard Peck because, some years before Bernard married his wife, Jimmy was dating her, and they parted on very good terms and Bernard was quite jealous of him as a result."*

A professional firefighter has been consulted.[206] His general comment is: *"Due to the material used in these buildings, it would be hard to set fire to one of them as a standalone structure. To burn one of these buildings you would need to introduce flammable material, such as mattresses, blankets, pillows and wooden furniture, which were in use in this building at the time."*

---

204 Email Goodwin-Miller dated 8 Feb 2023.
205 Email Goodwin-Miller 5 March 2023.
206 Courtesy of Philip Davis.

His answers to specific questions were:

- **Question 1**. Could the building have been set on fire accidentally?
- **Answer 1**. *No, it is highly unlikely that the fire was started due to faulty electrical issues, as highlighted, due to there being no electricity supplied to the building at that time. The peat boiler is not located close to where the fire started in Room 2, therefore that would suggest that it would be an unlikely source.*
- **Question 2**. Could the fire have been started deliberately?
- **Answer 2**.
  - *Yes, as fire is caused by a combination of an ignition source propelled by a fuel source. There is evidence to suggest there was enough fuel in Room 2 to sustain a fire, however, there is no evidence of a possible ignition source, but using something such as petrol would have accelerated the flames and made the fire take hold more quickly.*
  - *From the witness statement, it would suggest possible foul play, due to the destruction and removal of the building material so swiftly after a fatal fire. This would go against any modern-day fire investigations, as preserving the scene is key to determine possible causes of a fire.*
  - *Also, the actions taken/orders given to smash the windows to a building on fire with a person still in it are somewhat of concern, as this action would only introduce more oxygen to the fire and propel its intensity. Common sense would not need a professional understanding of fire behaviour to take such actions, especially as some of the people involved had undergone rudimentary training in firefighting.*

Biggs's body was slumped in the common room below the window. The possibilities appear to be that either he had been sleeping in Room 1, was woken by the shouting, but was unable to exit by the main door due to fire and/or smoke, and was trying to exit through the common room window when he was overcome by fumes and collapsed. Or, he had returned from the Social Club, sat down in the common room, fallen asleep there and was overcome by smoke/fumes without recovering consciousness.

The event was reported in *Penguin News*:

"FATAL BUNKHOUSE FIRE. A serious fire broke out in the Bunkhouse at North Arm on 20ᵗʰ August. There were two men in the building at the time and one, James Biggs, was (it is supposed) overcome by fumes and heat. He

was dead when found in the sitting room later. The flames were first noticed at 4.30am, and the blaze was soon being fought with all the appliances available. The building was gutted by the flames although the aluminium sheathing of the building was left standing. The Bunkhouse was a prefabricated building of the 'Coseley' type, of which there are several in Stanley and other parts of the Falklands. The victim of the blaze, James Biggs (better known as Jimmy) had been a Camper for most of his life and he will be sadly missed."[207]

DEATH

Looking through the window, Robin Goodwin could see that the common room was not yet fire-damaged and that the body of Jimmy Biggs was *"slumped under a window."* He and Titch Jaffray (his uncle) were told NOT to enter and rescue him, but they disobeyed, climbed through the window, grabbed the body and pulled it out, placing it on the ground a few metres away. Robin Goodwin makes no mention of Biggs's body or clothing being burnt and he and Lyn Blake, the manager's wife, felt that Biggs was unconscious or asleep rather than dead. Lyn Blake, who was a qualified nanny, whose training would have included many nursing duties, wanted to give him artificial respiration, but was physically prevented from doing so by her husband. Blake then produced a body bag, and Jimmy was quickly zipped inside and carried down to the woolshed, from where he was evacuated some hours later by Beaver floatplane to Stanley. Blake ordered that the fire be allowed to burn itself out, following which, the remains were cleared away, any movable debris being taken to the Settlement dump at Garden Point and the remainder hosed down. At about 1000, Robin Goodwin was ordered to wash the cement plinth using the hose and, when he went to start the water pump, it did so without hesitation.

Comments

- It is clear from Robin's description that Biggs was not burnt in any serious way and that the immediate treatment required was respiration, not dressing wounds.

---

207 *Penguin News*, 25 Sep 1980 Issue No 8.

- Why was Lyn Blake prevented from attempting to resuscitate Biggs?
- At what point did Biggs actually die?
- Why did Blake have a body bag so handy?
- Why was Blake so keen for the remains of Bunkhouse 3 to be totally eliminated to the extent of disposing of the debris and hosing down the plinth?
- Why did the water pump not work at 0430 but did so at 1000?
- Was a post-mortem carried out?

POLICE INVESTIGATION: 21 APRIL 1980

The first inquiry into the fire was conducted by the Falkland Islands Police, although their efforts were handicapped by the fact that the Chief Police Officer at the time was Inspector Toddy McMullen, who was terminally ill and absent from duty. Thus, the sole full-time police officer, WPC Livermore, was acting on her own when she flew to North Arm on the afternoon of 21 August to conduct an investigation.[208]

The Royal Marines Board of Inquiry into Addis's disappearance was ordered by HQTRF[209] in the UK on 13 August[210] and convened at Stanley on 22 September. It then moved to North Arm Settlement on 23–24 September. As Biggs had died on 21 August, it is clear that his visit to North Arm had nothing whatsoever with the Royal Marines Board of Inquiry.

Comments

The unchallenged facts are that:
- Biggs or Ruiz made regular trips to North Arm Settlement at approximately weekly intervals.
- Biggs could not have travelled to North Arm Settlement in order to give evidence to the police inquiry into Addis's disappearance because, on the day that he travelled, no such inquiry was in place.

---

208 At that time, the Chief of Police was also Chief Fire Officer.
209 HQTRF = Headquarters Training and Reserve Forces Royal Marines, located at Portsmouth.
210 Signal MGRM TRF 131419Z Aug 80.

FOLLOW-UP ACTION

According to Sarah Ann: "*The farm manager (Blake) sent a letter to the managing director of the farm assuring him that there was not then, and not likely to be in the future, any question of foul play regarding the missing Marine or the fire. This letter was dated 22nd August, the day after Mr Biggs died in the fire!*"[211] This letter is held by Marcel Theroux in his hand at *Island of Secrets*, 0.29.05. The Coroner subsequently ruled the death of Biggs 'an accident'. Even in such a remote place as the Falkland Islands and the even more remote Settlement of North Arm, Blake's letter seems to be a very casual way of dealing with a certain death.

COMMENTS

In some ways, Jimmy Biggs's death is even more difficult to explain than that of Alan Addis. Biggs was a true Kelper, born and bred by Kelper parents in the Falkland Islands. As far as is known, he had never travelled outside the Falklands.

Blake seems to have been very keen to eliminate all evidence of the fire as quickly as possible. Blake did not hesitate to describe the fire and Biggs's death as 'accidents' without explanation or justification.

The possibilities are:
- First, that the fire really was an accident and that Jimmy Biggs's death was an unrelated and unintended consequence.
- Second, the fire was started deliberately, but Jimmy Biggs's death was not intended, but why would that be? Perhaps a warning to someone; if so, to whom and why?
- Third, that someone (perhaps more than one?) in the Settlement killed Biggs and then started the fire in order to cover it up. But there were no wounds on his body to suggest that he had been attacked or involved in a fight.
- That Jimmy Biggs's death was intended, but for reasons that had nothing to do with the disappearance of Alan Addis.
- Either David Clarke or Bernard Peck may have felt jealous of Jimmy Biggs, but was that sufficient to cause either to kill him?

---

211 Addis, *Missing on Patrol*; p.36.

Whichever of those possibilities actually applied, it seems certain that:
- The fire was started deliberately, i.e., it was arson.
- The death of Jimmy Biggs may or may not have been intended, but in either case it was homicide.
- The manager, Blake, exceeded his authority in declaring both the fire and Biggs's death to have been 'accidents'.
- It is possible that Jimmy Biggs may have heard something at or after the party, but this has never been proven.
- The FIG authorities in Stanley were remiss in not holding Blake properly to account.

It is important to bear in mind that some events in investigations such as this have a suspicious feel, but may, in fact, be totally innocent.

Letter from Philip Davis

2–3 Gale Cottages,
Carriage Drive,
Littleborough,
Lancs.,
OL15 9JY
28/12/2022

Dear Mr Miller,

We have discussed my experiences in the Falkland Islands, and you have asked me to elaborate on one particular incident in writing. I served in the Royal Marines from 22/9/1970 to 1/9/1977. My service number was PO 28509 B. One of the postings during my Royal Marine service was to NP8901 in the Falkland Islands from 22/12/1973 to 15/2/1975. Our normal residence was the barracks at Moody Brook, but we paid numerous visits to various Settlements. During our off-duty hours, four of us got together to form a musical group and it was suggested by our CO Major Simon Cook that we should tour a number of the Settlements, which we duly did, starting on Thursday July 18th to Sunday July 28th. We named our concert party 'NAAFIROMFT' band, which stood for: No Ambition And Fuckall Interest. Roll On My Fucking Ticket.

We performed at nine Settlements with transport between them provided by MV *Forrest* and, on the night of Friday the 26th of July, we performed at the Social Club at North Arm Settlement. Before we started our performance, Al Keep, Steve Raw and I were standing together in the bar having a warm-up drink. Eddie Birch wasn't with us at that moment. A local (who we found out later was called Titch Jaffray) came over to the three of us, Al was on my left and Steve on my right. He stood in front of me and, without saying a word, nutted me on the forehead, not very hard I might add. I didn't react, so he did it again only harder this time. He was about to do it again when I said, "Stop doing that as you'll be the only one with a headache in the morning." He then leaned in towards me and said, "Right, you and me outside."

I could feel that Steve Raw was about to do something, when we noticed our boss, the farm manager Tony Blake, the Governor and his wife walking into the bar. At that point, the local turned around and went and stood at the bar. Titch Jaffray was about 5' 6" and I was 5' 7½" – just slightly taller. He was stocky, I am of a slim build. I found out later that Titch Jaffray had a reputation for this type of behaviour. We did our performance later and no further incidents took place. After a couple of drinks, all four of us headed back to the *Forrest*.

Sgd P. Davis.

Major Gilding's Order on Drinking[212]

Sarah Ann Addis Wrote:

"In April 1980, Alan sent me a copy of Daily Routine Orders from which I quote:

FORREST CONDUCT WHILST EMBARKED

During the short time we have been here, the OCRM has heard some very disturbing reports of previous detachments' behaviour whilst embarked on MV *Forrest*. This has been mostly due to excess drinking leading to unruly, tempestuous and disgusting behaviour. In the past, men have drunk themselves stupid – urinated on mattresses, been abusive and violent. In short, there have been drunken orgies. This is not to happen during our time here. You all know the OC's view on drinking. Drunkenness is to be considered a serious offence.

Whilst it is not intended to forbid the consumption of alcohol whilst embarked, the NCO in charge of the embarked force is to ensure that his section's behaviour is beyond reproach. Breaches of these guidelines will lead to disciplinary action and stoppage of alcohol.

NCOs are to ensure that Marines Quarters are left in a high state of cleanliness before disembarking.

The Master of the *Forrest* is an excellent seaman and is, of course, in command whilst you are embarked. His orders will be obeyed at all times."

---

212 Sarah Ann Addis, op. cit. p.62.

MAINSTREAM PUBLISHERS

Historical

1. **The Vietnam War**. Salamander, 1979. (Contributed 3 chapters) (also published in USA)
2. **The Wreck of the Isabella**, Pen & Sword (Leo Cooper), 1994 (also published by the US Naval Institute Press, USA)
3. **The Cold War, a Military History**. John Murray, 1998 (also published in USA). Republished as a paperback in UK by Pimlico, 2001.
4. **Samurai Warriors**. Pegasus, 2000 (also published in the USA by Brassey's).
5. **Lady De Lancey at Waterloo**. Spellmount. November 2000. Hardback, republished as a paperback by History Press, May 2008.
6. **The Crusades**. Pegasus, UK; Brassey's USA, 2001.
7. **Richard the Lionheart – The Mighty Crusader**. Weidenfeld & Nicholson, London, 2003. Hardback republished in paperback, 2005.
8. **The Duchess of Richmond's Ball**. Spellmount, 2005.
9. **Mercy Ships**. Continuum, July 2008.

Naval

1. **Modern Naval Combat** with Chris Miller. Salamander, 1986.
2. **Modern Submarine Warfare**. Salamander, 1987.
3. **Combat Arms: Submarines**. Salamander, 1989.
4. **The World's Navies**. Salamander, 1991.
5. **Submarines of the World**. Salamander, 1991.
6. **Modern Warships**. Salamander, 1992. (Complete rewrite.)
7. **Carriers: The Men and the Machines**. Salamander, 1992. With Lindsay Peacock.
8. **Jane's Major Warships, 1997. Volume 1**. Jane's Information Group, 1996.
9. **Jane's Major Warships, 1997. Volume 2**. Jane's Information Group, 1997.
10. **U-Boats. Hunters of the Deep**. Conway Maritime Press, 2000. Published in the USA [Brassey's, 2000]. Translated and published: Germany [Motor Buch Verlag, 2000], Denmark [2002] and Japan [2002].
11. **The World of Jack Aubrey**. Salamander, 2003.
12. **Patrick O'Brian's Navy**. Salamander 2003 (Contributed two chapters).

13. **Submarine Disasters**. Compendium, 2006
14. **Langsdorff and the Battle of the River Plate**. Pen & Sword, 2013.

Illustrated Guides/Directories; series published by Salamander

1. **Modern Submarines,** 1982.
2. **Modern Sub-Hunters,** 1984.
3. **Illustrated Directory of Modern Weapons Systems,** 1985.
4. **Modern Naval Warfare,** 1989.
5. **Modern Elite Forces,** 1984. (Published under nom-de-plume 'Max Walmer').
6. **Weapons of Special Forces,** 1988. (Published under nom-de-plume 'Max Walmer').
7. **Strategic Weapons Systems,** 1988.
8. **Modern Tanks.** 1991. (Complete rewrite).
9. **Tanks of the World.** 2000.
10. **The World's Surface Warships 1860-2001.** 2001.
11. **The World's Submarines, 1860-2001.** 2002.
12. **Uniforms, Weapons and Equipment of the US Civil War.** 2001 (edited).
13. **US Weapons Systems.** 2002.

Strategic and General

1. **Soviet War Machine.** Salamander, 1980. (Contributed 2 chapters).
2. **Balance of Military Power**. Salamander, 1982. (Coordinating editor and contributed 2 chapters).
3. **The Intelligence War.** Salamander, 1983. (Contributed naval section).

Translated into Japanese.
4. **Advanced Technology Warfare.** Salamander, 1985. (Contributed 2 sections).
5. **Modern Special Forces**. Salamander, 1999.
6. **A Century of War.** Greenhill, 1998.
7. **Great Battles of World War Two.** Greenhill, 1998.
8. **Commanding Officers.** John Murray, 2001. Translated into Chinese and published in Taiwan, 2004.
9. **Conflict Iraq.** Motor Books International, USA, 2003.
10. **Special Operations South-East Asia, 1942-1945.** Pen & Sword, 2015.

Land Warfare

1. **Modern Land Combat**. Salamander, 1987.
2. **Battlefield.** Brian Trodd, 1991.
3. **The World's Armies**. Salamander, 1991(Contributed).
4. **The Illustrated Book of Guns**. Salamander, 2000.
5. **Great Book of Tanks**. Salamander, 2002.

Children's Books

1. **Soviet Navy**. Rorke (USA), 1988.
2. **Battleships**. Rorke (USA), 1988.
3. **Soviet Submarines**. Rorke (USA), 1988.
4. **Soviet Rocket Forces**. Rorke (USA), 1988.
5. **Destroyers**. Rorke (USA), 1989.
6. **Frigates**. Rorke (USA), 1989.
7. **People In Action: Airline Pilot.** Salamander, 1992.

8. **People In Action: Fighter Pilot.**
   Salamander, 1992.

Colin Gower Enterprises (marketed in USA)

1. **Illustrated Directory of Guns**. 2006.
2. **John Moses Browning – Gun Designer**. 2006
3. **Fighting Men of World War II – Uniforms, Equipment and Weapons – Volume I Axis Forces.** Stackpole Books, USA, 2007. (via Colin Gower Enterprises, UK).
4. **Fighting Men of World War II – Uniforms, Equipment and Weapons – Volume II. Allied Forces.** Stackpole Books, USA, 2008 (via Colin Gower Enterprises, UK).

Photographic Monographs

1. **Deserts**. Compendium, 2006
2. **Bridges**. Compendium, 2006
3. **Oceans**. Compendium, 2006
4. **Las Vegas**. Compendium, 2007.
5. **US Churches**, Compendium, 2008

3. **Freedom We Died For You. Old Blues who died in World War Two**. Privately published by Christ's Hospital, 2011.
4. **In Their Own Words. Old Blues who fought in World War One.** Privately published by Christ's Hospital, 2014.
5. **Christ's Hospital and the V-1 1944.** Privately published by Christ's Hospital, 2011.
6. **True Blue, The Unusual Naval Career of Commander Lloyd Hirst.** Privately published by Christ's Hospital, 2022.

NON-MAINSTREAM PUBLICATIONS

1. **A Short History of the Office of the Master General of the Ordnance.** Ministry of Defence, London, 1973.
2. **Sir Barnes Wallis and the Christ's Hospital RAF Foundationers' Trust 1951-2003.** Privately published by the Christ's Hospital Club, 2003.

Printed in Dunstable, United Kingdom

66332515R00125